My First Ninety Years

Malinda Mae Yoder Everest

Mae Everest
1 Samuel 12:24

Acknowledgements

It it impossible to name everyone who deserves our thanks for their prayers and encouragement to write this book.

But it is my daughter, Cynthia McKee, and my grandaughter, Christine Veal, who printed the copies and the disk that I appreciate so much. To another daughter, Charlene Sherry, I thank for her part also in typing.

Most of all I'm grateful for the patient love, constant interest and support my husband showed to me. Long hours and several years kept me involved in handwriting these pages.

Mae, Cynthia, Christine

Printed by:

Evangel
PRESS

My Purpose of Writing

1. That children and their offspring might know the working of God's will in the lives of their parents, grandparents and great grandparents.

2. That although we cannot see the end from our beginning, God does.

3. That to be a Christian and true follower of the Lord Jesus Christ is far better than great earthly wealth and prestige.

4. That doing God's will from youth is an escape from many sorrows and griefs of old age.

5. That little prayer brings little results. That much prayer and trust brings mighty and often staggering results in the lives and events for which we pray.

6. That after many days or years, the bread we cast upon the water returns to bless and feed us.

7. That every phase and change of life is marvelous and with great advantages to those that love Him and His second appearing.

And now for the background and events of our lives, always for "the praise of His Glory."

Table of Contents

Mae with her father and mother

Chapter One

Joy and Sorrow

I was born in a new, small house near the end of Walnut Street in Nappanee, Indiana, but yet there were six rooms. Many of the houses in the early 1900's had a front porch with two doors in which to enter. The door most often used was the one that led into the dining room. And as you entered, you saw straight ahead into the kitchen, which led onto an enclosed back porch. The other door from the front porch entered the living room. To the right of it was a bedroom which was L-shaped and where Mama and Papa slept.

My sister, two and a half years older, and I slept in the other part of the "L." When our baby sister arrived three years later, we bravely climbed the stairway leading from the kitchen to a two-room upstairs.

But before we went to bed, Mama called us to her side at her rocking chair, talked to us and kissed us goodnight. One at a time, my sister and I knelt in front of Mama. With our faces in our hands, our hands resting on her knees, her hand on our head, we prayed. Then we said *"Goodnight."*

* * * * *

1

Our neighbors, nor we, had electricity, telephones, running water, furnaces or cars. Radios came to my home after I was married; much later, the television. I remember the day we were surprised to see some men come to our house to install a telephone. I didn't understand how this contraption worked, but it was surely fun to learn. We could call Papa at the store and order our groceries. Groceries were delivered to one's house usually by ten o'clock any day of the week.

We had a pump in our new house. Some people were still bringing in their water from an outside pump. Our pumps took some priming, but even I learned to do that before I went to school.

In the morning, Papa would build a fire in the big, black kitchen stove. Mama would help him by pumping water to fill the reservoir in the side of the kitchen stove. He started a fire in the little dining room stove and the large, round living room stove with the izing glass windows. While she made breakfast, he would wake us up. We dressed around the living room stove.

A housewife's work was very hard at the turn of the century. The wall-to-wall carpeting was swept with a hand broom, later with a Bissell sweeper. In the winter, Mama would bring in a pail of snow and sprinkle it over the carpet, then quickly sweep it out the door. The snow absorbed the dust and dirt.

Our conveniences were very few. The privy toilet was about seventy steps back of the house. Mama placed small white china pots with a handle under our beds. Of course, this meant she had to gather, empty and wash them each morning.

Mama baked our bread until Papa started working at Hartman's grocery store. That was a great help to have him carry bread home. On Monday mornings, she would always pump water, heat it and pour it in two large tubs. She scrubbed all the laundry by hand and had no wringer. Mama was a good cook, and I still have two of her cookbooks. One is a 1904 Gold Medal cookbook, and the other is one she compiled. They are most interesting!

I remember some dishes she used for certain things. One was a lovely white milkglass dish trimmed in blue. When she reached up to a high shelf in the cupboard for this dish, we knew what she was making for the next meal—walnut pudding covered with cookie crumbs. She had many pretty dishes that were no doubt given to her for wedding presents.

One day she asked Mary and me to go to the top of the stairs where there were sacks of nuts. *"Take along this flat stone. One of you can crack the nuts, and the other can pick the nutmeats out. If you get tired, change your work around. Here is a cup. I want it full,"* she said. We thought we knew what she was going to use it for—so we did not object—the delicious walnut pudding covered with cookie crumbs. After the nuts were cracked and cleaned, my sister returned to the kitchen with them.

I was alone, sitting on the floor by a stack of church papers along the wall under a window.

Being one of those children who read everything in sight that had print on it, even every word on the can of Dutch Cleanser, I began reading sentences here and there. Very short articles were easy for me. Suddenly I found a Sunday School Times Magazine and became intrigued with the "stick men" who illustrated the Sunday School lessons. My papa drew stickmen on the blackboard when he taught boys' Sunday School class.

I found a very meaningful poem. Oh, that rhythm and what an awakening to my mind and heart. My eyes filled with tears. I experienced a rush of urgency. It told of children across the sea who never heard of Jesus and would never know unless we (I) told them. This knowledge I kept to myself, never thinking of telling my mother or father about what I had learned. It seemed to be only between God and me. That was the beginning of my knowledge of the lost. But someone must tell children of God's love for other children. They must be made aware of it, or they grow up to be selfish adults.

Oh, that beautiful poem! Several times I went up to find it again. I wanted to keep it. I asked Mama what had become of those papers. She said they went with the trash. My little heart ached.

* * * * *

My very first recollection was when I was two years of age. Mama had moved my crib into the living room one morning. I stood up and watched her wash the dishes in the kitchen. I was very itchy and could not be quiet any longer. My hands were on the side of the crib. My body was shaking it so hard. Finally I started to cry. She came with some ointment and rubbed me all over. Instantly I felt good. I had chicken pox!

Another thing I remember was a wonderful day in March when I was nearly three years old. Mary and I had spent a few days with Grandma, who lived just a few blocks away at the very edge of town. Aunt Lynn, who was in nurse's training in Chicago and was home for a few days, took us back home. We walked into my mother's bedroom. She was lying in bed with a tiny baby beside her. I didn't know where she got it, but I was so very glad to see Mama! They named the baby Myrtle.

* * * * *

One day on April 3, 1912, which was my fourth birthday, Mama led me to the couch in the living room. *"Mae, you are old enough now to tie your shoes. I'll show you now, and then you do it,"* she said. We went through the process several times. I seemed to be willing to learn this great feat, because as I looked out through the screen door, I observed the silent falling of rain. Other children were in school. Knowing there wasn't anything exciting to do, I was willing to obey.

Outside our house, it was bare of trees, but we had a nice lawn. Papa bought and planted a tree called a Tree of Heaven, which grew nicely. We played under it as well as a huge oak tree across our street.

Our street was a plain dirt street until I was about four years old. Then bricks were laid one by one from our end of town, east to Main street. We neighbor children sat along side in the hot sun, bare-footed, never tiring of watching the men work. Bent and sweating, they never seemed to straighten their backs, and I felt sorry for them. There was a black man among them, the first one I had ever seen.

One day, Fred, a neighbor boy, called to me and said, *"Mae, this bubbly black pitch tar the men put between the bricks is good to chew."* He was chewing some; so I took some. I remember how it tasted. I chewed and chewed. That was all I remember about it.

But at suppertime, I got very sick and laid my head on my mother's lap under the table. Soon she asked me if I was sleepy. I sat up. And when she looked at me, she said, *"Are you sick? Did you eat something that I didn't give you?"* Well, I could not think of a thing except that pitch.

She was out of her chair in a moment, talking on the telephone to our doctor. She came back to the table, filled a glass with milk and said, *"The doctor said to drink all of this."* I gulped it all down. I did not know a person could feel that bad. I sat still. Suddenly it all came up. I determined I would not listen to Fred again. I probably swallowed it, and he spit his out! Mama did not scold me. She was very kind and sorry about the whole matter.

Papa had a chicken house built on the back of our property. In those days, people were

6

allowed to have chickens in town. Before Papa bought chickens to place in it, we girls used it for a playhouse. If Mama was baking pies, she would always use leftover dough to make us a small one. We had very few toys, but we used boxes and berry crates for furniture. We fed our dolls and rocked them back and forth, singing to them, too. Finally we were moved out, and little chicks occupied the little house.

* * * * *

The first six and a half years of my life were filled with play, laughter, love and learning many great lessons of my life. We were the average poor family, but my father and mother loved each other and knew their God, which took many of the burdens and stress out of life. I said six and a half years because this was all the time I had with my mother.

Mama taught me many lessons, which served me well in later years. She taught me the value of a minute. I loved to watch her sew on her new Singer sewing machine. Her feet went up and down on the treadle. She would stop to baste some more, then back to sewing on the machine again.

One day after the noon meal while I was watching her sew with a needle and thread, I asked her if I could sew, too. *"Well,"* she said, as she looked at the clock, *"it is five minutes of two. When the clock strikes two, what must little Mae do?"* *"Go take a nap,"* I said rather crossly. *"But it isn't two o'clock yet!"* *"All right. Here is a piece of material. I'll thread the needle, and you can sew*

7

until two o'clock." I looked at the clock. The long hand was only one mark before it would be straight up. I plunged the needle into the cloth when to my astonishment, the clock struck. I learned the value of a minute. I laid down my needle, thread and material and went upstairs to bed.

My first lesson in honesty came at the age of four. I can't remember of playing alone. I always involved others in play or they with me.

One particular day I was alone because my older sister and the neighborhood children were at school. All was too quiet out of doors; so I went skipping down the sidewalk and crossed the street. "Old Mary," a little old neighbor, was pumping water at the outside well in back of her house. We exchanged words, and I followed her into her house. Soon I heard Mama calling, *"Mae! Mae!"* So I ran home right away. But Mama was upset. With the little baby she was caring for, she had no time to run after me. She looked so worried that I immediately felt it necessary to make up a good story. So I said, *"Old Mary" broke her ankle, and I had to help her with her shoes.* "Oh," Mama said, *"I didn't know Mary broke her ankle!"* Whether she wanted to find out if indeed Mary needed help or if I was lying, she was about to find out. She checked to see if the baby was all right and then took my hand. We went hurriedly, I assure you, down Walnut Street to Mary's. Mary met us at the screen door. *"Good morning, Mary."* She paused. *"Why, Mae said you broke your ankle."* *"No, no, I'm all right,"* Mary replied.

With that short conversation, we headed for home. My hand was still in hers. We walked through our dining room, living room and into her bedroom. Then she let go of my hand. *"Mae,"* she said, *"why did you say such a thing?"* I said, *"I don't know."* And I didn't. She spared no words to tell me how wicked it was to lie and that it did not please Jesus any more than it pleased her. We were all the time kneeling by my bed. Then she prayed, and we both felt Jesus forgave me.

Do you wonder why it was always difficult afterward for me to tell the untruth?

Mama seemed to be wise enough to know that I needed more to occupy my time. One thing she did was to put her rocking chair facing the wall with me in it. She placed it close enough that the tips of my toes could touch the wall. That was so I could keep rocking. Then she placed a bed pillow on my lap and put the baby on the pillow. I can see Mama yet as she stood in the kitchen working. We could see and talk to each other as I rocked the baby.

Sometimes Mama would go to the bedroom, kneel at the bed to pray. I'd follow her and wait for her to finish. She'd tell me then what her burden was. Once she explained that her brother William could not be found. Grandma and Grandpa had worked with "Missing Persons" and even an international organization but without success. She told me that Uncle Will and Uncle Milo, who were grown boys, decided to take a trip to Chicago for a day. They left from Goshen on the Interurban. When they arrived at the Marshall Fields store, they made their arrangements for the day. They went their own ways. They planned to meet at a certain door of Marshall Fields at five o'clock, which would give them plenty of time to catch the train to return home.

William never showed up, and Milo had to come home alone. Years passed by. The family never heard from him for eighteen long years. Grandma and Grandpa suffered a great deal. My mother was the youngest of the family of seven children. My mother prayed and cried many tears for her brother. Their prayers were answered but not until after Milo, Grandma, Grandpa, Aunt Mary, and even my mother had died. William suddenly came home.

When I was ten years old, one morning we had an unexpected call from my father, who was at work in the grocery store. My stepmother answered the phone. Papa was doing all the talking; she was listening.

When she hung up the phone, she turned around and said, *"Your Uncle Will came back. He is in the store. He came back without a hint of his coming and is very shaken up about the death of his parents, his two sisters."* He especially grieved for my mother who was a very young girl when he left. When he asked about Milo, whom he left in Chicago, and learned that he too had died, he sobbed. My father was very upset over all this.

Eighteen years was a long time to be away from home and never allow his family to know where he was. I was very young, but I thought it was cruel. I never learned why he left. He did tell us – and we knew it to be true – that the western farmers were calling for young men to go west. The need for men was very great at harvesttime. They had no large machinery in those earlier years. So he did as so many young men did, went west. But why he did not write home, I do not know.

In my teens, I often visited my aunts in Goshen. One of them lived in my grandparents' home after they passed away, and Uncle Will would be there. He could not get a job because of an accident he had with a team of horses as he crossed a bridge. His elbow was severely crushed. He had pain continually.

He spent most of the rest of his days with his widowed sister, my Aunt Mattie Kingman. I believe she finally led him to the Lord.

* * * * *

Prayer was quite a prominent occurrence with us. It was a source of strength, and great peace came from it. I've been glad to know the power of prayer since childhood.

One of my friends in later years told me that she was not taught about prayer. She knew God loved her but not much more. But somehow she had an instinct within her that made her feel God knew everything. One day she wanted to tell Him something. So she wrote Him a letter. Out back of the garden, she dug a little hole by the fence, placed the letter in it and covered it up. If God knew everything, she figured, He would find it. Her heart was at peace then. She completely forgot it for years.

Mothers have a great responsibility to teach little children life's great lessons. Obedience, honesty, promptness, helpfulness and many other lessons we were taught in love by both Papa and Mama.

Mama was a humble woman and seemed to love everybody. She and I went shopping one day. As we came out of Lape-Ringenberg Department Store, she dropped my hand and rushed forward to meet a young Amish girl. She hugged her and said, *"I missed you so much last week. Are you feeling better?"* This was our egg lady who stopped regularly at our house.

* * * * *

I was playing outdoors one morning when I saw a policeman coming down the street. That was very unusual! When he turned into our yard, I ran ahead, slamming the screen door and called, *"Mama, a policeman is coming to our house!"*

He politely knocked, although he could see my mother ironing in the kitchen.

"Good morning," she said. *"Why are you here?"*

"Is Charles here?" he replied. Charlie was a young man she took in as a roomer, to make a little extra money, I thought.

"Yes. He's still in bed."

"May I go up to his room?"

"Yes," Mama said.

He wasn't upstairs but for a short time until down came the two of them. Well, off to jail went Charlie.

"Mama," I asked, *"why did the policeman take*

him?"

"Oh, Charlie has a bad temper. He has been work-ing for a farmer. They had an argument, and Charlie threw a pitchfork at him. Whether he really aimed directly at the farmer or not, it did hit him, and he was severely injured."

After his time in jail was completed, he came back to get his clothes. What I remember about that was that when he came down the stairs, Mama was ready for him in the dining room. *"Sit down, Charlie,"* she said, as he approached her. She sat side of him at the table with her Bible open. She explained to him the love of Jesus. How the conversation ended, I don't know. But I know she wanted to help him be saved.

* * * * *

As I ran to meet my father coming home from work one summer evening, he told me some-thing special. At a certain time that evening, the daughter of his boss was going to drive their new car past our house. While we were eating supper, suddenly we heard the sound of a motor. Each of us hurried out of the door and into the yard to wave at Miss Hartman. Now I realize she was driving very slowly, but that evening it seemed very fast. We rarely saw a car.

* * * * *

After each meal, Mama slid her hand into the metal handle of the cellar door in the kitchen floor, lifted the door back until it rested against the wall. Then she took the butter, milk and leftovers down the steps. In hot weather, this was the only way we had of keeping our milk and foods from spoiling.

Grandma Yoder had a different way of keeping things fresh. After a meal was finished, she put the leftovers, milk and butter into little porcelain-covered pails. We helped her carry them outdoors to the well. Nearby was a separate, small one-room house called the summer house. Somewhere between the two houses, we knelt on the sidewalk. Grandma lifted a large, round wooden lid that fit over the hole of the well. Then we each picked up our little porcelain-covered pail that the dish of food was in and hung it by the handle onto the hooks, which were fastened around the edge of the well. There was much water, but it did not reach the top of the well.

Grandma was always glad to see us. Although she didn't have toys, she did have games and a hammock. We often went to visit her on Sunday afternoons. Sometimes my cousins were there. That pleased me because I could not speak or understand her Deutch language.

My father was a teacher in a country one-room school before he became a preacher. His Deutch-speaking students found English grammar was very difficult. Therefore, he did not allow us to learn Deutch. My cousins would tell Grandmother what I wanted. She was always nice to me, but to me it was a great hindrance.

I loved to swing in the hammock. Wrapping it around me tightly and swinging while I looked up at the sky and clouds made me feel closer to God.

* * * * *

My father's brother, Uncle Amos, and his family of six children lived on the next street back of us. If the neighbor children were busy or not at home, there were always my cousins a block away with whom I played. Three boys and three girls can keep life quite interesting. If what the girls were doing became dull, I would watch the boys in their games and projects. I was very young, but I decided to try walking on their stilts. That was great fun. It made me tall. I never did fall while wearing them. But it was a bit scary. They had a fake monkey, too, with an organ grinder. What fun!

The songs of Uncle Josh were very funny and popular then. We had no phonograph at that time, but my cousins did. And they brought some great laughs. We'd all sit on the floor and rock back and forth laughing until our stomachs ached. The chorus of one was *"When Papa papered the parlor, you couldn't see Pa for paste. Dabbing it here, dabbing it there 'till there was paste and paper everywhere. Mother was stuck to the ceiling and the kids were stuck to the floor. You never saw such a bloomin' family so stuck up before, ha!"*

Another one was "Pa's Whiskers." *"Ma, she chewed them in her sleep and thought she was eating Shredded Wheat."*

* * * * *

My parents allowed us privileges of playing

with others nearby, but we were promptly brought into the house before nightfall.

One beautiful, snowy evening, my sister heard voices outside. Someone was tapping on the living room window. Mary pulled back the lace curtains. In our front yard, the older neighborhood children were playing Fox and Geese in our front yard. The snow was deep, and they were having a lot of fun. I rushed up beside her to see what was happening. I heard Mama scream! Just a few inches from Mary was a small table with a kerosene lamp on it. Had she been older than seven years, she would have been more careful. There were a couple of feet between the lamp and window. Mary had pulled the curtain over the lamp.

Papa was there in no time grabbing us out from under the flaming curtain, and Mama ran to the kitchen, grabbed a pail, then pumped water. Papa took the pail, threw the water on the curtains. He rushed out to pump more water while Mama called the fire department. I stood in one spot horrified.

Mama was exhausted when it was all over because she saw how near the flames were to Mary's hair. She was exhausted, too, from pumping water. The water had ruined the top of Mama's new Singer sewing machine. No one had time to cover it up. By the time the horses and water wagon came, the fire was put out.

* * * * *

My mother and father loved each other very much. She was so sensitive about his welfare. I remember her standing at the window as she watched him face a fierce storm to go feed the chickens.

And the time he walked home from the store with a broken collarbone, she looked so hurt, and I pitied them both. He had to walk home with his arm in a sling. We had no car until I was senior in high school.

If we wanted to visit out of town, Papa hired a rig from the town livery stable for a day. This was very infrequent because he worked long hours each day, six days each week. He preached every other Sunday.

One nice summer day, Mama, Papa and I went to Goshen in a rig to see my aunts and Grandpa Troyer. As we approached the bridge at Plymouth and Second Streets, we heard a commotion under the bridge. A rowboat had turned over, and a woman was about to drown. Suddenly a man came to her help with a rope. He threw it, she grabbed hold of it and was saved. He was pulling her into shore shouting, *"Help! Help!"* Papa gave the reins to Mama. He jumped down to help them. Then he was asked to take the lady to her home. Mama and I somehow made it the rest of the way. We probably walked about a half-mile.

We were used to walking – to school, church, town, and everywhere we were supposed to go. In twelve years of school, I never had a ride. At noon we always went home for dinner. I think walking in all kinds of weather was healthy. I can remember being sick only a few times because of mumps at age six, measles at seven, the 1918 "killer influenza" at ten, and the flu in my senior year.

* * * * *

Mama seemed to be a happy person, because I can, in my recollections, see and hear her whistle and sing around the house.

"Richer than I you will never be,
For I had a mother who sang to me."

Ralph Waldo Emerson

Mama often sang *"Love divine, all loves excelling, Joy of heav'n to earth come down! Fix in us Thy humble dwelling; All Thy faithful mercies crown."* I knew all these words because she rocked me as she sang this song.

Besides being a busy mother and housewife, she was a great blessing in the church. On Sunday evenings, she often called the children to the front seats and proceeded to give them an object lesson. I remember the book she used. It was titled, "From Eye Gate To Heart Gate." At home I would sometimes open the glass door of the bookcase and reach in for that interesting book. I thought, even as young as I was, that someday I'd like to teach children, too. I finally did—hundreds of them. That was a great joy in my life. I still pray for them. They are now fathers and mothers, scattered over many states, in many occupations and ministries. I pray for them as I do for my own children.

Mama's singing was not contained to the house, for she often sang in a mixed quartet. Two of their songs I keenly remember were

"They That Wait Upon the Lord," and "The Great Judgement Morning." Mama also taught a boy's class. My cousin said she was the best teacher he ever had.

* * * * *

One night the Bishop and the older preacher came to see Papa. They talked a long time. Mama held me on her lap and entertained me in the dining room by the dim light of a small lamp. No doubt she was keeping me from running to Papa, as I so often did.

* * * * *

Papa surprised Mama on her birthday. Two men came to deliver a lovely sideboard (buffet). Mother insisted they made a mistake with the address. The dreymen finally convinced her that Papa ordered it. I remember how very pleased she was.

One summer, a newly married couple moved in a house across the street from us. After supper they would come over and play croquet with my parents. They loved to play, but the darkness would come too soon. So my father wrapped all the arches with white cloth. This extended their playing time quite a bit.

* * * * *

I was five years old when Papa, Mama and I took our first long trip, to Iowa for a church conference. Papa bought Mama a new black seal coat and a red coat and leggings with shiny black buttons for me.

We stopped in Chicago to visit friends who were mission workers. They lived above the mission, which seemed very odd to me. The children took me down the back stairway to see the church. They had no yard to play in. I felt sad for them. They had a little tricycle. I had never seen one before; so I was anxious to try it out. Just along side of the dining and living rooms was a long hallway. The children wanted to see me ride it. All went well until I got to the end and wanted to turn around. I turned too sharply which caused me to fall off right in the doorway of the living room where the grownups were sitting. I was very embarrassed. However, they kept right on visiting.

Mama went calling with the minister's wife and later told Papa and me about her experiences. While in Chicago, our friends took us sightseeing.

I remember nothing about the conference that we attended in Iowa. But I clearly remember that Papa, Mama and I were taken to a farm where a mother was sick. She wanted my father to anoint and pray for her. I was much impressed with an old German song the people sang while standing around her bed. I never have heard it played or sung again until I was eighty-nine years old, although I have been able to sing it all these years.

* * * * *

I was very anxious to go to school. In the afternoon, after the first day of school, I ran into the house and found Mama in the kitchen. I called to her, *"Oh, Mama, I can read. We have Primers. This is my book, and I can read the first page. Just listen. 'See Carlo. See Carlo run.'"* Then I showed her the picture of a large Collie dog. That was the beginning of my love of reading. Mama smiled and joined in with my excitement.

I loved my little Bible and began reading it as soon as I could. We children memorized a Bible verse pertaining to the Sunday School lesson each week for many years. The first verse I remember was, *"Let the words of my mouth and the meditation of my heart be acceptable in Thy sight, oh Lord, my strength and my Redeemer."* We were taught to be responsible to learn our verses and lessons on our own.

Reading has always been a great experience for me. As I became elderly, books became my good friends. I like to read different kinds of books at the same time. I do not finish one book before I start another. Sometimes I would find one on the early history of our country, a missionary book, a devotional one, biography of great persons or sometimes a religious novel, books I can feel like a better person for having read them. For many years, I read my Bible through each year.

Books and music were my two great loves all of my life. When I started to school, Mama wrote down each song we learned. I can sing twenty-eight songs that I learned in the first, second and third grades:

- Good Morning Merry Sunshine

- Do You Wear a Pair of Rubbers on a Very Rainy Day?

- A Bumblebee Was Buzzing on a Yellow Hollyhock

- We'll All Go to See Granny Bobbin

- There's a Ship Sails Away at the Close of Each Day

- A Little Boy Went Walking One Lovely Summer Day

- Father, We Thank Thee for the Night

- There's a Wee Little Man in a Wee Little House

- Twinkle, Twinkle Little Star

- Mother Goose Invited Her Children Dear

- In the Rain or in the Sunshine

- One Beautiful Day in the Springtime

- A Riggedy Jig and Away We Go

- This is the Way We Wash Our Clothes

- Over the River and Through the Woods

Joy and Sorrow

- Old Jones was Gruff and Sour Enough, Ha, Ha, Ha, Ha, Ha, Ha, Ha

- Twenty Froggies Went to School

- October Gave a Party, the Leaves by Hundreds Came

- There's a Great Big Turkey on Grandpa's Farm

- One Day Last Week I Made a Kite (It was a fine one, too.)

- Mary Had a Little Lamb

- Hush, Be Still As Any Mouse, There's a Baby in the House

- Three Little Kittens

- Baby Bye, Here's a Fly, Let Us Watch Him, You and I

- Five Little Chickadees Sitting in a Row

- Oh, We are in the Kitchen

- John Brown Had a Little Indian

- When the Frost is on the Pumpkin

Music was continually a significant part of my whole life when I was a young child. However, at church, it was a different matter.

"Papa," my older sister said as we walked to Sunday School one Sunday morning. *"Mae doesn't sing in church."*

My father didn't answer. She was walking on the other side of him. I peeked over at her as she said again, *"Mae never sings."* Mary, two and a half years older, loved to sing.

"Well, Mae, why don't you sing?"

"I don't know," I said.

But in church that morning it dawned upon me why I did not often sing. It wasn't because I wasn't interested. It was because I was fascinated by the chorister and his tuning fork. He struck it on the top of the book and then put the fork to his ear. He followed this by humming, *"Do, me, sol, do."* He then proceeded to lead the congregation in song. In those days we had no piano or organ. I sat so close to him, I had to look straight up into his face. You see, I sat, always, on the second seat from the front at the middle aisle. In those days, the chorister never led the congregation from the platform but down on the level with the people. Sometimes I watched the saliva make a string from his upper lip to his lower one. He also wore pinched glasses on his nose. This talk on the way to church somehow awakened me to the joy of participating in the song service.

A few years later when the church purchased new songbooks, the drey (a wagon pulled by horses) delivered them at our house. Papa was

a preacher, and sometimes we had duties different than other families. Papa placed these packages in our little red wagon and entrusted them
to us. We pulled and pushed the wagon until
we arrived at the little white church.

The next Sunday, an announcement was made
concerning a "Sing" at 7:30 each Monday night
for the summer months. This was meant for
everyone who loved music and who wished to
learn parts – soprano, alto, tenor or bass. I was
so very interested that I did not consider my
young age but helped myself to this wonderful
learning of notation, tone, harmony, and the
reading of music in general.

In my teen years, I enjoyed singing soprano in
a mixed quartet and leading the singing Sunday
nights in the youth service.

But I always appreciated the very early training the church gave me as a very young child
just beginning to read.

* * * * *

We were a very close and happy family until
one Sunday morning in December, just before
Christmas. My father woke me up and asked
me to get Mama a drink of water. He was sitting
on the bed holding her. They looked very sad.
As the week wore on, she became worse. On
Wednesday and Thursday nights, they asked me
to sleep at the neighbors' across the street. I
remember standing at the window, in the darkness, looking over at our house wondering what
was going on.

One afternoon, all three of us girls – ages

three, six, and nine – were asked by Papa to sit on the couch in the living room. The doctor was coming to talk to us about Mama.

The doctor said, *"I'm sorry, but your Mama is going to die. She can't live any longer. We thought you'd want to say good-bye to her."*

I couldn't understand it. But I went to her bed, leaned over and kissed her goodbye. I was six, and I knew in my heart she was going to heaven, but I could not understand why. She was only thirty-three. She had given birth to a baby, but it died, too. She had just finished my Christmas dress of medium blue wool trimmed in plaid taffeta. How pretty! The funeral was just before Christmas. The doctor and his wife had us at their home for Christmas dinner.

Just before the funeral while we were still at home, the Bishop came to the stairway to talk to me. I had put on my red coat and leggings and was ready to go to the church. I did not know this preacher from Ohio, but he was a cousin of my father.

"Mae," he said, *"you are very sad about being without your mother. You cannot talk to her anymore. But always remember this. You can always talk to God."*

Oh, how that struck me. It has stayed with me like nothing else has. He certainly helped me more by giving me the assurance of that connection with God than anything else he could have said.

The helping neighbors told us girls that Mama prayed for us with her last breath.

After the funeral, neighbors had a nice meal

26

prepared for us. That was the first time I ate with sterling silver.

Uncle Daniel Brenneman

*Founder of the Missionary
Church*

Aunt Della Brenneman

Chapter Two

The Healing Process.

In a few days, Papa had packed our clothes and helped us get on the train to Milford Junction. We waited there for the Interurban, which took us to Goshen. My mother's sister, Della, and her husband, Daniel Brenneman, met us there. We would live with them for the last semester of school, which was in my first grade, and the following summer.

Papa told us much later that several church families wanted to each take one of us, but it would have divided us, and Papa could not bear that. Losing Mama was so severe and so sudden. We all were suffering very much. But God made a way to heal our broken hearts in time.

A businessman soon approached Papa about taking some Bible courses at the church college, which was located in the town where we were staying.

We knew our auntie very well and loved her dearly. She was a jolly, kind person and made our lives interesting. She had married at forty and had no children of her own. My uncle was a retired minister, Daniel Brenneman, who was seventy-five.

Each day he would read the Bible to us. Sometimes auntie would pray; sometimes he

29

would. Then he'd go to the organ to play a hymn, and we'd all sing. He was such a happy, kind man. I loved to sit on his lap and comb his hair and his little white goatee. I just loved to bring him things, especially so he could rest after a hard day in the summertime.

It was not easy to go to a school where I knew no other children. It was hard for me to keep my mind on what my teacher was saying. My aunt must have told her about my situation, for she was very kind to me.

In the summer, we learned to know the neighborhood children. We had great times together. Auntie often gave us chores or errands to do, too.

She gave us a package one day to take to uncle's son who lived many blocks from us. The boys and girls of the neighborhood went with us. There were probably six, as I remember. On the way, the boys said, *"Let's take the short cut."* We did not know what they meant, but we trusted them. Before long, we were all walking on the railroad tracks, then back onto a street again, which followed the river or large creek.

All at once, the boys saw a log across the stream. They started across it. Once on the other side, they begged us girls to follow, Mary whispered to me, *"We'll not cross on the log!"* I agreed with all my heart. We stood still. We never said a word. However, Marice Teeters, who was a bit older than my sister, heard the boys yelling at us saying that it was easy. So she dropped on her knees. When she crawled about half way across, she started to cry loudly. *"Oh,*

I'll never see my mother again. I'm turning back." She cried harder. Then we all said, *"Don't turn around and don't look down at the water. Look at the other shore and the boys."* I can see her yet as she struggled across.

* * * * *

My uncle had six lots of berries, strawberries, raspberries, and gooseberries. At the edge of town, he owned a melon farm. He had regular pickers come to fill the crates. The fruit was large and beautiful. The patches were clean and well cared for.

He would load the berry crates onto his spring wagon. Nellie, the horse, would be hitched to the wagon. Off he would go to the streets downtown, ring his bell and stop in the middle of a block. Women came from their houses to buy and chat with this dear old man. His fruit sold quickly, for housewives became acquainted with him and his lucious fruit. I enjoyed going with him a few times. However, the seat was hard and the hours too long for me. But I helped pick berries sometimes. I was seven years old that summer.

One day, as he was ready to drive away with his produce, I noticed Auntie detaining him. Holding the reins in his hands, he was explaining something to her. I ran and stood behind Auntie to listen. Something was said about berries being stolen from the patch. He had so many orders to supply to his customers. Would she keep her eyes on the patch occasionally to see who the thieves were? Well, the long chickenhouse was between the house and the berry lots. I turned to look around, felt a strange urge to be a spy myself. Barefooted, this seven-year-old was running fast, around the chickenhouse, the "outhouse," and then I slowed up. I could see down the long grassy path a man climbing my uncle's fence. In his hand was a kettle or pan. I slowed up until I saw surely that his intention was to steal berries from my good uncle. I ran toward him as fast as I could and yelled, *"Aren't you ashamed to steal berries from an old man?"*

He was shocked. He threw his leg back across the fence and climbed down. I watched him as I peeked around the barn. I saw him go into his back door. Now we knew who it was. He could have easily seen my uncle hitch up and drive toward the street and known my aunt was still at the house. With no pickers around so early, that was his chance. He knew I recognized him. That was the last they baked pies with my uncle's berries.

That summer we were very happy and well cared for. We had been well except for having mumps. Uncle Daniel got up one night and prayed for Myrtle, who had a high fever and was only three years old. I know we three little children were a great burden for them. But we did have a lot of fun with them. We learned many good lessons, too. God will certainly reward them.

Sometimes Mary and I walked to the south part of Goshen to Wilson Avenue to visit our other aunt, Mattie, her family, Uncle William and sons Ray and Allen. Ray was a wonderful portrait painter and earned his living all his life by his art. They took care of Grandma and Grandpa Troyer in their older years until they died. We loved Aunt Mattie's cooking and had good times there. It was a long distance to walk across town; so Mary and I counted the door-bells as we went down Main Street.

After the summer was over, Papa asked us to come home to live with him. But Auntie thought she should keep Myrtle, who was now four years old. Mary was ten, and I was seven.

Papa worked ten hours each day. The stores were open two nights during the week. He worked at the main grocery store. He also preached every other Sunday.

When Mary and I got up in the morning, our breakfast would be on the table. It usually consisted of corn flakes, cinnamon rolls and cocoa. Sometimes on weekends, he'd bring bananas from the store which otherwise would have spoiled. He'd bank the fire, then with good-byes, walk to work. After we ate, we would set two chairs side by side and put a dishpan on each one. Then we dipped a little water from the stove reservoir into each one. We washed and dried the dishes quickly and went to school. However, each morning my sister combed my hair, which was easy. Papa had my hair cut to my ear lobes after Mama died. It was parted on the side, and I wore a large ribbon bow on the other side. An older neighbor girl combed and braided Mary's hair for five cents per week. Then we all walked five blocks to school.

At noon, we went home for dinner. Papa often dipped hot water from the reservoir into a kettle, placed a couple cans of vegetables, and sometimes baked beans, in it. He set the kettle on the stove until the water boiled up good. He set the table. We gave thanks, ate, and back to school we went.

On Tuesday after school, we'd find the clothesbasket full and setting in our little red wagon. We pulled it down the sidewalk to our laundry-lady's house about five blocks away. On Friday, back we'd go to pick up our fresh laundered clothes. I think we paid her one dollar.

In the evening, again it was Papa who got our food ready. We always had something to fill our tummies.

Two nights each week he worked very late. One was Saturday night. Sometimes my sister was terrified to be alone, but I seemed less afraid, perhaps because she was older than I. One thing about Saturday nights we enjoyed. We had three things to do which would help pass the time. These were my father's instructions. One was to study our Sunday School lesson for the following morning. Another was to shine our shoes. And the third – what fun! – was to read the "funnies" that were in the Sunday South Bend paper which he would bring home to us on Saturday evening at six o'clock. Then we would jump into bed before it got too cold because of the banked fire.

How my father did all this and carried his grief for my mother, only God knows.

In the summertime, it was possible for him to find a hired girl or one of his cousins to stay with us. It was a great relief and a lot of fun for us.

One summer we had an Amish lady. If it thundered and the lightning flashed, she hurried us into the living room and gave us our rubbers to put on over our shoes. This was to keep us from getting struck by lightning. She set the chairs in a circle in the middle of the room. An elderly woman who lived directly across the street often came over to be with us because she was afraid of storms. The strange part of all this was that these two women told stories of the worst storms they had ever heard of or experienced.

The Amish girl cleaned the house, washed clothes and cooked. Still she had time to entertain us.

* * * * *

After two or more years had passed, we heard that Papa was dating. This was a great disturbance to my sister. She told me he should marry the Amish girl. She would surely change her way of dress. I knew I'd never feel I had any other mother, but what Papa did was his own "grown-up" choosing. But no one could take the place of my mother. I can still easily shed tears in my pillow for her. Maybe at ninety years of age it is more because of the joy of seeing her before many years pass.

* * * * *

There used to be tramps who came into our

community in the summer. When we were alone, my sister and I were very aware of any stranger who walked toward our house. We would lock the doors, pull down the window shades, and crawl under the dining room table until he had passed our house. I did not feel frightened. Mary just thought it was the thing to do.

* * * * *

One evening the phone rang. My father answered it, then hung up the receiver and said, *"Mrs. Miller is sick. She wants me to come anoint and pray for her."* I said, *"Oh, can I go with you?"* He said, *"Certainly."* So running along barefooted holding Papa's hand, we arrived at the Miller home. He read her some scripture, anointed her with oil, laid his hand upon her and prayed. God's presence was in the room. I was not surprised to see her leading the song service in Sunday School the following Sunday morning.

* * * * *

I grieved for my mother a lot. Papa surprised us one day when he brought home a little record player. Some songs were sacred like "The Unclouded Day." "The Thunderers" with Sousa's band was another piece.

Our church had a youth literary society. Before we were old enough to join, they invited Mary and me to sing special duets.

The church had a special speaker one Sunday morning. When I came into the sanctuary after Sunday School, it was filled. I came to the front of the church where we always sat. But there was no place for me. Mary was sitting with a friend of hers and her friend's mother. Suddenly my father was at my side conversing with a woman on the front seat. The women moved a bit so I could sit between them. I did not know who they were. I felt so small between them. I felt so unhappy and lonely without my mother. Papa saw tears roll down my face. So while the congregation was singing, he left the platform, took me by the hand and said, *"You may sit with me, Mae."* I was so bashful and timid, but this brought me such relief! I immediately stopped crying and sat myself down on one of the preacher's big chairs on the platform side of Papa. I was so relaxed that the service didn't seem long at all.

* * * * *

Once when I was eight or nine, we had an evangelist from Hesston College speak each night for one or two weeks. The messages were very good for me. My interest grew.

One night he preached on hell. That was something I knew about, but because I loved Jesus, as most little children do, I had given little thought to it.

The Holy Spirit that night brought my attention to Heaven, the holy angels and my mother with Jesus. I was deeply moved, and when the evangelist asked for all those who wanted to be Christians to stand up, I stood quickly. I knew immediately God was pulling me toward Him and Heaven. It was a new consciousness.

Something seemed new and happy inside me. Then we who stood were asked to come to the front. The congregation was dismissed. I walked to the front.

The evangelist talked kindly to us about accepting Christ as Savior and how to live for Him. Then the senior pastor of our church asked us to meet on a Saturday night for a convert's meeting. I went. We were lined up on the front seat. The girls and women on one side. The men and boys on the other side of the aisle.

Then the elderly pastor, after a short prayer, began asking us questions. Do you believe? All the questions were about God, Jesus and the Holy Spirit. I was sitting by the center aisle; so I was the first to be questioned. Of course they were easy questions for me. I believe the whole Bible. My heart responded, and I said, *"Yes."*

So down the line he walked and asked everyone the same questions.

Then he came back to me and asked some questions I did not know how to answer. When he asked, *"Will you wear a bonnet, hood or veil?"* I just sat there frozen. No answer came. He asked again, *"Will you wear a bonnet, hood or veil?"* No answer from me. So down the row he walked, and every other one said they would.

At the close of the session, he made it real plain that anyone who did not answer *"yes"* to that question could not be baptized Sunday morning.

When we arrived home, I took off my nice white wool cap with a thick tassel on top and my coat. I sat down on a chair and gave it all some thought.

Papa stopped in front of me and quietly asked, *"Why didn't you say yes as the others did?"* I said, *"I didn't say yes because I have no bonnet, hood or veil. Why should I lie?"* He half smiled and turned away. He knew I did the right thing, and I was happy. I didn't have a mother to talk to; so I did what the Bishop had told me to do: talk always to God.

The next Sunday morning, they had their sprinkling service. I sat several seats back of them and was quite content.

After the service, I made my way alone to the cloakroom to get my coat and cap. The senior pastor's married daughter came up behind me, put her arms around me and crying said, *"Mae, when you grow up, you will know what you have done this day."*

I felt so short and small beside her, but inside I felt quite grown up. I said nothing to her, but inside I said, *"They can't take Jesus from me. He is already inside me."* I've never doubted my conversion. It was so real. Later, when I was seventeen, I consecrated myself entirely to Him, and no doubt about it, He accepted me, cleansed and filled me with the Holy Spirit.

* * * * *

That summer Papa found another way to keep us busy. Ward's Bakery packaged their delicious cakes in decorative boxes. He purchased them by the dozen in different flavors. Mary and I put them in our little red wagon and went from door to door selling them for ten cents a box. We thought it better to canvas the next street south of us because the houses were larger. We figured they had more money and would be more apt to buy. Mary carried the money and made the change while I hurried down the steps to pick out the flavored cake the housewife wanted. The women usually smiled as I handed the cake to her. Next Saturday we would repeat this marketing. It was such fun.

At strawberry time, Papa bought crates of strawberries from a fruit grower. Again we used our little red wagon to sell strawberries by the quart box. How good they looked, but we knew better than to eat any.

Another thing we sold was horseradish. It grew wild in our garden. This was real work for Papa. He dug it out of the ground, washed it and put chunks through the grinder. He then seasoned it. We put it into new jelly glasses and went to ring doorbells again. My sister let me ring the doorbells. I liked that. She held the product we were selling and the money. This taught us many things. It taught us to be honest, to meet people, how to make change and to smile while we described our product. It was as much fun, too, as it would have been to stay at home and play.

* * * * *

The summer passed quickly. We girls were not bored, but we were glad to go back to school. The winter had just set in when the children in our school started getting the measles. Mary got the measles before I did. Papa could not take care of us. But my aunt on the next street in back of us was caring for all six of her children who had them. Then her husband, my uncle, who was the delivery man at the store where Papa worked, had pneumonia. So Aunt Mandy said, *"Better bring Mary here. I might as well have one more patient."*

I was sent to Grandma's house. I enjoyed that. My Aunt Lynn and Uncle Ike were still living at home. Aunt Lynn was now a nurse working for Doctors Willard and Delbert Price. That night when Uncle Ike called me for supper, he found me lying on the couch in the living room half asleep. He told Grandma and Aunt Lynn about it. They immediately came to question me. *"Are you sick?"* *"I don't feel very good,"* I said. Grandma unbuttoned my dress, looked me over and said in her language, *"Yes, she has measles, too."*

Aunt Lynn called Papa on the phone. He brought our little wagon to Grandma's house. By that time I had eaten a little supper. Grandma helped me with my coat and wrapped me in several blankets. Papa put me in the wagon. They laid me on a pillow. Uncle Ike helped Papa pull the wagon to "the measle house." I could barely see through and around the scarf tied over my face, but I peeked at the multitude of bright stars in the sky. It was a most beautiful night. About four blocks and we arrived. My aunt had set up a double bed in the living room for my sister. She told the men to just put me to bed with Mary. I soon learned this was going to be no fun because I was not as sick as she was. In the daytime, she wanted the blinds pulled, which made it hard for me to read.

Some of my cousins were almost well so that they could now be a help to their mother. Carrying trays and washing dishes helped her very much. Lester, the oldest of the boys, perhaps eleven years old, entertained me. He sat on the edge of the bed and showed me pictures of the terrible flood in Ohio. One man was sitting high up in a tree waiting to be rescued. We also cut out pictures from a catalog.

Papa brought groceries to the door, but we didn't see him for two weeks. I'm sure Aunt Mandy was glad when her nine patients were well again.

Left to Right: **Mae, age 7**
                       Myrtle, age 4
                       Mary, age 10

Chapter Three

*Cousins, first sight of a plane, and
my first job at age 13.*

Papa married again. I thought maybe it would be nice to sit beside of a lady and rest my sleepy head against her arm during Sunday night services. But it was not to be so. I did not know her. She did not know me. She was not used to being with children, which made me more timid and a bit fearful at times. I wanted to love her, but I did not know how to show it. But God often showed me ways to avoid trouble when she became angry. I did the work I was asked to do and then played the organ or read. However, she was a good seamstress and made us girls some nice dresses. We did housework while she sewed.

In two years, a baby boy was born. Robert was a delightful baby. I liked to take him for a ride in the baby cab.

He grew up to be a wonderful Christian young man. He married, but within five years, he died of cancer. He worked as an accountant. I missed him greatly.

We had moved into a new modern house nearer to the school but farther from church, Grandma and my six cousins.

Things were better in the house with modern

conveniences.

Edna, the cousin nearest my age, and I were often together on Sunday afternoons playing games and talking. My aunt and uncle went for a walk, perhaps to visit Grandma and Grandpa, as they often did. It was a lovely summer day. We were outdoors walking around where the beautiful flowers were in full bloom. Edna looked up at me and said, *"Do you ever wish you had some perfume?"*

"I don't know if I ever thought of having some for myself," I said, *"but it sure would be nice to have."*

"Well, I think we could make some out of rose petals," declared Edna. *"Let's get a pan and pick rose petals from the back of the bushes against the house. No one will see."*

So we did just that! We put just a little water in the pan and put the plucked rose petals in. Edna set the pan on the back of the old black cook stove. We went out to play again. We were so sure it would turn out all right. Maybe she would give me a little of the perfume to take home, I thought. Finally we went in the house to see how it was. We were shocked to see the petals and the water black. And how it stunk! So much for that project invention. We went back to our games.

* * * * *

One lovely summer night in my tenth year, Papa came to my bedside to ask if I was asleep. *"I was. What's the matter?" "Nothing. But do you hear a noise?" "Yes. What is it?"*

In a quiet town like Nappanee in the early

part of this century, there was little traffic except for pedestrians. Papa was in a hurry; so he helped me out of bed. Downstairs and through the library and living room we ran. Barefooted and in my nightgown I rushed to the outer sidewalk where the rest of the family and neighbors were all looking toward the sky. The noise was fading away. *"I'm too late,"* I thought. But as our family and friends were talking there in the darkness, we heard the plane coming back again. *"There it is. Do you see it?"* I saw it, or rather the light on the plane and a speck moving through the sky.

The following day, my sister Mary, my cousins and I walked out to a farm where the pilot had parked the plane overnight. How exciting to see a plane close up. The pilot told the people who had gathered there that he would take anyone for a flight over their town for five dollars. I don't know why I felt like I did about the challenge, but I did so much want to take that thrilling trip. I did not have the five dollars that day. Grownups went up and came down with the *"once-in-a-lifetime feeling."* Little did I know that in my adult life, I would be flying across the United States many times, into many countries and islands of the world.

* * * * *

In my tenth year, my stepmother asked Papa to buy an organ for us girls. We were delighted. We couldn't have lessons, but we knew the notes in our church hymnal. So we, each one, taught ourselves. In time we could play all of the

church songs. The first one of us girls who finished eating our meal got to the organ first. It
was being played most of the time after school.

* * * * *

In the fourth grade our teacher, Miss Pletcher,
taught the girls to knit sweaters for our soldier
boys. The teachers knitted the sleeves. We
made only the body of the sweater. The First
World War was severe. Most families had boys
or friends in training or over in France. The day
the war ended, we were in school. The principal
came to our schoolroom and made the
announcement and then dismissed us. That was
a great day for my Grandma and Grandpa
because the following day my Uncle Ike was to
leave the East Coast for the war in France. Not
only Ike, but his sister Lynn, had enlisted as a
nurse and was determined to go overseas, too, if
Ike went. It was a day of celebration, not only
on that day but the next day. Merchants set up
tables down Market Street for a block. Anyone
living in our town could eat all they wanted of
the meat sandwiches and other foods. There
was much talk and rejoicing. While this was
going on, the band was playing. Even the children were banging on cans, pans, or anything
they could find.

* * * * *

This was the year I became interested in
sketching, painting and story-writing. My
teacher was Miss Gee, a lovely young woman
who was interested in her pupils. Every Friday
afternoon she would read us stories like "Brer

Rabbit and The Tar Baby" or "Nights With Uncle Remus" or put a vase of flowers on her desk and ask us to do our best to sketch it. I liked to do that. Sometimes she would place a picture there and ask us how many things we could find in the picture. Then she'd say, *"Now write a story about it."* This stretched our imagination and caused us to think. There were some rather interesting stories written.

This reminds me of a paper I found in my yard one day many years later. An elementary school was located just a block away from our house. On the way home, a child had lost or thrown away a paper with a picture and a story on it. The story was: *"I WENT TO TOWN TO BUY A HAT. I PUT IT ON MY HEAD. ON THE WAY HOME A LITTLE WIND BLEW IT OFF MY HEAD. IT BLEW OVER THE FENCE AND LANDED ON THE HEAD OF A COW. IT LOOKED BETTER ON THE COW."*

How I laughed! I kept it.

* * * * *

I had just finished my seventh grade of school. The summer seemed so long. There was no library in our town. We did have chores to do. We were expected to wash dishes. We cleaned our rooms. Whatever was told us to do, we did. But I was restless and lonely. I often asked, *"What can I do now?"*

Once a summer Dad would put me on the train and send me to my Aunt Della again. The train station was very close to the store in which he worked.

47

While with Auntie that spring, she read an ad in the Goshen newspaper one evening. Dr. Becknel desired a young girl to stay with his wife as a companion. We talked it over, and I said it sounded right for me. I went with Auntie to talk with Mrs. Becknel. They talked. I listened. They talked freely about me and of my duties I would have to perform. All the while I was listening, but at the same time I was looking at all the beautiful volumes of books in the library. After ringing the large doorbell, this nice lady had led us into the library. Little did I know then that much later in my life I would have a husband with a larger library and almost two thousand books.

Oh, what a large home they had. A large porch with large white pillars, columns, that extended from the downstairs porch to the roof of the upper porch. Mrs. Becknel had a housekeeper who cleaned the whole house every other week. My cleaning would be the dusting of all the rooms, except their personal bedroom and bathroom, and a young intern's bedroom. He was seldom there. He left early in the morning and came in too late at night. I believe I saw him only twice that summer. I had always taken the maid's back stairway from the kitchen up to my room. The entrance had a beautiful spiral stairway, which looked very elegant to me. This was to be dusted, too. But the daily work was minimal. I prepared the vegetables and learned to make salads. Mrs. Becknel did all the cooking, and I set the table. The dining room was much larger than the parlor. Actually it was the largest dining room I would ever see in all my travels. We always ate in the dining room, both noon and evening.

After breakfast Dr. Becknel would always say, *"Now, you'll keep the leftover coffee in the refrigerator, won't you, Mae? I'll come home at ten o'clock for a glass of iced coffee."* His office was just across the street. I sat between them at the table. They were very kind to me.

My duties were few. I came to realize that she was growing lonely, for they had no children and were now in their seventies. So we often just sat and talked in the afternoons. Sometimes she'd give me something to read while she did her stitchery.

Dr. Becknell purchased an electric car. It was high and almost square. He would sometimes ask me to go along on an evening call to a patient who lived alone. I'd hold the soup or other nutrients of some kind he thought was needed. I thought it was very kind of him, and it was certainly a great pleasure for me to help a sick person.

I stayed with them all summer until it was time for me to go back to school. They paid me three dollars a week. I bought some shoes and clothes for school. As I left the Becknels, I hoped my life lived in that home brought glory to God, for I had opportunities to discuss spiritual things with them. I was a bashful girl, but as I grew up, I had a great desire to please my Savior.

Chapter Four

*High School, music opportunities,
and dating.*

The summer previous to becoming a freshman in high school, we moved to another town.
We had to make choices of different sorts. One
was a church to attend. A schoolgirl asked me to
visit her Sunday School the first week I was in
town. My father approved of my going with
her. My older sister also accompanied us. We
liked the pastor and his message very much and
urged the whole family to go with us next
Sunday. We were all very happy to join what
turned out in later years to be the Missionary
Church.

My freshman year had many new experiences
for me: new friends, new principal and teachers
with new subjects such as Latin, literature, algebra and home economics. The only subject that
gave me trouble was algebra. But I loved to
learn, and the winter months passed quickly.
However, I missed my friends in Nappanee. It
would be seventy years before I would see some
of my classmates again. Several of us lived our
later years at Hubbard Hill Estates, a residence
for senior citizens.

Soon after school was out in the spring, my
father asked me a very exciting and surprising

question. He had taken a job with Slosser's Creamery Company and needed an assistant. He wanted me to handle it for the summer. I perked up immediately and answered, *"Oh, yes, but what does that mean?"* So he explained. While he was out on the route gathering up the farmer's cream, I was to stay in the cream station to wait on customers. People came in to buy butter, ice cream, and in the spring we sold vegetable plants such as tomato and cabbage plants.

But he also wanted me to test the cream. To do that, I must study a book, then go to Fort Wayne Courthouse to pass an examination before an official. I did. I came home having answered all the questions correctly and was presented with my license.

At first I figured I was only fourteen, too young to do that. But Dad said he knew I could do it and my age did not matter. My Dad was a kind man to work for. I can't remember a cross word he ever spoke to me. He worked hard. Sometimes he'd come back from his route with a funny happening or news from a farmer. When I heard the truck drive in, I would go to the testing room, put on a black leather apron, and be ready to receive the test tubes into which he partially filled with cream. In the course of testing, I had to use carbolic acid. I found the percent of fat in each farmer's test tube, multiplied it by the pounds of cream in the ten-gallon can which Dad had weighed, then figured with the current price what the farmer's check would be. Usually on Saturday they would come in for the checks I had prepared. I met many people, and I thoroughly enjoyed my work that summer. I was growing up fast.

My father would encourage me in anything that I was asked to do. He never pleaded with me. He didn't just say, *"Do it."* He'd say, *"You can do it."* And he'd always tell me how to get started and then walk away. This he did once when I was supposed to speak on a certain subject in church. He gave me a commentary and a Bible. Then he said, *"You can do it."*

Another time in High School literature class, I was one of the students selected for a debate. I couldn't say *"No."* What would my Dad say about that? So I argued my point. Lo and behold, when Miss Sears chose persons to give rebuttals, she called on me. Scared me nearly stiff. Then I suddenly changed my attitude and enjoyed it. I think she gave me a responsibility she thought I needed. We won the debate! Maybe I was not as timid as I thought.

It was difficult to find work in our small town. But I was not too concerned. I was still too young for a real job, I thought; so I helped my stepmother around the house. I was only fifteen. But less than two weeks after school closed, a classmate of mine called on the telephone to ask if I wanted to work. *"Sure,"* I said.

"Well, if you'll be at the square at 6:30 each morning, you can go with me and two others to Elkhart. They have jobs open at the Doll Cab Company. I hope you will go with us."

"I'll ask Dad and let you know right away."

That evening I asked my father. Of course he

wanted to know who was driving the car. All I knew was that he was a country Mennonite boy who was older and seemed to be a responsible person. I had Dad's permission and called my friend. Then I heard more of the particulars. I was to bring my lunch, and we would work ten hours, standing, packing doll cabs in good-sized boxes. We worked on the third floor away from any windows, a half hour break in the morning but no where to go, for the restroom was full of smokers. We were also allowed half an hour at noon to eat our lunch. What a relief to sit down! Then back to work again. The more boxes we packed, the more money we made, which in those days was called "piece work." I was strong and did not mind it as much as some girls did.

However, after a few weeks, my "straw boss" told me to go to the end of the line to do a different job. As the packers shoved their boxes along the bench, I was to close the flaps and with wide tape that I first put through a contraption to wet it, seal the boxes, one long tape lengthwise and one across each end, then slip a corner of the address label under a bit of the wet tape and quickly put it on a large cart until they were stacked probably six feet high. I was to push the cart to the elevator across the room, grab another cart and wheel it back to our work place. I couldn't lose much time because I had to keep up with the line of packed boxes that was being shoved down the line.

Of course I made more money. How good it was to hear the whistle blow at five o'clock.

How relaxing it was to ride those twelve miles home. And how good it was to sit down to a hot prepared supper with the family. The most I ever made in a week was twelve dollars. Three dollars went to the driver of the car, five dollars to my family, and a dollar twenty cents to my church. What I had left for myself was not very much. But I bought a heavy, beautiful sweater for school and a pair of shoes.

My father always insisted that he pay for my schoolbooks and fees. With so many youth quitting school at sixteen years of age, he did not want us to get any idea like that. He needed not to worry, we told him. I loved school, especially literature, Latin, business and art.

God taught me many things that summer. I learned to be helpful and kind to the other workers. I learned to take responsibilities, to know who I was, and to take my place as a Christian in the secular world. The factory was not conducive to good health or good relationships. I aimed for higher things.

A year or so later, the "Child Labor Law" was put into effect.

* * * * *

As to the activities of my teenage years. They were quite limited in our little town. Some of the town young people went to Elkhart at times where there was a theatre. We grew up in a religious community where movies were not approved of. I was satisfied with church, occasional parties and basketball. One fall my father bought me a season ticket. I was so pleased. My older sister was working as a switchboard operator for the telephone company. So she purchased her own ticket. How I loved the game! We went together to the games.

* * * * *

By the time I was sixteen, I wondered if I would soon be asked for a date. Who in the world would it be?

The basketball tournament time came, and who should ask me to go with him but the boy who seemed to me like a brother. He was always advising me that this fellow was not as good or that one would not be right for me. I never asked his advice. He just gave it.

I found that he wanted to date me himself. I asked Dad. He said that since it was a daytime affair, I could go. We double-dated, enjoyed the games, and had lunch. It was a fun day. That was it. As far as I was concerned, he made no impression on me.

In study periods, he would write notes to me because I was assigned to the seat in front of him. I was afraid that the assembly teacher would see it and embarrass us. I never answered the notes. So I told him one day that if he did not quit, I would pass them on to the girl sitting in front of me. He did it once more, and I gave the note to her without reading it. To this day, I don't know what was on it, but it must have been interesting. In time they married each other. I certainly approved, and we were friends for life!

When I was a junior, my music teacher surprised me by handing me two songs to sing for the Junior-Senior Banquet at the new Hotel Elkhart. "Trees" and "Glow Worm" were the titles of them. How nervous I was in the preparation of it. The girl next door to me was an accomplished artist and wanted to practice with me. She was a great help. As the time approached, she also helped select my clothes and arrange my hair.

One of the steady, brainy boys of my class asked me for a date. I was very happy. Having a date and singing solos was very exciting. However, I thoroughly enjoyed the evening. It was again a double date. The boy was a gentleman, but I did not wish to go with him again. I began to sense that God had a certain plan for my life, and I was very willing to wait for the right young man.

* * * * *

Soon after school was out and I had not yet found a summer job, I noticed my stepmother was pregnant. I had just turned seventeen. She was usually sitting at her sewing machine, but this morning she stopped me as I passed her sitting on the davenport in the living room. She asked, *"Would you go downtown and buy a spool of thread? I ran out of white No. 50."*

"Sure," I said. I always liked to do anything that took me out of doors. We lived on the avenue just two and a half blocks from the "square."

So in May, a baby sister, Lois Arlene, was born. She brought more work but much enjoyment and fun.

Lois grew up to be a talented girl, married and has children who have good occupations and ministries.

* * * * *

One Sunday afternoon the telephone rang. I happened to answer. A boy was calling from Elkhart whom I had seen at our family camp, but I had never met him. He wanted to see me that evening. I was still so young that I hated to ask my dad. So I told him I was the songleader for our Sunday night youth service this year. *"Well,"* he said, *"that's fine. I'll go with you."* But I said, *"No, I don't think so."*

The next Sunday afternoon another young fellow called. My sister answered. He asked for me. Oh, I was so thrilled with his call because I had seen him, too, at camp. He came late to that service because of helping his father with chores, he told me years later. I had looked at him then and said to myself – but mostly to the Lord—*"There, that's the kind of friend I want, a good-looking, well built fellow who is brave enough to come to camp alone. He must be a Christian."*

However, I gave him the same pat answer, *"I don't know that I can. You see, I have to lead the singing tonight."* Same answer from him. I hung up and suddenly felt so very sad.

Dad called from the living room and asked if I knew who these boys were who had been calling.

"Well," I said, *"the boy who called last Sunday is a son of one of our preachers. The one who just called*

I don't know much about."

"Mae," he said, *"you can date once in a while if you know they are nice boys."*

"Oh, goody," I thought. *"Now I'm on my own. I have permission! I'll take the next one who calls next Sunday, if they call again. I wouldn't blame them, though, if they didn't."*

I did not know until years later that they were together when they called and that they had dared each other that I would go with them. So the next Sunday, sure enough, one of them did call. It was getting to be quite funny. I think I really shocked him when I said yes, but that I must be on time for the youth service. It was the first boy that had called me, and this was his third call. It was the preacher's son. We dated every other week—which was his father's arrangement—for a whole winter. He was very nice to me and very funny. I never criticized him to others, but I knew he was not for me.

One day I prayed on my knees that God would never let me love a young man who was not God's choice for me. God knew the life I was to live, and I felt a special desire to know and to do His will. I felt so relaxed and never again worried or fretted about the future. You see, I remembered what the Bishop said.

In the spring, I told this young man that I was not interested enough in him to take his time and asked him not to come again. We exchanged nice letters the following week.

The same evening we quit, my sister's boyfriend, although he approved my decision, was surprised and said he had four tickets for the next Friday night's operetta at a distant high school. *"Oh, well,"* he said, *"leave it to me. I know who I'll get for you."* I strongly objected because he would not tell me who he had in mind. But he assured me that I'd be pleased. So I consented.

Friday night soon came. I could barely wait for the doorbell to ring. When I opened the door, there stood the other young fellow who had called me on the phone six months ago. A few weeks before this he had seen me on the street downtown. He wanted to take me home. But I was clerking in a department store every day plus two nights until very late. One night was band concert night and also on Saturday nights. I was ready to go home and go to bed.

But finally we were both happy to be together. Neither one of us ever accepted the company of another. We were married three and a half years later after we finished our education.

* * * * *

My father bought the first family car when I was a junior in high school. He took us three girls to Ohio for a week to visit his relatives. It was a Model T Ford. We thought it was beautiful. We took our lunch along and sat on a hillside to eat it. It was a real fun time with our Dad. We visited in several homes of his cousins. They were very excited to see him after many years. They were very pleased to show off their families, and Dad his.

They were all farmers, and we ate some very delicious food. The strange thing to us was that every morning they served different kinds of cheese at each corner of the table. To me it was an interesting trip. To my knowledge, I never saw them again.

* * * * *

My senior year was quite uneventful. I worked hard at my school lessons and liked to do more outside reading than was necessary. I enjoyed Les Miserables very much. It is a story of the French Revolution, a 1,492–page book. Sometimes I read until midnight to get it finished in time.

On Senior night, our graduation class was to entertain our parents, neighbors, friends, in fact, the townspeople in general. Again I was asked to sing. I cannot remember what I sang. The program was held in the gym. My friend, Quinton, was not able to be there because he was attending Fort Wayne Bible Institute in my senior year of high school. But almost every day I received a letter or note in the mail from him.

Senior Night I felt alone. What I remember most of that night's rendition was that a very gracious lady, who was herself a beautiful singer, approached me immediately after the program. With a smile and words of encouragement she said, *"Mae, that was lovely. You have a talent God wants to use. Sing for His Glory."* I've never forgotten that. Perhaps she did not know I was singing in a mixed quartet in my church. I began thinking seriously that I must be more aware of doing all that I do for the Glory of God.

* * * * *

At the family camp the summer of my seventeenth year, I spent every evening and most of the days enjoying the deep, rich ministry of noted Godly speakers. My heart was thrilled as I drank in the spiritual truths. I knew I was saved when I was very young. Jesus was my Savior and friend. I talked to Him often. I loved to read my Bible and follow Him wherever that would take me. I often felt like crying when the congregation would sing "I'll Go Where You Want Me To Go, Dear Lord. I'll Be What You Want Me To Be." Other girls had their own mothers to talk over intimate things. Oh, how much I missed my mother! No one can take the place of one's own mother. Often times, though, I would suddenly remember what the Bishop said to me the day of her funeral. *"Mae, you miss your mother and you cannot talk with her anymore. But remember you can always talk to God."* It was a very personal thing with me that I never shared with anyone else. What peace He brought to me as I often wet my pillow at night with my tears as I was growing up.

There were and are to this day many of God's people who have helped me in my Christian walk. Many people have made a great impression on my life by their consistent spiritual lives and by their prayers. I praise God for this.

Chapter Five

Assistant teacher for a day.

After I would graduate from high school, my greatest ambition was to attend the Fort Wayne Bible Institute. I did not know why, although my father would rather have had me go to an accredited college so that I would be prepared to teach school. My older sister was teaching at that time. She had attended Bluffton College. I was very interested in teaching, but my heart was drawing me to Bible training, not because Quinton, my friend, was there, for I was making my plans before I knew he was going.

One incident may have influenced my father that I, too, should teach. In my senior year, I had a surprising opportunity. I had just arrived at school, entered the assembly and put my books into my desk. A male student came up to me and said, *"Mae, Principal Gerber wants to see you in his office."* Mr. Gerber was also my botany teacher. So I went to his office rather stiffly and anxious. He looked worried. He said, *"Mae, I had a telephone call from Miss Brunk, and she said her father died last night. She tells me her day's work is all outlined laying on her desk. Would you like to take her place this morning?"* Miss Brunk was the first grade teacher.

How thrilled I was that he considered me to

take this responsibility. I was nervous as I walked down the hall, but it happened so fast that I had little time to think about my emotions. I opened the door, and there was a room of quiet, cute little children. They responded so well to me, that I supposed Mr. Gerber told them why Miss Brunk couldn't be there that day.

After school was dismissed, he walked with me to the center of town. Then our ways parted. While we were walking, he asked me if I ever thought seriously about teaching school. This brought a little conflict to my mind because my pastor's wife walked with me home from church one night and asked me if I had a desire to be a missionary. It gave me a feeling of urgency. I reasoned that I must be close to the time when young people are called of God for special work. This was a very personal realization that I kept to myself. My Aunt Della, knowing of my spiritual concerns, approached me about my education and strongly advised me to go to Bible Institute.

That summer I gave myself completely to the Lord. He always listened to me, guided me and gave me peace. Finding a summer job was difficult. I settled down to waitress work in Goshen. I liked serving people and used my instruction from home economics. But I did not know where to find lodging. The restaurant was not far from Dr. Becknel's home and office. I suddenly thought maybe they would take me in. I wanted so much to see them again. It was five years since I had lived with them for a summer. I walked over to that lovely house. A strange woman answered the doorbell. The lady was kind but said Mrs. Becknell had died and that the doctor lived above his office. I went across the street, rang the bell and waited awhile. He finally came to the door. I told him who I was. He smiled, and then as if he knew I would listen to his sad story, told me of his loss as tears flowed. I told him how sorry I was and asked him if I could do anything for him. He was not well himself but was glad to see me again. I told him I was working nearby and wished so much that I could have had a room in his big house. Immediately he told me he sold it but that I should go back across the street and ask the lady if she could possibly rent me a bedroom. She did, and I stayed until school began in the fall. The Lord again answered my prayers and took care of my needs.

Chapter Six

*Education at Fort Wayne Bible Institute,
and Quinton's first pastorate.*

Now in September 1926, I was settled in the
dorm room at Fort Wayne Bible Institute with a
girl whom I had known for many years. My
schedule and classes were excellent. I felt I was
in a bit of heaven. Church history, Apologetics,
Bible I, Homiletics, Doctrine, Music Notation,
and Choir, Book of John and one semester of
Ezekial, one of Daniel, one of Revelation, the
three missionary journeys of Paul, and Child
Psychology.

Each student took his or her turn giving a
chapel message. Each day it was exciting to
learn who was to bring the message that day.

The school had a requirement that each of us
must do an hour of work each day because the
tuition, board and room was very low.

They didn't know me before I came but put
me in the kitchen after breakfast to wash the
large kettles and frying pans. After a few weeks,
the cook came to me and said, *"I think you would
be a good missionary. You do what you are told and
do it well."*

The next semester I wiped the breakfast dishes for a male student dishwasher. He was a very
funny fellow, Earl Leonard.

Another volunteer job I had was to iron four shirts for Quinton. The fellows were allowed to put only two in the laundry. He could not get along with less than four because he was out on quartet work so often. The President's wife, whom we called Mother Ramseyer, sometimes came through the laundry when I was ironing Quinton's shirts. She would smile and say, *"There's 'May bird.' She's doing her love work again."* She always called me "May bird."

Many times Quinton moved pianos for a piano company for one dollar a job. At times he mowed lawns for fifty cents an hour, or beat carpets for the same amount. The boys usually worked for fifty cents and the girls for thirty cents.

* * * * *

The second week I was placed in a girl's quartet. We traveled weekends to sing in different churches and towns and occasionally at the Friday night Missionary Band.

I wasn't there more than ten days until I received a letter from my high school music teacher telling me she had arranged to get me a scholarship at American School of Music in Chicago. Would I please inform her of my wishes? Well, it wasn't even a temptation. I was so satisfied that I was in the place God wanted me.

* * * * *

The rules of the school were very strict, and our dates did not come often. The daily arrangement was that the boys went west one day; the girls went east. The following day was the opposite. If you had a job that interfered, that was all right. But if you wanted to go to the drug store, you would go to the office and get permission. I had certain girlfriends who walked with me and exchanged questions about our exams. I always got good grades. This association helped us all.

We also had to call each male person by Mister, plus their last name. If Quinton or I would pass each other, we would smile and say *"good morning."* That was all. Then as we passed, we would exchange notes very quickly. Someone told me the first part of the first year that we must send them through the mail. I never asked an authority about it. We just kept doing it.

Once in a hallway near the chapel, we passed notes, when suddenly music Professor Gerber appeared and saw us. He smiled broadly. That cheered us!

Quinton was in a very busy, popular quartet that traveled weekends and often sang in shop meetings at noon. Because we had dated for over a year before we came to school, the faculty finally had compassion on us. One professor asked Quinton to stop at his office. The matter of dating was brought up. I guess he knew how difficult it was for us and that we had not broken rules.

He gave Quinton the key to the reception room for two hours. *"Pull the drapes and lock the door,"* he said. We were to tell no one. These were evening study hours. Students were to be in their rooms or in the library.

Quinton and I sneaked in without being seen, but in less than half an hour we were receiving notes and poems under the door.

My roommate did not know where I was. Others were paying no attention until the curiosity became so great, they couldn't settle down to study. What an evening! We had a good time, and they did, too.

The giveaway? It was Quinton's hat. The hat was placed on a rack in a hallway. He roomed down the street at the home of a brother of the professor's.

The next morning in chapel, a long poem was sent around. We did not know who wrote it. It finally reached me, and I kept it for many years. I've lost it, but not the memory of our special date. The professor gave us a key another time for the office. No one ever knew about that!

A number of years after graduation, Quinton was elected as a board member and had the pleasure of helping to change some of the rules for the betterment of the students.

Now most colleges lack the good rules.

We were thrilled when holidays arrived so we could go back home and be together. The years went quickly.

* * * * *

One special experience we had before graduation was an invitation for me and the wife of one of the men's quartet members to accompany Dr. S. A. Witmer to Peoria, Illinois to a large church for meetings over the weekend. We were about to graduate; so Dr. Witmer thought it nice for us to go along. It was a lovely trip with fun and pleasant conversation.

On Saturday morning we were told that a certain man had planned an unusual day for us. He wanted to take us to Pekin for a look at a coal mine. I don't know what the professor thought about it. The group seemed to think it would be quite a new experience and decided to go. I don't know why Lorraine and I went, only that we were too ignorant about the whole thing to refuse.

When we arrived, it was misting and chilly. The guide said, as he arranged his cap with the little light on it, *"We'll be going down 850 feet into the earth on this elevator."* No one said anything. We just followed him. Down this old shaft we traveled.

This was on Saturday; so the workmen were not down there.

We walked awhile, standing straight, but after several turns, we bent over and had to go slower. It seemed to me it was getting harder to breathe. I finally said to Lorraine, *"I believe I'm getting sick!"*

The men heard me. The guide said, *"Why don't you sit here until we come back. Be sure to sit right there."*

"How long will it take?" I asked. I don't remember what he said. But Lorraine was a very pleasant person. I was so glad to have her with me. On the way up the elevator, the guide said that since the men were not working, the air shaft was not on. No wonder I felt as I did.

Lorraine admitted, too, she was glad to sit it out. How wonderful it felt to be on top of the solid earth and breathe deeply, even of the misty air.

* * * * *

Finally graduation came. Quinton was class president. He had responsibilities and activities at the close of school. His quartet and mine sang at the graduation commencement ceremony. Before our class said our last good-byes, we were called together for prayer. Each prayed a short prayer. Each seemed to be sure of their calling and thanked God for it. But Quinton and I did not have the assurance of what or where God would lead us.

I remembered then of an experience I had a couple of months before. It was in the afternoon when I was very tired of studying that I suddenly stopped and laid on my bed. I did not nap but was wide awake thinking of the future and wanting to be certain not to make unwise choices. I mentioned this to the Lord. I suddenly saw a picture on the closet door of Quinton and I holding hands and walking upward toward a bright light. Back, below and all around as far as I could see were people. It was as if I had been somewhere and now saw this crowded scene again.

I said in my thoughts to the Lord, *"What does this picture mean? Why am I seeing this?"* And these words came to me. *"These are the souls you are going to win for me."*

I could hardly take it all in. That was between the Lord and me, and I didn't tell anyone about it, only Quinton, after many years. I suppose it was a vision. I had such peace and felt our lives were in God's hands. I never was surprised at the great opportunities that were sent to us after we were married.

However, after the commencement service was over, our District Superintendent came to Quinton, congratulated him and promptly asked him to preach for the next two Sundays at a little church in Union, Michigan. He indicated that the church may soon be closed if he could not find a pastor for it. But Quinton said, *"I've never preached one sermon. I've taught a Sunday School class only three times. I've only given my testimony as our quartet traveled."*

"All right. Then give your testimony. Surely after you've studied the Bible these years, you can fill in for two Sundays."

We were not married yet. I worked at the Bethel Publishing Company for eight months, filling orders of Sunday School supplies and books. I loved my job. I wanted to work to pay off my school debt of ninety dollars first. Quinton bought a truck and bread route to earn money for our marriage. He was free of debt.

I had been working as I had opportunity during the school months by doing anything I was able to do, but the pay was very low. For example, Mondays I ironed twenty starched white shirts for a businessman and his three sons. His wife expected me to do six in one hour, at thirty cents per hour.

One day one of my friends asked me to help her dish up plates and serve several courses at a women's club dinner that evening at seven o'clock. It was not far from the school. It sounded like quite a job, but she encouraged me with, *"Oh, it will be fun."* It probably will be, I thought, because she was a funny girl.

The hostess came for us. Then she told us when to start serving. Now we were on our own. Flora said she would fill the plates while I served. Then she would serve while I dished up. Of course, when they were eating their dessert, we were washing dishes and cleaning up the kitchen. She was very pleased with our work and paid us well.

When she took us back to the school, she held me back in the car to talk to me about my Christian life. I gave her my testimony and encouraged her to give her life to Christ.

* * * * *

For two weeks, Quinton traveled eighteen miles to the little white church preaching Sunday mornings and evenings. On Wednesday evenings, he traveled again to conduct the Bible study and prayer meetings. Oh, how he studied and prayed! It was a real testing time. At the end of two weeks, the District Superintendent did not contact him. By the end of the week, his mother became very concerned. *"Are you going up to Chapel Hill next Sunday or not? If you don't go, maybe there will be no preacher there."*

So Quinton said he would go see if another showed up. There was no other to take the services; so he continued on for two and a half years! When he first went there, only nineteen people were present. The few children and young people liked the new preacher because he preached only seven and a half minutes in the first service. His first sermon text was *"If God be for us, who can be against us?"* The young people liked him for his short sermons.

As a result of his faithfulness to the Lord and to the people, it grew rapidly. In the summer he had tent meetings and Daily Vacation Bible School. In the winter, he would have a special evangelist come for a two-week revival meeting. God used Quinton in many ways because he learned to know the people by visiting homes, every home. Many people were being saved.

Quinton and Mae, *"Our Wedding Day."*

Chapter Seven

Marriage and Honeymoon.

Our wedding took place in the home of my sister Mary in Wakarusa on February 16th, 1929, at six o'clock on Saturday evening. There were thirty-two in attendance.

My bridesmaid was Arveda Wooliman, and the best man was Clifford Grabill. He brought her, which turned out to be their first date. Later they, too, were married. She had been a member of my quartet. Clifford had been Quinton's roommate.

We were married by Rev. A. B. Yoder. Quinton's sister Pauline played "The Wedding March" as we came down the open stairway.

My dress was white crepe with long sleeves and butterfly pleats in the skirt. The bride's bouquet was made up with white rosebuds and baby's breath. Arveda wore a lovely blue crepe dress.

Immediately after opening the gifts and having refreshments, we drove to Elkhart for picture taking. It was eleven o'clock when we were finished.

On Sunday morning, our attendants accompanied us to Chapel Hill Church where Quinton preached, and they gave their testimonies. Because of his job and his church, there was no possibility for a honeymoon for two years.

We lived with Quinton's parents after our wedding day until September. They were very kind to us, but we needed to have our own home. We found a little bungalow on Lane Avenue that rented for $35.00. We lived there from September until spring. To save money, we moved five times in seven years, the duration of the time we lived in Elkhart and were at the Zion church. Later we found a house on Pleasant Plain for $28.00. This was a very nice house. We were very happy there. But the people of our congregation were losing their jobs. Some people stood in long lines downtown for staple foods from a government subsidy called a commissary. It was in the middle of the Depression.

So we moved again. Just next door the house was empty and rented for $14.00. This was a great help to us financially, but it had only a bathroom stool. We had to go back to our childhood of bathing in a washtub. We put up with it for a year. During this time our first child, Betty Charlene, was born. She was born in the hospital on Labor Day while the Elkhart City Band was playing in the McNaughton Park beneath the window. I felt like a million dollars. How beautiful she was and precious.

But soon we were moving again, always closer to the church. Now we were paying eleven dollars per month. The owner was a lady who owned nineteen houses. Many of them were empty. There were many empty houses all over the city because young couples were going home to their parents to live, or parents were living with their children. Our landlady asked my husband if he would paint the house. She would give him three months rent-free. He readily consented. It was quite new and very adequate.

* * * * *

It was two years after our marriage that we decided to take our honeymoon. Most couples had to wait a while because of finances. We had no children yet; so we saved and planned until we had the date set. Our car was too old and unreliable. So Quinton bought a new four-door, soft green Chevrolet. He bought a small camp stove.

Near the time to leave, Quinton's parents said to him one day, "If you'll take your two sisters along, we'll give you twenty-five dollars." So Marie and Pauline shared our honeymoon!

In 1931, there weren't many tourists making long trips. We had a map and a few instructions from his father. A few years before, his parents had made a trip to his cousins' ranch thirty miles south of Pueblo, Colorado.

It was quite an adventure. Quinton and I were twenty-three years old, his sisters Pauline and Marie, eighteen and fifteen. But we were all anxious to get started on this "fun" trip. Quinton had always worked very hard, as had I, which made it so exciting and relaxing to think of riding "West" to see our country and enjoy the fresh air. Our aim was to see Yellowstone Park, the Black Hills and his cousin Kreider's big ranch.

There were no motels in those days. We drove until we observed a "Tourist Home" sign. We were careful to stop in a clean community and always found a welcome among reputable people. Usually they would serve us suppers as well as breakfasts. The cost was about five dollars including supper and breakfast for the four of us. The first thing we did was to scrub up. Oh, how good it felt after driving all day on the dusty gravel roads. After crossing Illinois, it was either dusty or muddy. Beyond Illinois the main highways were not yet paved. At the end of the day we would often look at each other and say, *"My, you look funny."* Then we'd look in the mirror and realize we all looked strange. So we'd start laughing, stop laughing, and then start laughing again, because the laugh-lines made deep tracks on our faces.

Kansas was a hot state. We could see miles of golden wheat. All but the driver would sometimes hang their bare feet out the car windows. Sometimes in some states we would drive for forty miles without seeing a house. So we had to watch the time and plan ahead for an hour or two.

On the first morning after the day's journey, Quinton got out the camp stove and made breakfast for us, bacon and eggs. I cleaned up the mess, and he packed the things back in the trunk.

Sometimes the day was a bit boring, but, oh, the lift we got from the first view of the mountains. All I had seen, up to that time, were pictures.

Our first destination was to be the Floyd Kreider Ranch. We drove thirty-two miles on a gravel road south, out from Pueblo, Colorado, nothing to see along the way but a fence on the right side of the road, the telephone wire stretched along the fence. We had no idea the area would be that bleak.

When we arrived, they were so happy to see us, for they seldom ever saw family members. It was nearly suppertime. The father, Floyd, and son, Bill, were already in from chores. Their married daughter from a neighboring ranch was also there to get acquainted with her relatives.

They seemed anxious to sit down to eat supper. We soon understood the reason. We were not eating as hurriedly as they were. Mrs. Kreider explained that by dusk the moths would get so thick on the screen doors and windows that no air could get into the house. She needed to blow out the lamps. We hurried to get the dishes washed. Then we finished the evening in darkness. The family was very gracious to us and asked us many questions. Some of us slept on the floor in front of the door. The weather was very warm. There were no trees but cotton trees in that whole area. The white cotton balls were in the air everywhere.

The next day we needed to get on our way again. The girls wanted to ride the ponies. They were up by the house; so the men helped them on. They did not go far. At least they could say they had a horseride. Then everyone was calling Quinton, telling him to get on the little horse.

Horseriding was not new to him, for he had grown up on a farm and rode his father's horses. But his animal did not "take" to him. It balked and threw him off to the ground quickly, and before he could manage to get up, the horse fell on his lap. I was so scared. I had the camera in my hands, but so quickly did it happen that I failed to take the picture. He was not hurt!

We were packed; so soon we gave our good-byes and left. They were so glad to have some of their family come to visit. They kissed, hugged us, then cried and waved. Years ago they had moved out there from Elkhart County for health reasons.

It was so good to be on our way again. Denver, Colorado Springs, the Garden of the Gods with mountains all around were so delightful.

Quinton took a trip up Pikes Peak. We didn't go with him. We were glad we didn't.

As we neared Yellowstone and came to Cody Road, we saw the mountains we were to climb, but the beauty of it all seemed to take the fear away. It was gorgeous to be right in the mountains.

As we drove up to the cabin we were to occupy, a man came up to Quinton with a good-sized pan of fresh fish. He acted as if he was our friend and glad to see us. He said, *"I know it's suppertime. You must be hungry. We thought you'd like some fish I caught today."*

Well, we heartily thanked him. I got busy and fried fish. How very good it was. I believe we had fish, bread and fruit that evening.

80

After supper I said, *"I'm going down to the restroom."* This was down a path quite away from the cabin. Marie went with me. When we came out and started to walk back to the cabin, we felt the ground shake, looked up and saw a large bear tearing down the path straight at us. I whispered, *"Just be quiet and walk slowly."* We were scared. It thundered straight on past us, on past the "outhouse." Suddenly it stopped. There were her little cubs, and she was protecting them. We turned to see where the bear was and then hurried to the cabin.

It was very cold that night. We used all the covers and coats we had. Later Quinton got up and lit the camp stove.

"Old Faithful" and the other attractions were most interesting, but we hurried on to the Black Hills of South Dakota. Every day we saw new and beautiful things. This is the handiwork of God, I thought. What marvelous things are made for our enjoyment.

Perhaps it was six years later when Quinton and I took Charlene, age four, to see the Kreiders again at the ranch.

The first morning after breakfast we all went out to see the Kreider men and their neighbors brand a lot of cattle.

The Kreiders had miles of land (sections). Bill's job was to periodically ride out to count the newborn and see about their health.

In the afternoon they took us to a parade and rodeo where Billy turned out to be the winner.

Billy and his wife had a little girl the same age as Charlene.

Chapter Eight

Revivals, beginning of 50 years
of broadcasting the Gospel.
The Depression.

News got around, and when conference time came, the Zion church in Elkhart, Indiana, asked if Quinton would consent to be their pastor. He prayed about it and felt there was a great need in the south part of Elkhart.

In the two and a half years of preaching, he had never felt a clear call of God to preach. But doors for service kept him busy, and his heart and mind were open to God's will. That was what he wanted most in life, to do God's will.

Zion church was struggling to exist. The opportunities were tremendous because of the population of children in the area. The Sunday School was growing over one hundred, but there were very few adults.

The Depression was on. This was 1932. Jobs were scarce. However, there was very little thievery. People planted large gardens and canned hundreds of quarts of fruits and vegetables each summer. We all shared food and clothes. Quinton and I were so happy, we didn't think of being poor. Our free will offerings were given us on Sunday nights in hard cash. No dollar bills until later on. We could not afford a phone for a while. The young people finally had one installed for us at the price of $1.25 per month. The sanctuary needed to be painted. Quinton did it by himself. One man handed him a dollar bill. It was my father.

Quinton's sermons were improving, but he felt he did not have a definite call from the Lord to preach. So he took three days off work to fast and pray about it. One morning he felt relieved of this great burden. A great desire came over him to sell his bread route and give full time to study, pray, preach, and visit every home in the Zion area. This meeting of the people in their homes was very beneficial.

About noon that day, a young man came to our door. Quinton knew him well. *"Quinton,"* he said, *"I heard you want to sell your bread route."*

"Well, I don't know how you heard that, but I do."

"How much do you want for it?"

Quinton stated the amount he wanted, and Willy said, *"Good. I'll be back this afternoon with a check for that amount."*

What a turning point in our lives. We would now live on faith. Nothing hindering from the work of the Kingdom. Because we had no money for gasoline, he rode his bicycle up and down the streets.

* * * * *

For food, we planted a large garden. One summer he also planted the vacant lot next to our house. Every other day he bicycled two miles to his parents' home in the country to get milk. They had a dairy farm. Fruit we got from the farm, too. In the fall when his father butchered, we were given meat. With it we made beef vegetable soup and canned one hundred quarts. I had five hundred quarts of soup, vegetables and fruit.

I seldom went shopping unless for fabric to make clothes. If Quinton needed better undershorts, I'd go to the "rag bag" upstairs, find two that had holes, then make one good one. If he had holes in his socks, I darned them. One year I became very anemic and stopped sewing for awhile. Charlene, our first child, was two or three years old when I bought her dresses at McClelean's Dime Store for twenty cents. For a Sunday dress with a white collar, I paid twenty-five cents. Feed sacks that were made of flowered cotton we also used to make little girl's dresses.

* * * * *

Another problem we had was the need of refrigeration. So far we had none. There was an iceman that served the homes with ice every other day, but we had no refrigerator. Well, the basement was quite cool; so Quinton chopped a hole in the basement floor, and we placed butter and milk in there.

Later in that house, we did get an ice refrigerator.

When Charlene was four years old, Quinton James Jr. was born. It was a very hot August night when I was awakened by pain. Quinton had to go about eight miles to bring the attending nurse. So while he was gone, I dusted the furniture and floors. The night was so hot that my husband dismantled our bed, brought it downstairs, and reassembled it in the dining room. At five o'clock, we called Dr. Work who told us he'd come immediately, no reason to go to the hospital. By six o'clock in the morning, we welcomed a handsome ten-pound baby boy into our family.

At age sixty, Quinton James, Jr. still likes to tell people he was born in the dining room.

* * * * *

This was the year of the dust storms in the mid-western states. Even in our town, it was visible in the air, and the housewives would dust their furniture every day. Hundreds of farmers in the west lost their farms because of the loss of the topsoil. We had no trees. It was a miserable summer, but we were happy.

Quinton was becoming well acquainted with the community. By this time, the church leaders were feeling the need of revival. One retired minister of our congregation came to him privately and urged him to be their evangelist. Usually we had special outside speakers who were full-time evangelists. Quinton declined the invitation, feeling he was too young, at twenty-five, and inexperienced. The man later asked him again, saying that he had been praying much about this. Others felt the same way. After seeking the Lord's will in prayer, he finally consented.

A great burden for lost souls came upon him. He preached night after night for two or three weeks. As he gave the call to accept Jesus as Savior, many came to do just that. Many railroad men hardened by sin and whole families were born into the Kingdom of God. Forty-two converts were added to the church. This was, no doubt, the beginning of his great love for souls and pull toward evangelism. People stood around the walls and filled the lobby. The church was packed.

He formed a men's quartet, of which he was a part, that sang on radio station WTRC for half an hour each Sunday afternoon from 5:00 to 5:30.

One day the manager called Quinton and said he would like him to put on a religious program. Radio was new, and WTRC had just opened up shortly before this. *"Oh, Mr. Baker, I'm not a radio preacher."*

"Well, we think you are. Think about it."

Later he asked him again.

"How much would it cost to broadcast a half hour?" Quinton finally asked Mr. Baker.

"Five dollars," he said.

"That's more than I get in the Sunday offering. But I'll ask the Board." He asked the church Board, and they said it would be impossible. So Quinton went to his study room, got on his knees and asked God again about this. He finally opened his Bible, and his eyes fell upon Jeremiah 33:3. *"Call upon me, and I will answer thee and show thee great and mighty things which thou knowest not."* This became his special lifetime verse. That seemed clear enough to him. If it was the money that was the hindrance, then God would take care of that.

THE WAY WILL OPEN

Child of my love, fear not the unknown
morrow,
Dread not the new demand life makes
of thee;
Thy ignorance doth hold no cause for
sorrow
Since what thou knowest not is known
to me.

Thou canst not see today the hidden
meaning
Of my command, but thou the light
shall gain;
Walk on in faith, upon My promise lean-
ing,
And as thou goest all shall be made
plain.

One step thou seest—then go forward
boldly,
One step is far enough for faith to see;
Take that, and thy next duty shall be
told thee,
For step by step thy Lord is leading
thee.

Stand not in fear thy adversaries count-
ing,
Dare every peril, save to disobey;
Thou shalt march on, all obstacles sur-
mounting,
For I, the Strong, will open up the way.

Therefore go gladly to the task assigned
thee,
Having My promise, needing nothing
more
Than just to know, where 'er the future
find thee
In all thy journeys I go before.

* * * * *

Quinton got on his bicycle and started for the
mayor's office. He told Mr. Paxton his great
concern. *"Sure,"* said the mayor, *"I'll give you
seventy-five cents."*

From there, he got the attention and interest of
other people who gave twenty-five cents or fifty
cents. Nothing larger than fifty cents until he
had four dollars. Not far from our house was a
dairy. The Cook brothers owned it, and he knew
them quite well. He thought of them one day.
The first one he encountered was Claude. The
men were unsaved, but Claude said, *"Sure, I'll
make up the last dollar."*

Now the work of studying and praying for
another sermon each week increased his burden.
Besides that, he must go collect these radio offerings. Mr. Baker was delighted. Later on we had
a revival meeting for several weeks, and Mr.
Baker gladly gave from 7:30 to 9:00 of broadcast
time for $16.50 per night. The men of the church
said it cost too much. Anyway, they thought
people would stay at home to listen. But before
the meetings ever began, Quinton announced on
his Sunday broadcast the coming revival meetings and the cost for airtime. The bill was paid

before the meetings started.

This was a time of proving the promises of God. The church again was filled every night with people standing in the foyer. Many were the answers to prayer in those days. One revival lasted six weeks.

In the summers, we conducted two weeks of Daily Vacation Bible School for the community children. These programs were set up for much memorizing of scripture, singing and Bible teaching. On the night of the last day, the children gave a program to their parents and relatives. The church was always crowded, and the children performed well. How thrilling for us to hear the great number of children quoting chapters and long portions of scripture.

The last year we were there, the church bought a parsonage. Quinton was asked to hold a revival meeting in a distant place. Before he arrived home, the leaders of the church told me that they were going to move our furniture into the property that they had bought. I had not the privilege to see it before we moved there. I was thankful they took the responsibility, but I did not know where or how they would arrange things. However, I had the two young children to concern myself with, without worrying about that.

The house was brick and quite adequate. But I was amazed when I went into the kitchen and found no water there. The water sink and faucets were on the enclosed back porch, which was cold in the winter. Or we could go down the hall past the stairway and bedroom to the bathroom and fill the teakettle there.

So we were in strange circumstances when the day came for me to go to the train station to pick up Quinton. When we drove south on Morton Avenue I said, *"I'll take you down to see the new parsonage the church bought."* So we went on to Main Street. I drove into the driveway. He got a strange feeling. *"You don't mean we are living here?"*

"Yes," I said. *"The men thought it would save you a lot of time and effort if they would have us settled in by the time you came home."* He was grateful for their kindness. But when he learned of the lack of water in the kitchen, he was very concerned for the inconvenience I had daily.

Another revival was soon scheduled, and in those days the evangelists usually stayed at the parsonage. This time not only did he bring his wife, which was fine for me, but his secretary also. Getting three meals each day, washing dishes, sharing the bathroom, bathing my little ones and doing the laundry was quite a burden for me. Of course, being in the church on time to find a seat for the children and myself was a trick in itself. But, oh, how I did enjoy the meetings. And just to sit back and relax. My strength was renewed, and I felt God was so good to me, for I had great blessings from being hospitable to these special servants of the Lord.

* * * * *

At our District Conference one year, Quinton was voted to be the Youth Director. In those early years, not much attention was given to the youth at our family camps. He was determined to get the attention and interest of the youth. Most of them attended only on Sundays. The tabernacle seated two thousand people. Many of the young people came with their families but stayed outside.

After dinner on Sundays, the adults and small children would gather in the Tabernacle, but the youth would walk back and forth down the wooded drive where the cars were parked. Some sat in the cars.

So Quinton thought, *"If they won't come into the Tabernacle, I'll go to them."*

He contacted a few of our best youth singers in our conference, and with his trombone to lead the singing, went to the beautiful driveway where scores and scores of the youth were.

The music drew their attention. Everyone started singing. Then Quinton preached to them. This was a success, but what about the other ten days of the camp?

Soon afterwards, we, as a family, traveled to Stayner, Ontario, where Quinton was the evangelist at their family camp. We were amazed at the number of youth attending the camp and were determined to find out what interested them so much that they spent all ten days and nights there.

We noticed, first of all, that a much older man than Quinton was the director. He was Dr. Erb, a prominent doctor, in the province. He really had a big heart for the youth and took great interest in the unsaved ones.

He set up many tents. He held Bible studies

mornings. In the afternoons, they played ball. Then they cleaned up before supper. They were all required to attend the evening meetings.

We were thrilled with what we saw and the bond of love for each other and for the doctor.

Quinton came back and told those over him what he wanted to do. They said it wouldn't work!

He said, *"I'll try it."* He did, and the first camp they set up nine tents. They were full. It rained most of the time with water running into the tents. No one went home.

In a few years they built dormitories and showers. A great number of our youth have been saved, some called to the ministry or mission fields, at our camps. Our Prairie Camp has been in existence for 118 years.

* * * * *

Other churches were engaging Quinton for evangelistic meetings, so often that he made it a rule to be in his own church on Sunday mornings. One of the churches he served as evangelist was in the Brenneman Memorial Church in Goshen. After that wonderful outpouring of the Holy Spirit in saving and sanctifying power, other churches began looking to him for leadership.

Chapter Nine

Scarlet Fever, chicken pox, polio,
tornadoes and World War II.

The following spring, the Annual Conference moved Quinton to Goshen, Indiana, to become their new pastor. The attendance at Zion was then around 340 when we left Elkhart. He had ministered at Zion for seven and a half years.

Quinton talked to the leaders of the Brenneman Memorial Church of Goshen about the parsonage. They promised to build an additional bedroom and half bath downstairs. Quinton preferred having his study room upstairs. The new bedroom would be used for the many guests we entertained.

We loved the house. However, a factory was next door. This required scrubbing the long front porch every Saturday. There was also a train track one block away. Many tramps jumped off at our street and headed for our house at mealtime. We never turned them away hungry. They sat on the back steps to eat and then went away. We kept a set of silverware and a plate especially for them.

There was no hot water heater. This required me to carry a tea kettle of boiling water through the kitchen, dining room, living room, up the stairs and down the hall to the bathroom for the children's baths. In a few months, we had a water heater installed. What a wonderful help!

Now we needed to get rid of the rats living in the basement. They were burrowing in under the new bedroom, then running around the laundry room. Quinton put poison where they were coming in and finally got rid of them. How relieved I was when it was time to do the family washing. In those days, we boiled the rinsed-out diapers. No "throw-aways" in the 1930's. Washing was a chore!

We had a lovely garden each summer. My husband was a great gardener. He also loved to plant flowers. All through our married life I had plenty of vases of flowers. And the vegetables kept us healthy with well-balanced meals.

Quinton bought white sugar sand and built a sandbox for the children. Each spring he would buy clean sand.

Young Q.J., Jr. was four years old when he began begging for a dog. A farmer friend of ours heard about his love for puppies and gave him one. That meant a fence for the back yard. There were no boys in the neighborhood, but we supplied him with boyish things with which to play. Also he liked to help his father in the garden with his own little garden tools. I loved to watch them working together.

The children loved to hear the stories I read to them before they could read for themselves. Charlene seemed especially attentive one day while I was reading about Jesus, when He was twelve years old and talking to the priests in the temple. She stopped me, put her finger on the head of one of the men in the picture and said, *"My daddy wears his hair on his head."* She must have never seen a bald head with long hair on a chin.

* * * * *

When Charlene was six years old, we desired so much to find a piano teacher for her. Having been in the town for less than a year, we didn't know how to start searching for one. We wanted the best piano instructor we could find. One Sunday night after church, we were visiting with people outside the church building. Mrs. Ella Moyer came to me and said, *"I hear you are looking for a piano teacher. My neighbor has been teaching for many years and has been very successful with the Robyn Course. Her students have become noted for their touch and technique. She has sixty students now. I do hope she can take Charlene."*

I was so astonished. I thanked her profusely.

That very week we called on Mrs. Pletcher, and she accepted her. For the remaining years we lived in Goshen, the three children took lessons of her, and for several years after we moved to South Bend, we traveled back and forth, summer and winter, to Mrs. Pletcher's studio, which was in her home. A beautiful and kind person with such patience I had never seen. She certainly loved children but was very exact in her teaching.

Our children were soon studying under Professor Ray Weaver. He often said he would rather teach advanced students from Mrs. Pletcher than any other teacher he knew.

Charlene first heard Professor Raymond Weaver at a concert and was so impressed that she stood in the aisle the whole time to see his fingers. She always wanted to play like that. She was then four years old.

The lovely Wellington piano that Quinton bought for my first Christmas present after we were married was certainly put to good use for many years.

* * * * *

The spring we moved to Goshen little Q.J. got very sick. He was not quite two years old. His dad was in Detroit conducting evangelistic meetings. I was six months pregnant. His fever climbed higher each day, and I expected him to break out with measles, for he was exposed to them. The pediatrician said as the fever approached 105 degrees that I should give him hot tea to drink. He said it would drive the measles out and the fever would go down. I gasped and asked him twice if he didn't mean cold tea. *"No,"* He again said *"hot tea."* I quickly called my Elkhart doctor, but he was out of town. However, Dr. Todd, who worked with our Dr. Work, said firmly, *"Mrs. Everest, it makes no difference what the pediatrician said. Please put a chair close to his bed, sit on it, and every fifteen minutes throughout the night give him cold water to drink. Don't go to sleep. Lay your head on the railing of his crib."*

I prayed with great earnestness that God would help us through the night. My love went out to him as I prayed and tried to trust the

96

Lord. I watched the clock, and every fifteen minutes I raised his head, and he gulped down some more cold water.

By daylight I could see his skin turning pink. I had bathed his face in cold water, too. Throughout the day, the measles showed more and more. How I thanked God. But he was sick for some time. We spent much time together entertaining each other. When Quinton was still in Detroit, he kept in touch with me by telephone concerning Q.J.'s progress. He was sorry to be away from home.

After we thought he was doing very well, we were given a week to spend at a cottage at Wawasee Lake by one of our church families. It was lovely weather, and the four of us could be together playing and resting from the duties of church and parsonage.

But the second morning we had a shock. Little Q.J. got up. I started to dress him for breakfast. Suddenly I saw a lump as large as half a baseball in back of his ear. I wanted to cry out for help, but I forced myself to quietly ask him if it hurt him. He said, *"No."* Then I carried him out to the kitchen to show his daddy. We both knew it was a mastoid. We finished our breakfast but did not take time to do anything that was not necessary. All of us got into the car and started for Elkhart. I held him tightly all the way. We were so frightened but only told him we must ask the doctor about it.

Our good family doctor sent us immediately to a specialist. After examining him and learning that he had had measles, he gave us some information about a new drug called sulfa. He told us how to administer the medicine. The specialist said he had a fifty-fifty chance that he would not need surgery. Oh, how we prayed.

One day he broke out with hives. It was a side effect of the sulfa, the doctor said. That night Quinton wrapped a blanket around himself and headed for the study room to pray. This had to be settled. We were doing all we could for our little boy whom we loved so dearly, but we needed help and healing from the One who has all power. He spent most of the night seeking God's will. God answers prayer and gives peace. We became more confident and were happy knowing God had taken the case. Although the sulfa had brought his hemoglobin down for a while, he gradually built up the red blood cells, and strength returned. Later another medicine was added to sulfa which did away with the worst of the side effects.

* * * * *

Another joy was ours when little Sharon Jeanne came into our lives. The night she was born, I got up at 1:00 a. m. to swat at the mosquitoes. Couldn't sleep with them buzzing around. Quinton woke up and saw me standing on the bed with a rolled-up magazine trying to reach the ceiling. He got up quickly and helped me. Then pain started to interfere with my work; so I stopped. By seven o'clock, the good Dr. Work from Elkhart had come and an attending nurse. *"Another 10 ¹/₂ pound baby girl! What will you name this one?"* the doctor asked.

A Rose of Sharon bush was growing just outside our bedroom window. *"Let's call her Sharon,"* I said. Then Quinton said, *"Jeanne would sound well with Sharon."* He had just come home from a distant city where he preached at a citywide campaign. A beautiful nine-year-old girl was saved. He thought at that time if it was to be a girl he would want her named Jeanne. She was our curly blond. Charlene and Quinton James were out on the farm with Grandpa and Grandma Everest. Little Q.J. was lonesome for his mother, and I for them. It was so nice to be together again.

> *"One beautiful day in the summertime*
> *When the scent of the flowers filled the air,*
> *A princess came into the kingdom*
> *A princess with gold hair.*
>
> *Her eyes were as blue as the summer sky*
> *Her cheeks like the roses so fair.*
> *And even the angels loved her*
> *And gave her gifts so rare."*

It did seem that Sharon had the gift of music from birth, as did all our children. I was giving her daily baths on my lap yet when at ten months she was singing the chorus of Jesus Loves Me, just the tune with *"da, da, da, da,"* etc. By the age of two, she often stood in front of the piano. With our family looking on amazed, she found harmony by putting her left forefinger on a note, held it down, and with the right forefinger pressed down on one key after another until she found one that harmonized with the left one. Then she'd play both keys again and again with a happy face. She would change then to another key with her left hand and try again to find a key to harmonize with the right hand.

We had a radio, too, that interested her. She turned the knob, dialed around to hear some music. We often laughed when she stopped quickly to hear an opera singer. There she stood facing the radio so very interested.

Though we had more illness and tragedies at Goshen, we were very happy and loved to serve the people there. Several great missionary conventions occurred with outstanding speakers. Q.J., Jr. was very impressed with Dr. George Warner of World Gospel Missions. His messages tugged on his heart. He loved the man and wanted to sit side of him at the table.

We always had family worship every day, which helped our children spiritually. The atmosphere in a home has so much influence on children as they mature. As they reached the age when they could read, we allowed them to take their turn to read the Bible and pray. Oh, how we loved to hear them. We all prayed for each of the family and help for the day.

* * * * *

Charlene was saved when she was four years old. That happened at Zion Church in Elkhart. When the evangelist gave the altar call, she was suddenly crying. She asked me for a hanky and rushed to the altar. I was holding our baby Q.J. and stayed in the pew when I saw her daddy kneel in front of her. She prayed, and Quinton prayed. She stood then and smiled. That was the beginning of her Christian life.

The next Sunday, her little girlfriend went to the altar, and Charlene quickly followed her. They knelt, and I saw Charlene put her arm around Patsy and began praying for her. What a blessing it was to see this concern for her friend.

Her Sunday School teacher came to tell me after service one morning that Charlene was like a little mother to her classmates. If their shoes needed tying, she tied them. If their nose ran, she gave them a hanky!

* * * * *

Q.J. was saved when he was seven years old. I had been sick with anemia and in bed for six weeks. At that time the family doctors seemed to have little knowledge of help for a low hemoglobin. Drink lots of milk, eat beefsteak every day, and get plenty of rest. Rest, I did, for I was so weak I could barely turn myself over in bed. We had hired a girl to cook, clean and do laundry. But I ached to care for my children.

While I was so weak, little Q.J. came rushing to my bed one Sunday night after church was over. He must have run all the way home, for he seemed out of breath. He bent over me and said excitedly, *"Mama, do you know who got saved tonight?"* As I looked into his sparkling eyes, I started to ask, *"Was it you?"* But he didn't wait a bit. He just said crisply, *"I did."* Then he told me all about the meeting. *"Oh, I wish I had been there,"* I said.

There were many times after a Sunday morning church service that he would run ahead of us and go to his bedroom. This went on for sometime. I finally took the courage to go to his room when he was downstairs. There I found a little bunch of papers folded to look a bit like his daddy's sermon notes. He hurried home to write down a few thoughts and sentences that he wanted to remember. He was ready for the second grade when we left Goshen. He was very young to try organizing his thoughts on scripture.

During the week, he would preach his little sermons to Charlene, Sharon, and a neighbor girl while they sat on the porch swing. Once Sharon put up her hand. He asked her what she wanted, rather crossly. She said whimpering, *"But I'm not!"* I guess she got under conviction by his preaching.

* * * * *

Now the Second World War was on. Hitler was making drastic headway in Europe. He was on radio trying to overthrow many countries. Certain stations were allowing him to blast away. He sounded to us like a mad man.

One summer every home, store, church and businessplace dared not have lights on for fear of the enemy's potential striking power. It was a real "black out." Sunday nights we all sat in the dark, and Quinton preached by flashlight. The service was shortened so they could get home before complete darkness.

Sugar, gasoline, metals of all kinds were rationed. This was the first time we ever bought sliced bread. It was sliced at the bakery because there were no knives for sale. We all salvaged everything possible. We didn't suffer, except so many things were rationed that it was sometimes difficult to get enough gasoline for traveling to an evangelistic meeting. But Quinton often went by train.

* * * * *

Polio was rampant one summer. It was a real devourer. It brought much fear into our town and community. Praise God that our children were not plagued with it. It killed many and crippled others for life.

My cousin's beautiful little five-year-old girl died in an iron lung. Quinton and I went to the hospital while Janet was sick to pray for and try to encourage the parents. After we had prayer, they asked us if we would like to go in and pray with Janet. We had thought that would be impossible, but the nurses said we could if we would follow their instructions carefully. We had to put on gowns, gloves and touch nothing. Then after our visit, we were to go out without touching the door or handle and strip off the gown and gloves. Janet had been begging for her mother to take her out of the iron lung and hold her. She wanted to be rocked. My heart ached so badly for her parents and Janet. It was one of the most heart-rending things I have ever witnessed.

We couldn't take our children to church. No

one could until the law said so. When freezing weather came, it died out. Our son-in-law's father died in an iron lung. He took sick when preaching in an evangelistic meeting. He lived in California, was a pastor and teacher of Greek in a university. This we learned many years later.

Between the contagious diseases, we held revival meetings and missionary conventions. Lives were changed. In those days, unsaved people attended special meetings. They must have had their minds and hearts awakened as the war raged on. Thousands of American boys were giving their lives for our country's freedom. There was much sorrow in many homes. We comforted and helped all we could. One family would give their hearts to Christ, and it would spread to other relatives or neighbors. Quinton still visited unsaved homes, too. Some men were under such conviction; as a result, they made life very hard for their Christian wives.

One man hid in the coal bin in the cellar all night to make his wife think he left home. He must have done a lot of thinking that night, for he had his wife call Quinton the next morning at seven o'clock to ask him to hurry over to pray for him.

Another man suddenly felt so miserable he wanted the pastor right away. *"But he can't come now,"* his wife said. *"You are hearing him on the radio. You'll have to wait until he gets home."* He walked back and forth. Finally, he got out all his liquor and poured it out in the back yard. I always wondered if it killed the grass. His wife called Quinton as soon as she supposed he'd be home. Quinton rushed over and found the man still pacing the floor. When he saw Quinton come in, he threw himself down on his knees and began sobbing. There was much confessing and praying, then laughing, rejoicing and hugging.

God was glorified again. These men were sick of their sinful lives and were faithful to God all the rest of their lives. Many more accounts could be told.

* * * * *

We enjoyed having a large group of young people who became Christians. Some of these served the Lord in Nigeria and India. John Blouser and Wayne Brenneman come to mind. Some girls became minister's wives.

"Only serve the Lord in truth with all your heart, for consider what great things He has done for you." I Samuel 12:24 was my special verse in my teen years.

* * * * *

We were still in Goshen the day the Japanese struck Pearl Harbor. I remember the day very well. The church was in the midst of a wonderful missionary convention. That awful tragedy occurred on Sunday, December 7, 1941. The news came to our attention by radio at noon.

Mrs. Lettie Cowman, the author of "Streams in the Desert," was our speaker that morning. We were all in the living room when the message came to us. It was such a shock to her because she just had arrived from Japan. Her husband and she represented the Oriental Missionary Society, which they had established. Hundreds of missionaries and their helpers had just finished placing Bible literature in every home of Japan. She was now seventy-five years old and had a great love for the people of Japan. When she heard the news, she dropped to her knees in the middle of the floor and called earnestly on the Lord to protect the Christian people there. The news was agonizing to her.

I never forgot that day, nor the prayer she prayed for me before she left our home. I was so weak but had so many responsibilities. She told me of her serious heart attack. Her doctor said she could never preach again, nor climb steps. And of all things, she dared not fly or travel anymore. She asked that a large world map be placed on the wall of her recovery room. She prayed daily for the people in all countries.

"Since then," she said, *"I've preached in twenty-five countries, and still at seventy-five I am here in this convention. Mae, God is not overlooking you. Help will come from Him."*

Then she prayed a special prayer for me. Oh, how she prayed. I knew she was sent to me from God. My faith increased. God soon brought me help and strength to my body as I repeated and repeated promises that He made real to me. One was *"The name of the Lord is a high tower. The righteous runneth into it and is safe."*

Another was, *"Delight thyself in the Lord, and*

He shall give thee the desires of thine heart."

Lettie is in Heaven now. I wish I could tell her that God answered her prayer and I, too, traveled with my husband into many countries and islands visiting and preaching the glorious Gospel.

I like the verse in Psalm 66:9, *"He holds our lives in His hands. And He holds our feet to the path."* Living Bible.

* * * * *

It was a busy day, and I had not noticed the approaching storm. Then suddenly a strong wind came up, and I opened the screen door to take a peek. Right then a large tree, much taller than the neighbor's house, simply fell over like a matchstick. It lay across the street. I backed myself inside to see where all three children were. Oh, of course, they were in the house. Charlene was in her bedroom quarantined with scarlet fever, and young Q.J. and the baby were with me. Daddy was quarantined "out" since he was the evangelist in a citywide crusade in Berne, Indiana.

Edna, the hired girl, was sick in bed with the "flu." I myself had been down for six weeks, so weak with anemia that I could not care for myself, let alone care for my family.

While Quinton was gone in a previous meeting, another hired girl and I thought I was dying in the middle of the night. I asked her to call the good doctor I had in Elkhart. She told him of my condition and how I felt. Knowing my past record years ago, he called my present doctor in

Goshen to instruct him to get on the case immediately. He was to send his nurse to our home each day for two weeks and give me an injection, 1 c.c. of reticulogen (liver shots). After that, I was to go to the doctor's office twice each week for my shot. After several months my strength gradually increased so that I could care for the children and take some of the other responsibilities. This was the third time in my young married life that my hemoglobin had become dangerously low.

Now Charlene had scarlet fever. Dear Charlene was a very good patient. No television in those days, but we gave her a radio. Of course all cards, books and anything she handled would have to be burned at the end of her sick time. But she was not seriously ill, for which I was very grateful to the Lord. I was required to scrub my hands thoroughly and put on a special gown before I entered her room. Then I removed it as I left and washed my hands again. I was the only one who could enter her room for four weeks. We did have some nice chats. She was not moody but pleasant and easy to care for. My lack of strength and the long distance between the kitchen and upstairs room was the difficulty.

One evening after putting Q.J. to bed in his father's study room, I threw myself onto my bed and cried to the Lord to strengthen me. I felt too tired to live. I had made baby Sharon's formula, set juice and water at the hired girl's bedside and said *"Goodnight"* to my scarlet fever patient. Now, if I could just close my eyes and sleep, even if I could not undress.

About that time, Q.J. called me whining that he itched. There was nothing I could do but go get him quieted down. He was quiet again, and I went back to my bed. I finally relaxed saying over and over *"The name of the Lord is a strong tower. The righteous runneth into it and is safe." "I am safe. I am safe."* I dozed off. It must have been about eleven o'clock.

Near midnight I awoke suddenly by the clanging noise of fire trucks one by one rushing past our house. On the next street the ambulances were screeching. Back and forth they went, coming and going all night. During all of this noise from midnight on until seven o'clock, we slept peacefully. Then the telephone rang. *"Is Pastor Everest there?"* Or, *"Please have Pastor Everest come to the hospital."*

"Why? What's wrong?"

I was so sorry that I didn't know of the tragedies of the night. Between calls, I prepared breakfast, fed the baby, Q.J., and took trays to Charlene and Edna, the hired girl.

The telephone interrupted several times. My energy was getting low; so I placed two chairs next to each other under the wall phone and laid down on a sofa pillow. Every time I was through with an activity, I again took advantage of this resting place. Every caller wanted to know how someone was. I finally asked what had happened. I had not known that a tornado had struck Goshen just six blocks south of the parsonage during the night.

So that was the cause of all the noise of ambu-

lances and fire trucks. Many of our church people and friends were hospitalized, and many
were without homes.

One family had just moved into their new
house. The father was a builder. The mother
was putting some of the younger children to bed
upstairs. The father was helping the older children with their homework around the dining
room table. Suddenly the tornado struck sending the family flying and the new house disinte-
grating. In days to come, they could not identi-
fy anything that belonged to them except the
bathtub. No one was seriously hurt. One boy
had one heel cut off. But there were long lasting
emotions to be dealt with. One of the children
composed a beautiful poem about their experience giving God much praise for His care over
them in that awful storm.

Another couple had moved recently into their
new house. The wind picked it up and set it
down in the middle of the street, as if, on second
thought, it should not be destroyed!

The hospital beds were full, and temporary
beds were set up in the halls.

Since the telephone continued to ring, I had
no one to answer it for me, and since I must care
for my patients and little ones, I wondered how
I could ever make a nourishing dinner for us all.

While I was agonizing over this, the Lord
brought the name of a man to my mind whom I
had not thought of for years. He had been my
substitute math teacher in Nappanee when I
was in the eighth grade, Bob Stemen. Now he
owned a good restaurant in Goshen. I called

him. I told him of my dilemma. He immediately put me at ease, telling me that he remembered me. He said I should not worry. When noon came, he would have dinner delivered to my front porch. He named all the good foods I could imagine and more. A huge box was set at the door of the parsonage at twelve o'clock. I heard a rap, but the person saw a large "SCARLET FEVER" sign and was gone before I could open the door. Besides the hot food, which was enough for days, there was plenty of ice cream for all.

I told Mr. Stemen that my husband would pay the bill when he arrived home the following week. But when Quinton tried to pay him, Bob would not accept anything. How thankful we were for his kindness to us. It gave the children a real lift, and I got more rest for a couple of days.

Quinton's parents drove around that very night trying to find someone to come and help me, but no one wanted to take the chance, since we had scarlet fever.

One evening little Q.J. complained of itching. I looked him over. He had red spots and fever. I called the doctor. He said, *"Oh, Mrs. Everest, I have so many patients yet tonight, I'll be over right away tomorrow morning. Can you set up a bed in Charlene's room?"*

"Yes," I said. *"Do you think he has scarlet fever?"*

"Yes," he said.

When the doctor came early the next morning, he examined Q.J., threw up his hands and said, *"This child does not have scarlet fever. He has chicken pox!"*

We hurriedly took him out of Charlene's room hoping he wasn't exposed to scarlet fever too long. Now his bed was set up in his daddy's study room again. Oh, how I prayed he would not get scarlet fever, too. He didn't. But the day the officials took down the quarantine sign, we were shocked again. That day I scrubbed the room, burned whatever Charlene had handled, washed her bedding, and we all rejoiced that dear Charlene was downstairs having a fun time with all in the family. That very night, she took a high fever and broke out with the chicken pox, all because our doctor thought Q.J. had scarlet fever.

Then Charlene was very sick and itchy. How sorry we all felt for her. My grief was almost more than I could bear. The doctor said her chicken pox were the largest he had ever seen.

Quinton's mother came then to help me with the cooking, which helped me greatly.

When Daddy came home, it was a great day. Q.J., Jr. had marked off the days of the calendar until he returned. Quinton had written letters to us about every day, but we could not send mail to him. I talked to him a few times on the phone. The children were always excited to see what he had brought for them in his suitcase on his return home.

* * * * *

During these five years of pastoring the Brenneman Memorial Church at Goshen, the radio work prospered. It enlarged in scope until we were soon broadcasting on South Bend WSBT, WLS and WMAZ Chicago, a Hammond station, CKLW Detroit-Windsor, which reached Ontario, Boston, Shenendoah, Iowa, KMA in Long Beach, California, Seattle, and several stations in Florida.

When the mail started coming in, we were amazed and hurriedly set up an office in our dining room. Quinton persuaded Harold Moyer, a very godly man who was an accountant in Elkhart and a brother-in-law to Quinton, to be our first secretary and treasurer. He also sang a solo on the half-hour broadcast, *"Lead me to some soul today. Oh, teach me Lord just what to say. Friends of mine are lost in sin and cannot find their way. Few there are who seem to care, and few there are who pray. Melt my heart and fill my life. Give me one soul today."* That was a very touching song. People often wrote about the impression that it made upon them. This song followed Quinton's prayer.

We soon felt that the broadcast should be identified by a name instead of a local church, for it was covering a large part of the United States, Ontario, and a few stations in Alberta. After much discussion and prayer, it was decided to call it "Your Worship Hour." In years to come, we realized the wisdom of this choice.

A pastor friend in Detroit, Rev. Ray Pannabecker, strongly suggested that Quinton should have a radio agent. The agent knew better what stations were best to take on. There were no Christian stations back in the 1930's. His friend suggested a certain agent. They met

and worked together for some time until the
agent became very critical of his reading of certain scriptures. He wanted Quinton to forward
his sermons ahead of the time of broadcasting.
That was unbearable. God answered prayer. He
was soon introduced to a wonderful Christian
agent, Mr. Walter Bennett, who said, *"Quinton,
you preach the Word. Have no fear."* They worked
together for the rest of the fifty years of
Quinton's radio ministry.

Our dining room was no longer adequate for
an office. A house one half block from the parsonage was for rent, just what we needed.

Quinton was very fortunate to become
acquainted with the first radio convert that we
knew. Eunice Robbins of South Bend was so
enthused with the Bible preaching that she
offered her time working for "Your Worship
Hour." She had an excellent position with
Bendix Corporation, was speedy at shorthand,
and trustworthy. She wanted to be a missionary,
but God did not call her. She was a great help in
the preparation of his sermon books in years to
come. God surely planned her life around "Your
Worship Hour" for the next thirty-six years,
before the Lord took her home to Heaven. There
were other secretaries and announcers who
would spend from fifteen to twenty-six years in
this far-reaching ministry. The overseas broadcasting would come later.

Chapter Ten

*Another move, another burden
and a vision for a college.*

After five years at the Goshen Church, a new burden for souls in another area was pressed upon Quinton. Years before when he had operated a bread route in South Bend, he had become anxious to start a new work for Christ in that city.

Now that he was getting mail from South Bend, he again saw the need. We did not tell others about this but felt it would be the leading of the Lord in the near future. Our decisions must come from Him. How wonderful to be in His plan for our lives. The greater the opportunities, the greater the enemy tried to hinder us. But through rough times, we learned to know how great our God really is.

Then came time for our church's annual conference. The church voted for a pastor. Quinton got a unanimous vote again. We were very grateful for that. But they were still ignorant of his feeling of being called by God to minister in South Bend. For three months, we prayed for a sign of the Lord's leading us in that direction.

One evening about seven o'clock, a man named Ernest Duncan, with a delegation of members from a failing church project in South

Bend, came to our door. I knew they had come with some heavy burden on their hearts. Since I felt the three children and I might disrupt the meeting, I told Quinton we would go walking or take a ride. The session was long and serious. Quinton related to me their concerns after I put the children to bed.

It seemed a small group of people, earnest in their faith, had bought a lot and started to build. Rather low in funds, they started worshipping in the basement before trying to finish the entire structure. Then they had to dismiss the pastor for immoral reasons, which broke their hearts. Another young preacher came for a year but could not or did not have the vision for this place. So he left.

Not knowing which way to turn, they gave themselves to prayer. They could not possibly close the doors, for one hundred children and perhaps two dozen adults were depending on the church board to find a way to continue.

One of the board members brought up the name of Quinton J. Everest, whom they had been listening to on WSBT "Your Worship Hour" broadcast. The other members said that would be foolish to think that he would give it consideration. But Mr. Duncan said he believed if it was of the Lord, Quinton would come. The group offered him $40 per week with more as soon as possible.

A truck farmer promised Quinton food for his family if he would come. From the very beginning, he brought washed clean fruits and vegetables every week, all we could eat. Such a variety of foods as we had never enjoyed before, even though we always had a large garden. Then he helped us get a freezer and meat the first winter. He had been listening to Quinton preach on the radio. He set out from the beginning to help with his offerings as if he were a Christian. Many prayers with God's divine love finally reached his soul.

So Quinton met with the church board about his great burden for South Bend. They, at first, did not consider his leaving when so many people were being saved. They needed more parking space and soon would enlarge the sanctuary.

Finally, a godly man, Forrest Robinson said, *"I will not hinder our pastor from doing the Lord's will in starting a new church in South Bend."* Suddenly all agreed. Then the congregation really showed their love to us. We were invited to homes for dinner and for supper every day until we moved. We had to turn some invitations down.

The district home mission committee was not favorable for Quinton to leave the Goshen Church; so they voted it down. But he still felt it was God's plan.

* * * * *

Sometimes we had conflicting schedules. The summer family camp meetings were in August. The year we moved to South Bend, Quinton was to be the evangelist at Ludlow Falls, Ohio. Before he left home, we had gone to South Bend and placed a down payment on a house near Indiana University. But just before he left home for Ohio, the owners called and informed us that they had changed their minds about selling. They were sending back the down payment to us. I well remember how we looked at each other after Quinton hung up the phone. I said, *"I know this is right. God has something more adequate for us."* And so we smiled and then prayed about it.

Then we got very serious about it. *"It is nearly time for school to begin. We must find a home before that." "Maybe Mr. Duncan will help you to find one. Also, the mission board has not helped me in this venture in any way. Surely the chairman, Rev. Rassi and his wife could accompany you."*

They were delighted to assist me. They came to get me at nine o'clock one morning. It rained the entire day. We had Mr. Duncan guide us to the locations of houses for sale in the classified section of the Tribune. We drove up and down streets in the vicinity of the school the children would attend, and the place we were starting a church. We went through many houses, but none were adequate.

It was getting very late. We were tired, but no one was complaining. Mr. Duncan finally said, *"I know of a well-built house a block and a half from the church. There had been a 'For Sale' sign, but it has been taken down. It is only two and a half blocks from a very fine school of fifteen hundred students. There wouldn't be any harm in going to see it. Mr. Clifford Gould, the owner, I know him."*

I felt relaxed immediately.

"Mr. Gould purchased an acreage on McKinley and Logan Street, developed it and now lives in one of those new houses. He has rented out the house we

118

want."

Mr. Duncan rang the doorbell. Mr. Gould opened the door and at once invited us in. We explained our reason for being there. Mr. Duncan told him of our experiences of the day. Then he asked if the house had really been sold.

"No," he said. *"I'm not interested in selling it. It is just fifteen years old, a well-built house. We enjoyed living there with our boys. But if you want it for a parsonage, I'm willing to sell it to you."*

We four looked at each other, took a deep breath, and started smiling. *"But you haven't seen it yet,"* he said.

I said, "It is almost time for school to begin, and we must move in as soon as possible."

"Well," Cliff said, *"the occupants will be back soon. They are on vacation. I wouldn't want to unlock the door to show you, but I will take a large flashlight to show you the inside from the windows."* Through each window we liked what we saw.

We again met at the Gould home and signed a temporary agreement to buy it and paid fifty dollars to hold it for us. The price was $7,500. Again God was guiding us. How we thanked Mr. Gould for his kindness and generosity!

We left there at 11:00 p.m., tired but very happy, and praising our Lord for answering prayer. We lived in that house for twenty-two years. Charlene, Q.J., Jr., Sharon and Cynthia all loved that home. That was the house we lived in when Cynthia was born four years later.

School began two weeks before we got the walls washed and moved our furniture. During that time, I took the children to school and then went to the empty house to clean.

I had brought our lunch from Goshen. We sat down on the floor and boxes. One noon after Quinton came home, he went with us. He made a nice fire in the fireplace, and we had roasted wieners with buns, some fruit and milk. It was fun for us all.

Where the children grew up —22 years

The very first day of school, Q.J., Jr. lost his way home. It was so unusual to see a big clock on the corner that he (and we) thought he would see that. We pointed this out to him when we took him to school in the morning. But he was not used to all the traffic; so he walked down the avenue, past the clock for three more blocks. He was getting nervous because he realized he had walked longer than he had in the morning. So he asked a man where 833-31st Street was. The man said, *"You walked past it. Turn around. Do you see that large clock down there? That's 31st Street."*

"Thank you," Q.J. said and ran to his new home. I felt so sorry for my little boy. He was a second-grader.

In a few days, he had another problem. A boy who was a bit larger than he wanted to pick a fight with him at recess. Q.J. wasn't used to being picked on and did not know how to get rid of him. Finally the boy started following Q.J. home, and I once saw him hiding in the bushes along our driveway. Maybe the fellow just wanted to see where Q.J. lived. When he came into the house, he said, *"Mother, now he's following me home. What will I do?"*

"I believe we'd better pray and ask God what you can do for him."

The next morning I chose two large shiny red apples, polished them well and said, *"Put one in each pocket. At recess, look for him. At the first sign of him, walk toward him with your arm stretched out holding the apple and say, 'This is for you', and smile. Don't be afraid."*

When Q.J. came home, he rushed into the kitchen and said, *"Mother, I offered him the apple, but he turned away from me as if he was shocked."* Maybe he was. But he never bothered the new boy, Q.J., in school again.

The girls seemed to fare all right. Betty Charlene was our oldest child. We had always called her Betty in Goshen. Now we were living in a new city where we knew no one. So she decided she would not be Betty any longer. In church, school and the neighborhood she was Charlene. Strange, but we did not realize it until test papers came home signed "Charlene Everest"—also report cards. Well, we were all surprised, but if that is the name she wants for a lifetime, let her enjoy it. Her Uncle Wilson had suggested that name before she was brought home from the hospital. If her uncle would not have suggested Charlene for a name, it would have been Arlene.

Sharon Jeanne, our little blondie with natural curls, was ready for kindergarten. She was anxious to go to school like her brother and sister.

The first Sunday we went to church was a tremendous change for our children as well as for us. There was water on the floor of the auditorium. They showed me to the Primary Department room. The floor was dirt. Nothing seemed to be ready for a worship service, until the hundred or more neighborhood children came. What a sight! How glad I was to see them. Probably twenty-five adults were present. Our whole family agreed that we were in mission work and that the Lord had a big task for us all.

Quinton preached as if he had a houseful. He never embarrassed the people about their small beginning.

As soon as we moved to South Bend, Quinton made an appointment with Mr. Swintz, manager of WSBT radio station. We wanted to be on WSBT, not only on Sunday with "Your Worship Hour" but on a daily time for a fifteen-minute devotional period, Monday through Friday. "Your Worship Hour" was a half-hour program on Sunday.

"I can't possibly do that. There are nineteen other ministers who want time. I have their letters in my files. You already have a half-hour each Sunday night from 9:30 to 10:00." But Quinton felt deeply about getting acquainted with the city in a more personal way.

The second time he was turned down again.

But Quinton could not give up. Finally Mr. Swintz said, *"I tell you what I'll do. We now open the station at 6:30 a. m. for the News. We decided if you want to broadcast that early, we'll open at 6:15 a.m., and we'll never take it away from you."*

From then on, Quinton broadcasted what we called "Sunrise Meditations" for twenty-two years, the length of his pastorate in South Bend.

Every morning he hurried through the alley to the church, one block, and did a "wake-up call" for the city and surrounding communities. Some people said they were eating breakfast, some getting dressed, others heard it on their car radios as they were traveling to work.

The program began with the hymn "Take Time To Be Holy," then a scripture verse, a prayer for the listeners, some pointed thoughts, an illustration or a very meaningful poem.

We soon learned some of the results. In less than a year, we needed better and more seating in this church basement. A businessman in Elkhart learned of our dilemma and told Quinton to contact the American Seating Company to supply us with comfortable theatre chairs. Quinton was to send the bill to him. It then seated 347 chairs. Also, the platform had been extended for a fifteen-voice choir. The Lord was sending in some Christian talent, and we all did what we could to help with our talents.

Quinton was then signing off the early morning broadcast with an invitation to anyone who wished to have counsel and prayer to come to the church immediately. He would stay there for an hour before going home for breakfast. There were many interesting experiences as a result.

This meant more study, more prayer, and more counseling. There were Sunday morning and Sunday evening sermons. He taught the adult Bible Sunday School class; the "Your Worship Hour" broadcast sermon; and the Wednesday evening prayer meeting devotional talk. Besides these responsibilities, the five daily "Sunrise Meditation" talks had to be prepared.

Duties of being on Missionary Church boards of different kinds and president of the Foreign Missionary Society took him abroad at times. Nevertheless, we as a family, felt these were the open doors God was giving to my husband and their father.

Living in a parsonage is not the same as the ordinary home. To be together, we ate three meals at scheduled times and had family worship every day. Ours was not a quarrelsome family, nor a loud one. The neighbors' house to the north of us was only fifteen feet away from ours. As the husband or wife washed dishes, they could look out their window through our dining room window to our kitchen. As we'd walk through, we'd wave at each other.

One evening these neighbors invited me over just to sit and visit, I thought, because I was alone. But as soon as I was seated, they brought up the subject of child training. They were married, in their late thirties, and had one boy. He was perhaps twelve years old at that time, and he hated any discipline. They bought a book to help them. They were disappointed. Their problem continued. I asked if the author was a father. The fact that I had all the answers, because we were raising four children, was not sufficient for me. But I said almost immediately, *"Everyone is under authority of someone else, whether you are a child or an adult. You have a parent, a teacher, a boss, or someone you are accountable to. Greater authority than these is God Himself, if you like it or not. The child should learn this soon, the sooner the better. Tell him that you, too, are under authority every day. Be sure he understands this."* His mother was a schoolteacher. They thanked me and were always friendly to us.

* * * * *

When Quinton was the evangelist at the Ohio family camp, he met Helen Keller, the children's worker, from Detroit. She had a big heart for children, was a good storyteller and lovely singer. Her calling was from God. Children should come to know the Savior early in life, she felt, as did we.

In their conversation one day, he asked her if she would consider coming to South Bend as a full-time worker. Her duties would be children's Bible clubs during school months and Daily Vacation Bible School for two weeks in the summer. She would also lead the church music, sing solos, and sing in the radio choir. The first thing she asked was, *"How many children are there now in your Sunday School?"*

"Over one hundred now," said Quinton. That was exciting news to her, for she had fewer chil-

dren than that in Detroit.

She said she would pray about the offer he made her, for she wanted to be sure the Lord was leading her in that direction.

Before many weeks passed, she moved to South Bend and became a tremendous asset to our work. A large elementary school was a block and a half from the church. Helen started a Bible Club on Thursdays after school for one hour. First a mother at the door took the names and addresses of the new children. Then they were seated in the basement sanctuary. The sessions were opened with wonderful children's songs that she taught them, then a flannel-graph Bible story with another story to illustrate it. After a prayer for the children, they would be divided into groups their own age and grade. Mothers would take each grade into a different room. The mothers would help them memorize a Bible verse that was in their Bible lesson. Helen had a Bible Study course that was well known at that time. Each child had a folder to take home that had blanks they filled out. These were checked by the mothers the next week. When each child finished the eight grades of material, they graduated and were given a certificate. My four children all profited greatly from this course.

The names and addresses were followed up by Helen. She would visit each home and inquire if the parents were attending church anywhere. Those people who were going to no church were then visited by the pastor.

Our church services were growing rapidly.

The Wednesday night prayer meetings as well.

The high school age group swelled with newly saved boys and girls. A youth service was held by them and for them. The children, though young, were told stories, and then they were encouraged to pray. I loved to hear them pray so earnestly.

The young people became burdened for the lost. They rolled tracts in cellophane, took them down to a main corner of the city, two by two, and passed them out to passersby. Then they would go back to the church and have Sloppy Joes or something else of their liking and exchange experiences.

They voted for their youth leader out of their own group. As yet we could not afford to hire a youth leader. The leader and committee would plan things to do for others that would be of real spiritual work. One was to hold services on Sunday afternoon one Sunday each month at the County Home. Another Sunday they would sing, speak and have prayer with the unfortunate young people at Parkview Detention Center on Riverside Drive.

Soon after we arrived at the Gospel Center Church, I was made superintendent of the Primary Department. About twenty-five children of the first, second and third grades were given me. How thrilled I was with this responsibility! I selected a good pianist. I printed words of songs on a large blackboard. Children love to sing. We came to know each other quite well, and they soon brought other children with them. In about two years, we built more classrooms all around the former basement. Before many years, the primary department had nine classes. The teachers cooperated well. It was a happy eleven years that I served them. I enjoyed working with the teachers developing programs for Easter, Thanksgiving Day, Christmas, Mother's Day and Father's Day. For plays, recitations and songs, it took much time in planning and practicing. The Sunday School material we all used was Gospel Light by Henrietta Mears.

One year during our great Missionary Convention (we had them every year), I told the children I thought it was time for us to be involved in helping a missionary. We chose a little woman, Bessie Cordell, who had been a missionary in China for many years until the war with Japan. They house-arrested her at first but later told her to get out of the country. She loved the Chinese people. So instead of going back to the United States, she found her way to Taiwan. Here she found plenty to do. She cared for a group of soldiers who had been blinded by war and fled from their homeland. She taught them of Jesus' love for them and that He could forgive them of their sins. They were good listeners. They came to respect her very highly. She provided food and clothing for them and taught them many things in their regular Bible studies.

Our primary children were all excited when I read a letter from her in which she said, *"These men drink goats milk, but I need one more goat so that they all can have some."*

And I said, *"Children, how would you like to*

*bring an extra offering to Sunday School for Bessie
Cordell so she can get another goat?"*

They all agreed loudly. So I searched and
searched for a large picture of a goat. At last I
found one and hung it up in front of the department. We even prayed for the goat, Bessie and
the soldiers that they would do as she admon-
ished them to do, to give their hearts to the Lord.
It had nice results, and my children found it to
be pleasant to serve the Lord.

One Sunday our secretary took a picture of
our department children with the teachers and
their substitutes standing along the walls. There
were ninety children. The total Sunday School
then had reached to between 600-700 in attendance.

One Easter I was so burdened for the children
that I asked the teachers for permission to keep
the children all together in the main room. I felt
an unusual urge to preach a little sermonette on
the real meaning of Easter. They all consented.
I asked them to be ready immediately after my
talk to take the children who wanted to take
Jesus as their Savior to one of the classrooms.
Here they should pray for them, each one indi-
vidually, and suggest they pray, too. They
should see that each one had help. The Holy
Spirit surely worked in their hearts that day. I
was convinced of the Lord's will in this.

We did have several troublemakers. One
teacher walked out of her class to tell me she
was so disturbed by one boy that she could not
continue teaching. I said, *"That cannot be. Just
tell him to come to me."* I don't know what he

expected, but I'm sure he wasn't prepared for what was to take place. When he came out, I just informed him that since he doesn't allow his teacher to talk, we will talk out here. Just the two of us. But maybe it would be better to go up on the main floor to my husband's study room. He wasn't there. He was teaching a Bible class in the sanctuary. We went in, closed the door, and I started asking questions.

"Tell me why you do the talking in class? Why do you pick on others?"

"I don't know," he would say.

"Do you want to come to Sunday School?"

"Yes."

"Do you know John Dillinger?"

"I know about him. Yes, he was a mean one."

"Yes, and you know what happened to him?"

"Yes."

"Well, he went to Sunday School, too. But he disturbed the class so much that the teacher told him to never come back again. I'm not going to tell you that because we want you here. But we want you to listen so that you will understand God's love for you. Are you happy?"

He looked at me so funny. *"No, I guess not."*

"Do you know why you're not happy?"

He looked and looked at me. He finally said, *"Because I have three mamas."*

I almost blurted the next words out. *"Larry,"* as I took his two hands in mine and slid down on my knees, *"I love you, Jesus loves you, JESUS LOVES YOU. Kneel down with me here and let's talk to Him."*

So I prayed for his father, for his real mother,

and the other mothers. Then I asked Jesus to forgive him of his sins. I asked him if he felt Jesus did. He shook his head up and down.

I asked his teacher if he made any trouble after that, and she said he did not.

Many years later, perhaps fifteen years later, I received a letter from an officer in a Dallas prison asking me if I knew the reason that Larry would choose my name if he was permitted to write to just one person. I answered the best I could. That I was a friend, his Sunday School superintendent and would certainly answer if he wrote to me. I never heard from him. Some years later, he came to South Bend. He called and said he was in need, could we give him five dollars. We did, but that was all we ever heard from him. Sad. But if he is still living, I pray God will yet save him.

Another thing happened one Sunday morning while classes were in session. A boy slipped out of class, went to the bell and rang it. I had stepped out of the room for a minute but was just returning when I saw, through the glass door, this boy taking his hand off the bell and grinning from ear to ear.

"What have you done?" I said. But off he ran, and just as soon as the bell rang, all nine classes came rushing out and started for the stairway. All the older departments of juniors, junior high, high school and adults were still in session. What a distraction! My teachers and myself did all we could to get most of the children to return back to class. Class time was only half over.

* * * * *

131

I often visited the homes of these children, especially for the teachers who had to work.

Once I got a big idea, too big for me, but with my Lord's help, I did what I first thought was impossible. A sit-down dinner banquet in my home for 65 invited mothers of my children.

Men of the church brought long tables and folding chairs. They set them up through the living room, dining room and redwood room, all in a straight line. Rolls of white paper covered the tables. High school girls came in after school to set the tables and serve as waitresses. Two older women had cooked and cut up the chicken. Gravy was made for the chicken in our kitchen. The menu was to be creamed chicken on biscuits, peas, salad, homemade pie, coffee and tea. The supper was scheduled for six o'clock. They would need to be escorted right to the table since the rooms were so full. I intended to be at the door to greet my guests, but at 5:45 the cooks asked, *"Where are the biscuits?"* The side dishes, salad and pie were on the table so that the waitresses need only to serve the filled plates and the drinks. But where were the biscuits?

So hurriedly I told one of the teachers to take my place at the door. I was not nervous for once in my life. I could make fluffy biscuits for my family. So I rushed to the kitchen, multiplied the Crisco recipe by ten, got out two large mixing bowls, measured the flour, baking powder, salt and started sifting, half of it in one bowl and half in the other. The Crisco was hurriedly cut in and then the amount of cold water. Working it quickly, I rolled them out on my floured table. Everyone was helping me do something, turning on the oven and finding the right size of glasses to cut the circles. As soon as we had enough cut to fill two large pans, we put them in the oven. In twelve minutes, they were baked and lovely. In went the two filled pans again, and they were baked by the time the girls had served the others. There was plenty of chicken in the gravy, which made it look so good. We kitchen crew all smiled at each other.

I said, *"You cooks and waitresses deserve a good dinner, too. Help yourselves and eat your fill."* How I appreciated my helpers.

I went into the dining room and ate with my guests. After we were finished eating, I had them introduce themselves. They had come from different parts of the city, and a few of them had never been inside Gospel Center Church. But their children had.

Next I had one of my teachers pretend we were her Sunday School pupils. She taught last Sunday's lesson to us. It was a very interesting fifteen minutes. She certainly had their attention.

After that I showed a film of a beautiful family having family worship, and the effect upon the mothers clearly showed.

It was an evening I shall never forget.

Many years later, my husband and I were seated in a restaurant in Fort Myers, Florida. I felt someone staring at us. Their table was very close to ours. One of the ladies smiled and asked, *"Are you the Everests from South Bend?"*

"Yes," I said. *"Should we know you?"*

"Yes. I was at your home years ago at a mother's banquet." Then she introduced us to those sitting with her. She paused and then said, *"I'll never forget that."*

* * * * *

Our time together on Sunday mornings was planned and varied, joyous, yet serious and meaningful. We opened with singing good children's songs. Then I prayed for the children and teachers and for all children of the world. As soon as I prayed, we sang this:

"Father we will quiet be, As we listen
now to Thee " (pause)
"As we raise our heads we'll sing,
Thank you God for everything."

We worked well together and periodically met to inspire and support one another. Another thing that helped us tremendously was to attend the State Sunday School Teacher's Convention in Indianapolis. I received many excellent ideas from speakers like Henrietta Mears. For twenty-two years, we used her publications of Sunday School material. God blessed her with tremendous insight of His Word and gift of speaking.

* * * * *

As much as I loved singing in the radio choir, church choir and once in a while a solo, plus my primary children, my greater love and responsibility was for my own husband and children.

We all had our duties at home, but there were fun times, too. I loved to read stories to my young children and play games. Once a summer we'd spend a couple of days at a lake fishing. Our son always enjoyed that.

* * * * *

One day, since our children became a little older and I was nearing forty, I had a strange lonely feeling. I had always loved my three babies so very much. *"Oh, I'll never have that wonderful feeling of holding and caressing a little baby again,"* I thought. Then the thought left me entirely.

Next Sunday morning as I came into the sanctuary, Mrs. Duncan motioned me to come to her. She was already seated in her accustomed pew. It was fifteen minutes before time to begin. (It was the custom for all superintendents and teachers to be in their places before their students arrived so they could greet them.) So I went to her. She said, *"Sister Everest, I dreamed last night you are pregnant,"* and smiled.

"Me?" I said. And I hurried on. In two weeks I indeed had a report that this was true. Quinton and I were both very happy.

I felt better, worked harder, did my spring cleaning early, even washing the walls of the living room, dining room and kitchen. Everything was normal, except we, as a family, didn't go to family camps with Quinton as we usually did once a summer. When it was time for our own Prairie Camp near Elkhart, he moved us out to our cabin. Then he left for a camp in Kitchener,

Ontario, Canada, where he was to be the evangelist for ten days. He took Charlene with him because she was asked to be the pianist. This was a month before the baby arrived. Young Q.J. and Sharon wanted so much to be at our camp. So I managed to go and thoroughly enjoyed it.

* * * * *

The two years previous to this time, Quinton was burdened with another vision and task from the Lord. He was very concerned about our young men, who were called of God, getting their education from schools not of our own. We had two Bible Institutes in Canada but not one in the United States. Our Missionary Church boys were often marrying girls from other denominations or they were often offered places to preach before graduating for "practice preaching experience." For years, Quinton had been on our Indiana educational board. For some reason, they made him chairman of the board.

The board became serious and prayerful about the reason for having such a board. Quinton's burden for a school to train ministers and missionaries intensified. Finally, they started looking and praying for a suitable campus. They gathered with board members from our Michigan and Ohio conferences. These men traveled to different locations in these three states. Once they gave money for a down payment on an old school in Michigan. It was not long until a school official sent the money back.

They had changed their minds about selling. As a result, the Ohio and Michigan men resigned, leaving our five men in Indiana to "carry the ball." They were getting discouraged as well. Not long thereafter, two of the Indiana men resigned, leaving three. Not Quinton. He, more likely, thought it was impatience or not God's time. He never lost the vision and burden.

One evening the phone rang. I answered. Quinton was in his study at the church. When he came home, I told him the other two men of the board were together. They wanted him to call.

Quinton called, and they said they, too, wanted to resign. He asked them if they would stay there until he could drive over. They said they would.

After talking a little while about the impossibilities of starting a college, Quinton said, *"Let's pray again before we make this closure final. Each of us pray."* They all knelt and one after another asked God to open the way if it was really His will. Surely if it was His divine will, there would soon be a location available. When they arose from prayer, Quinton asked each one to be a committee of one to find a campus and report as soon as possible. They went to their homes and retired.

Quinton got up for the early morning 6:15 broadcast. After he had signed off, he suddenly thought of the name Clifford Gould, the insurance man from whom the church bought the parsonage.

"Mr. Gould," he asked, *"do you know any piece*

of land that would make a good college campus?"

"Yes, I can think of two places. One is on Jefferson Street, and the other is across Logan Street near us." After a short conversation, they hung up, and Quinton first called the owner of the land on Jefferson. The owner said he would not sell to any church or religious group. So that shortened the selection!

Then he called the owner of the thirty-five acres on Logan Street who was owner of Buick Sales Corporation. Quinton also knew him but had no idea his beautiful wooded riding trails were for sale. After a short visit, a time was set for them to meet with the other Indiana board members to view this lovely place. Quinton invited the two members who had resigned to join the three of them to survey the property. All the men were thrilled with this prospect, so close to home in our Indiana Missionary Church headquarters territory.

They asked how much down payment he wanted to hold it for them. *"Five hundred dollars,"* he said. Of course none of the men had cash like that with them, except one had his checkbook and hurriedly wrote a check for five hundred dollars. The full price was $35,000. There was a small house, a horse stable, and a clubhouse on the property. It was a time of rejoicing and praising God for answered prayer.

Now the struggles began. Trees must be cleared, the first building constructed, a godly intellectual man must be found for the presidency, professors, and a curriculum. Would it take a year or two or three? And will our young people respond? Much prayer and consulting was to take place.

At this time our Gospel Center Church was seeing much progress. Also, the broadcast was being listened to over many more stations. As money came in, more time was purchased on other stations.

Walter Bennett was recommended to Quinton by Dr. Myron Boyd as an excellent Christian radio agent. Radio was quite new yet and certainly Christian broadcasting was just getting a good start. We started broadcasting before there were many Christian stations. This meant we were paying commercial prices for airtime, which was often very high. However, we felt we were reaching more unchurched with the Gospel on commercial stations than on Christian stations at that time.

The urgency became greater, and more and more doors were opening. Which stations to take on as the letters poured into the office was difficult to decide. Mr. Bennett was thrilled to meet Quinton, for he had heard "Your Worship Hour" program himself. Mr. Bennett was very knowledgeable about the outreach of stations and the probable response Quinton would receive from that area. Mr. Bennett and Quinton had a most unique Christian fellowship in the Lord's work for over forty years. He had faith in Quinton's passion for souls, reaching out into more and more countries of the world. Mr. Bennett took care of the United States schedule; Quinton took care of Trans World Radio, Far Eastern Broadcast, H.C.J.B., Veeqes, 4VEH, and others beyond Canada and the U.S. He also claimed Quinton operated on a "shoestring," which meant he, our board and staff spent no money foolishly. Besides that, Quinton, for the first twenty-five years, never took a salary or traveling expenses from the "Your Worship Hour" fund. This was a missionary venture. Our family knew this, too.

Although we had come to South Bend for half the salary (in offerings) that we had received in the Goshen church, we never heard our children complain. I remembered the song "I'm On The Mission Field For My Lord." We were happy in what we were doing.

How could it be otherwise? The encouraging letters of parents and children who were being saved. And as Quinton and I traveled in radio rallies and evangelistic meetings, we heard many testimonies and stories of how God changed lives. Also his radio sermons were now being printed and were in many countries of the world. Thousands of pastors have read the books and used them in their churches. Over four million have been printed.

A medical doctor in India taught the book of Revelation to his medical students on his veranda on Saturday mornings. He sent for more books that Quinton had published from sermons on each chapter of Revelation. Many boxes of sermon books were sent to our theological seminary in Ilorin, Nigeria at their request.

Someone gave an African man a sermon booklet. He could read English. It made him so angry that he threw it in the fire. It burned, but the messages he read burned in his heart until he became so convicted he could not sleep. Finally he allowed Christ to come into his heart. Then he was so very happy.

Our broadcast was on Elwa station, and the missionaries as well as the natives jumped for joy as it came over the air.

One student from Thessalanica was so convicted by the Word of God preached on "Your Worship Hour" that he wrote, *"I am so miserable since I heard you preach. You got me into this condition; you are responsible to get me out. Now pray for me that I will become saved."* We surely did. The office staff prayed daily for the requests that came in each day.

A theological student in the Vatican wrote that the Worship Hour sermons were food to his soul. He never missed listening to them. Several nuns in Ohio wrote that his messages were food for their souls.

Quinton usually preached through an entire Bible book; thus he was teaching as well as proclaiming the way of salvation.

One of our pastors was on a plane. As they flew, the man next to him finally asked him where his home was. *"In South Bend"* he told him.

"Oh," he said, *"do you know a Rev. Quinton J. Everest?"*

"Yes," the pastor said. *"He is my friend. We have known each other a long time."*

"Well," said the man, *"I took a load of trash to the city dump site, and as I was ready to drive away, I saw a highly colored book. I stopped, got out of my*

vehicle and picked it up. As I read a bit of it, I thought the book was good enough to take home. I did, and the truth of God's Word in it caused me to see my lost condition. God saved me as a result."

The daily broadcast called "Sunrise Meditations" awakened South Bend-Mishawaka people at 6:15 a.m. However, many were sitting at their breakfast tables or already driving to work. One day I went to the Public Library, and on showing my card, the lady behind the desk asked, *"Are you the broadcaster's wife?"*

"Yes, I am,"

"I must tell you," she said, *"we have never had anyone pray for us or with us until your husband began the early morning program. We hurry around, and the whole family sits at the breakfast table to eat and listen. When he prays for the listeners, we think he means us. We bow our heads. He prays God will encourage us in our faith, for strength for the day and to be a blessing to others."*

As she said this, tears came to her eyes. She was so glad to be able to thank me. It was very touching to me.

A man who was urged by his wife to attend our church services, but was never interested, was such a disappointment to her. He worked at Bendix. On his way, he always listened to "Sunrise Meditations." One morning the Holy Spirit spoke to him so personally that he couldn't get out of his car. He struggled with the awfulness of his sins until he cried to the Lord for mercy. His confession was real and sincere. God did a wonderful work in his heart. He is a

142

happy man and a good husband. Praise God for the results of Quinton's labors of love and passion for lost souls.

Then there was a day when I went shopping for a dress. I had been in this shop only a few times before. I was not acquainted with any of the clerks, as I was in some places. After selecting a dress and was signing a check, the clerk looked at me and asked if I was the wife of the broadcaster. *"Yes,"* I said I was. She seemed so excited and suddenly grabbed my hand, pulling me back across the floor to the dressing room. She pulled the curtain and said softly, *"Now tell me about Jesus. What can you explain to me that I can know why you think he is our Messiah?"*

Quinton had preached many months on Isaiah and prophetic books of the Bible. How my heart went out to her. I quickly asked the Holy Spirit to enlighten her and help me to speak the right words. It was a very moving five minutes. But she said, *"I must go now. Please come back. I want you to tell me more."*

In two or three weeks, the store closed. I was so shocked. I failed to get her name. All I could do was to pray that she would keep listening and pray to be saved.

Quinton often told the listeners as he signed off the early morning broadcast that he would stay in his study room at the church for an hour before he would go home for breakfast. If any one would like counseling and prayer, he would be glad to help them. He had some unusual experiences as a result.

A man who was in the police force for many

years came in crying one morning after having heard the broadcast. His wife always turned on the radio at 6:15. As he sobbed, he told Quinton of his sinful life. At least part of his sins he confessed. Later we learned he was unfaithful to his good Christian wife. But what he told Quinton was that he gambled away so much money in a nearby tavern. Quinton told him of the power of Jesus to change his life and desires. Then he prayed earnestly for God to forgive him, but all the man would do was cry and say, *"I'm supposed to help people to be good, and I can't be good myself."*

Another day he came back. It was the same thing. His drinking had something to do with the unclearness of his mind. On Good Friday afternoon, we had just come home from services at the church. The doorbell rang. There was the broken-hearted policeman, remorseful that he had been gambling away $600.00 instead of being at church. He readily knelt down at the davenport while Quinton prayed for his soul. He talked very plainly, but kindly, quoting scriptures and encouraging him all he could. Sometimes I thought the man expected Quinton to wipe his slate clean but not understanding that it was God who could forgive and change him. He always said as he left, *"Oh, I wish I could be a good man like you are."*

Quinton would always tell him that he himself could not live right without the Lord. It was not long before Quinton received a call that he was in the hospital and wanted Quinton to come see him. At that visit, he said he accepted Christ.

Quinton visited him periodically. The nurses claimed he was a different man than when he came in. He had been a chain smoker and did not ask for any cigarettes. After a month in the hospital, he died.

* * * * *

I was just leaving Quinton's study at the church one afternoon when a middle-aged policeman walked in, sat on the corner of his desk and said, *"Pastor Everest, I've wanted to meet you. River Park is my beat, and I've seen a great difference since you are here. You have made my work much easier. I don't know what you are doing, but keep it up."* They had a nice visit, and I went on home.

My neighbor lady, who together with her husband owned the 5 & 10 cent store, called to me as I crossed the street one day.

"Mrs. Everest, what is your husband preaching about lately? The children and young people are bringing articles back to the store which they picked up and didn't pay for."

"Good," I said. *"They are getting under conviction and giving their hearts to the Lord."*

She looked amazed, and I just smiled.

Another morning on Sunrise Meditation, Quinton spoke on "the home" and the responsibilities of parents. Soon after signing off, the phone rang. It was Mr. Miller, the owner of the South Bend Tribune.

"Pastor Everest," he said, *"I'd like a copy of the talk you gave this morning. I want to print it in the Tribune. It is so vital for our times."*

"But I had no script. I only spoke from my heart."

"Could you write it out, as nearly as possible, as you gave it this morning?"

"I'll try," he said.

In only a few minutes, there was a knock at the door. *"Come in."* The door opened. A woman stood there with flushed face. Quinton asked her to sit down. She gave him her name and said she taught at our nearby school. She heard his talk on family life, and his comments made her very angry. She told him she didn't agree with him at all.

"That's strange," Quinton told her. *"Mr. Miller of the Tribune just called. He wants a copy of it to print in the paper."*

"Oh, that Mr. Miller," she said, and stalked out of the room. Mr. Miller printed the article, which was a full-length column.

Gospel Center Missionary Church
South Bend, IN

Chapter Eleven

Cynthia born Sept, 7, 1947,
Bethel College began Sept. 8, 1947.

The Gospel Center Church basement was now crowded. Nearly every Sunday people were being saved. Sunday evening attendance was only a bit less than in the mornings. And the Wednesday night prayer meetings were very well attended. The upper structure needed to be built, although money was scarce in those days. The congregation was so willing to do all they could. The construction company was chosen, and the architect made up the plans, which delighted the Board. But it was a tremendous venture. Much prayer was made, sometimes nights of prayer. Our faith was increasing because we all saw the need. How God was going to help us accomplish it was not known to us then.

Soon after the renewal of the basement, with the paying off of our debts, we started a building fund. We worshipped in the basement for seven years. Every New Year's Eve we had a special meeting from eight o'clock to twelve midnight. The evening consisted of special singers, choir, quartets, and a strong special speaker. There were testimonies and other ways of including many persons during the evening. Before midnight, we had a communion service followed with a mighty surge of prayer on our knees. This meeting was always well advertised. What a blessed time!

The altar was lined with candles; also the windowsills. Weeks before this meeting would take place, the church families would pledge so much for the building fund. Fifty, one hundred, five hundred and one thousand dollars would all be represented by a candle of different sizes. It was a beautiful sight. Happy and grateful the people were as the ushers counted the offering and reported, yet that night, how much came in toward the building of an upper sanctuary.

It was to seat 1200. Many of our officials of the District of the Missionary Church were very anxious about building so large. However, the people quoted promise after promise. We knew there was a great work to be done. The pastor, radio staff, church board and Sunday School teachers were all helping us bring to pass the vision that seemed so clear.

As an example, our Cradle Roll superintendent drove back and forth on the streets of River Park on Monday mornings. She was looking for diapers hanging on the clotheslines. If she saw a home where there were some, she stopped, introduced herself and told whom she represented. She asked to see the baby and take its picture. She dearly loved babies, and the mothers loved her. At one time we had a large frame on the wall at the back of the sanctuary with ninety baby faces on it. Each month she returned to these homes with literature for mothering and spiritual help. This brought families into the church and to know Christ ultimately.

I, myself, as a superintendent for eleven years in the primary department and eleven years in the Junior High department, drove up and down the streets while classes were in session. I'd look for children playing out of doors during that time. Then I would write down the addresses and hand them to our mission workers. The visits I made were to the homes of my department children to show the parents the Sunday School material. I always let them know that I loved their children and wished very much for them a Christian home. Only once did a burly father slam the door in my face. On Tuesday nights, Quinton and I would visit in the homes of newcomers. I began doing this after our children were grown.

As to the building of the church, it took seven years before we could really start. Trinity Builders were hired. Then we ran out of money before it was finished.

At this same time, the Bethel College board was looking for a construction company to begin their building immediately. Quinton talked to Trinity Builders and the church and college boards about loaning the builders to the college for a year while Quinton raised more finances for the completion of the church.

So the builders proceeded to construct the first floor of the administration building. (Q.J., Jr. got a job there that summer.) It was a flexible place for dining room, classes, chapel and

149

library. This was the first part of what would be called the Administration Building. Great excitement filled the campus as they hurried to make ready for students by Monday, September 8th, 1947. The new professors were coming in to occupy the steel, one-floor houses. Because of the war, many things were scarce and expensive. The metal houses took the place of lumber. Some of the students were to occupy the same kind of housing in a different area. Many students were living in family homes for several years. Washers and dryers were installed; kitchen equipment and furniture for classrooms were all in place.

Quinton was to be chairman of the college board for the first six years, which added greatly to his responsibilities. It seemed not to be an interference of his church work and radio broadcasting but an added "open door" that the Lord had given him. He had great joy working 12-14 hours a day. It seemed always to be so. Things were never dull at our house. We all took an interest in what was going on.

The day before classes were to open was a Sunday. I did not go to Sunday School and morning church service because we were certain this was the day our fourth child was going to be born. Two of our office girls came home with the family for dinner and to stay with the children while Quinton took me to the Elkhart Hospital.

All went well until two o'clock when I grabbed my bag and said goodbye to the children. That was one time that I didn't tell

Quinton to slow down. Soon after arriving at the hospital, a bad storm with hard rain occurred. My doctor was out of town, but his wife knew where to reach him. However, the telephone lines were down, so he didn't get her message until almost seven o'clock.

At five o'clock, Dr. Goodman, president-to-be of Bethel College, and his wife, Marie, who is Quinton's sister, came to the labor room to have a consultation with Quinton. Marie came in to stay with me while Quinton walked the hall with Goodman discussing some last minute matters and procedures concerning the opening of Bethel the following morning.

This over, Quinton came back in where I was hoping and praying my doctor would arrive. Instead, an altogether new doctor, to me, came in, examined me and said, *"I'm thinking of sending you home, to come back later."*

"What?" I said.

He asked, *"Is this your first one?"*

"No. I'm nearly forty, and I've had three. And I know it won't be long until I'll have our fourth!"

With that, he left the room. Almost at once, I called for the nurses. They came running with the cart, transferred me over onto it, and ran down the hall. Almost immediately, my own Dr. James A. Work ran in, scrubbed up, and beautiful baby, Cynthia Sue, was born right away. Dr. Work's words were, *"Mae, she's ten pounds. How do you do it? Three, ten-pound babies."* It was eight o'clock.

At that very time, the professor—whose name I do not remember but who was to preach that evening at Gospel Center for Quinton—said to the people, *"We all know why the pastor is not here this evening. Let us all pray for Mrs. Everest before I start to preach."* People told us that he was praying for me at eight o'clock. I often say, if you don't remember the date for the opening of Bethel College, ask me.

* * * * *

Praise God! Ninety-one students registered for college that first year. And one young man, Marcus Krake, from Michigan, who already had three years of college, graduated at the close of that first year.

* * * * *

One Sunday morning after service was dismissed, a strange man asked Quinton if he was in need of money for the building of the upper structure. He told of a burden the Lord laid upon him for this ministry after he had listened to his messages for a long time. Quinton had not begged for money. But he let this man know our circumstances. *"Please go out with me for dinner,"* the man asked him.

"I'm sorry," Quinton replied. *"We are in the last day of our week-long missionary convention. The wonderful message you heard this morning was given by Miss Yoe from Nigeria. My wife is serving dinner for the missionaries today. They will expect me to be with them."*

"Then can we find a side room to talk? I won't take much of your time."

"Surely, just as soon as I shake hands with the rest

of the people," Quinton said.

So the two of them had a good conversation. He was a businessman from Ohio, came to South Bend with the purpose of seeing the pastor of Your Worship Hour. He finally took out of his pocket a small sugar sack with $2,500 in cash. He was an old man encouraging a young man.

Quinton then came home to dinner with a wonderful story to tell us. *"And,"* Quinton said, *"the man said he'd be back with more."* And he did.

One week later, he called from a downtown hotel and said, *"Tell your Daddy I'd like him to come see me. This happened after much prayer about the building of the church."* He unrolled a newspaper containing a sugar sack of cash with $15,000. God blessed and encouraged the faithful praying people. Quinton asked him to stay over and come to dinner.

* * * * *

After about a year, the Trinity Builders, in a much smaller group, came back to the Gospel Center for about a year. The seventy-foot trusses, two lines of steel surrounding the building, and ceiling joists were in place. Trinity men were then assigned to another job by the company since the church was low on money again.

Some men of our congregation were very qualified builders themselves. They met with Quinton to offer their free services to finish the upper structure. How well they worked together! One man designed the ceiling with indirect lighting and a long cross from the platform to the rear of the sanctuary. Many men and a few women put on the lathe. Quinton designed the altar in sections. The tops could be opened and communion cups were inserted. Small trays would hold the bread. Then the lids would be closed again until time for participation.

* * * * *

In September 1950, the Gospel Center Church was dedicated. Dr. John Church was the speaker that day. What a wonderful time of rejoicing! Dr. Willard Hallman was head of the college music department, director of the radio choir and also director of music of the church. Attendance in the first Sunday morning service that was held in the upper sanctuary looked indeed small. Three hundred and fifty people in the basement church was a crowd, but in the upper structure that could hold 1200, it looked rather empty.

As Quinton and Dr. Willard Hallman took their places on the platform, Willard leaned over and asked, *"What are we going to do?"*

Quinton said, *"What do you mean?"*

"Well," said Willard, *"there are so many empty pews."*

"Oh, we're going to fill them."

There were many times in later missionary conventions, Music Week and meetings for special speakers we had well over 1,200 present.

These were exciting years. How we prayed and then rejoiced as unsaved people were so convicted of their sins that they called for help.

* * * * *

One Sunday afternoon, a sixteen-year-old boy called our home to tell Quinton he didn't know what to do. His parents were trying to commit suicide. They had often listened to Quinton's messages on radio but never went to church. Smart boy to call a preacher instead of the police. He asked Quinton to please come and gave him their address. He went immediately.

On entering the home, he soon said, *"I'm a minister of God. The only way I can help you is if you want Jesus as your Savior."*

"Oh, yes," they both said as they fell on their knees at the davenport. Quinton knelt to pray for them as they were sobbing and confessing their sins. They were a happy family after that, their lives were definitely changed, and they were faithful in their Christian walk and behavior.

One Wednesday evening while we were singing at the beginning of the prayer meeting, a strange lady walked in. Quinton was about to give a Bible lesson before we divided up into prayer groups. Before he could say a word, this lady stood up and said earnestly, *"Would it be out of the way for me to go to the altar? I want to be saved!"*

"Oh, that is in order. That's what we are here for. We want to help you." He didn't have to ask her to go. She was walking down to the altar as he was speaking. Some gathered around her, and we all earnestly prayed God would enlighten and give her the desires of her heart. Her husband and two boys were also converted as a result.

* * * * *

Quinton was often called in the night to other homes and hospitals. Life in the parsonage was a busy place, too. The trustees decided to add another room onto the dining room, which became a family room and for overnight guests. The room contained our children's musical instruments, a hide-a-bed and a desk and two chairs. Now we could sleep more visitors. If they stayed more than one night, Q. J. would give up his upstairs room to them. Before, Q. J., Jr. often slept on a rollaway bed in the dining room or upstairs in the storeroom. He says he liked the storeroom because it had windows on three sides, and he could see much of the neighborhood.

One day, Q. J., Jr. came home from school and hurried toward the stairway. I just caught him in time. *"Quinton James, there is a girl in your room. We don't know her, but she has mumps."*

"What?" he said.

"Yes, Mrs. Shupe, the girl's dorm mother, called to ask us if we would take her in."

"Have you all had the mumps? The college will be closed over the Christmas vacation, and I don't have anyone to house and feed her."

"What could I do? Poor girl. She is far from her home and so sick." She was a good patient. The children took turns with my delivering her trays. Many years later, we met again. She was so grateful. Another time a home burned, and Q.J. moved out of his room again until the parents could find a place to live. It was a matter of only a few days. But Q. J. always went through

these moves in stride. I guess we all got used to the unusual.

There were all kinds of characters in the long procession of visitors who passed through the doors of the parsonage. One month Quinton counted one hundred extra meals that I served. I was born in a pastor's home. Then twenty years later I married a pastor.

Like most days at this time of the morning, I began preparing the noon meal. We were raising our children when most mothers were still feeding their own families. Three meals a day, no pizzas, no short cuts, but cooking fresh foods was the rule. It took much more time but was a much better way to good health. It took at least an hour, but mothers were well repaid with remarks like, *"What's cooking? Something smells good! May I set the table now?"*

* * * * *

The screen door slammed. Charlene hopped upstairs to the bathroom to wash for dinner. Then I heard a male voice singing, *"Oh, my darling, Oh, my darling, Oh, my darling Clementine."* I sneaked into the dining room, listened, and then proceeded to the living room. Down came Charlene.

I asked, *"Who's that?"* as I pointed to a boy on our porch swing, swinging about as far as it would take him. He was near the window, but he didn't look to the right or to the left. When he was through singing, he just got up and went home.

"Who is that?" I laughed.

*"He is just a boy that follows me home. I don't
know where he lives."*

I laughed again. *"He must have a crush on you."*
It happened again and again. But there was no
response to the music from Charlene. He finally quit coming.

* * * * *

The characteristics of a parsonage, or for any
Christian home, for that matter, is having a daily
schedule for parents and children with three bal-
anced meals each day, rotation of a few regular
chores, preparing school assignments, and the
practicing of musical instruments, and finally
family worship each day. Believe me, you know
where your children are if they are musical.
They were also in John Adams High School's
wonderful choir. Their instruments were piano,
violin, cello, viola, and trumpet. The three older
children all began teaching piano or violin at age
sixteen under the suggestion and direction of
Professor Raymond Weaver.

Before the family scattered after supper, we
gathered in the living room. This has been our
habit for over sixty-nine years now. We took
turns reading the Bible and praying for each
other and anything that was on our minds.

One evening, our next door neighbor lady, the
dentist's wife, rang our doorbell as we were
engaged in family worship. I was holding baby
Cynthia while I was reading the Bible. Quinton
went to the door and asked her to come in. She
declined when she saw us all together, but he
said we'd soon be through. She did not sit down

but stood by the door. After I had finished praying—for her family, too—she remarked, *"I have never seen anything so beautiful in all my life."*

* * * * *

One problem I had while the children were in school and Quinton was in the radio office or his study was that often the phone rang while the doorbell was bound to have my attention, too. I could choose to get frustrated or take care of both callers. I'd hurry to the phone and say, *"Hello, please hold. There is someone at the door."* Then I'd hurry to the door and say, *"Please come in. Have a chair. Someone just called on the phone."*

Listeners to our daily broadcast sometimes came to our house to talk over their problems. We always finished with prayer. Q.J., Jr. reminded me recently that he remembers me counseling and praying with women on the phone.

A lovely high school girl stopped at the parsonage on her way home from school one afternoon. She wanted me to pray with her. My children were home. So I said, *"Let's go upstairs to my bedroom."* Her fear of getting too popular was disturbing her. She had given her life to Christ, and she was determined that God had a special ministry for her. She could not see the future, but she did not want to miss God's best. After we discussed the matter and after each of us prayed, we got up off our knees and smiled at each other. We were both confident the Lord was in control. Her parents were unsaved, and I was superintendent of the intermediates of the Sunday School. Now she and her husband have been officers in the Salvation Army for thirty years. An evangelist at our Prairie Camp told us he knows them well and gives much praise to her speaking ability.

* * * * *

Praise God for all the witnessing that our children did, too, as they were growing up. Young Q. J. won his eighth grade teacher to the Lord. His teacher was teaching on creation. He knew it was not the truth as he read it in the Bible. So he stayed after class and told her. She wanted him to explain it to her as he understood it. He did, but finally said, *"You should come to our church on Sunday nights. My Dad is preaching on Revelation."* He knew that there were no services at her church on Sunday nights. She came week after week. Her hunger for the Word of God increased, and her mind and heart were enlightened. She went to Quinton's study one day after school and poured out her thoughts and experience to him. It was a joyful time, now that she understood salvation and could testify to His saving grace.

Once she came to his study with forty dollars to give toward anything we needed. Quinton was surprised. He said he never takes money for counseling. *"But, oh,"* she said, *"you could use it for dental bills or something."* She never got over the joy the Lord gave her through the Everest children.

* * * * *

Several years after Charlene was married, one

160

of the girls she graduated with from high school came back to South Bend from California for a visit. She was in trouble with her marriage and almost frantic. Charlene was not a special friend of hers, but the dear girl couldn't think of anyone she could go to for help. Young people never know how great an impression their Christian lives make on others until years go by. The girl spent a day or two with Charlene to get the help she needed.

Sharon was very sensitive about the salvation of her school friends. At one time she told me she had such a strong, heavy burden for a neighbor girl, that she had to go to her house and pray with her. She couldn't sleep at night. I listened to her. I told her if she feels it was from the Lord, He would go with her and would tell her what to say. I added that I would quit working and pray for her while she was gone. (I think she was about fifteen at this time.) When she came back, she told me the girl and her mother were there alone. Sharon told her in simple words the plan of salvation, that the Lord loved and died for her. She said, *"I am so concerned about you that I had to come over and pray for you."*

So Sharon knelt and poured out her heart in prayer for her. Neither her mother nor the girl said a word to her. So Sharon just came home a little mystified but, oh, so relieved.

I said, *"Sharon, you obeyed the Lord's promptings. She knows you care for her soul. And if she doesn't respond, believe me, she will never forget that as long as she lives."*

Our obedience to the Lord is of much more

value than the work we try to do for Him in our own strength. Sometimes people did not accept Jesus' teaching either. People set their own minds to do as the worldly ones do.

* * * * *

Monday was wash day at our house. The second batch of clothes was in the wash machine. It was a busy morning. As soon as I was through with the laundry, it would be time to start preparing the noon meal. All the children came home at noon and needed to have it ready as soon as they arrived. Their time was limited. But I suddenly thought of a family whom Quinton had visited and for whom we had been earnestly praying. God impressed upon me to go see the mother while she was alone. I prayed as I worked but became so uncomfortable about it that I felt pressured. I was to go now.

"Shut off the washer and go now," He seemed to say. I really was afraid not to go. So I went down the Avenue about four blocks, rang the doorbell. She opened it immediately as if she were there waiting for me. I had never been to her home up to that time. She looked at me and started to sob before I could say a word.

"I just got back from the dentist five minutes ago. Oh, Mae, I know why you are here."

"You do?"

"Yes," she said, as she turned and knelt at the davenport. *"I want to be saved. I'm so miserable, and I know my boys need a Christian mother."*

She did most of the praying. I then prayed for her, her husband and the two boys. One of them

162

was in my Sunday School department. As she arose, I saw a woman with a shining face and a love for my Savior, and for me. And I had a new friend, too.

* * * * *

There was a man in a nearby town who often called at the office and at our home. I think he was a lonely man. But he always said the same things and took too much of our time. Many times he would end up by saying, *"Mrs. Everest, tell your husband to talk louder on the radio."* Then I would always say, *"Just turn the volume up a little."* But he'd say, *"If I turn the volume up, the neighbors upstairs don't like it. They knock on my ceiling."* This went on for years. It was just a trial for the office girls and myself. *"Poor fellow,"* I'd always say.

* * * * *

Our children were quite uniquely spaced. When Cynthia was born, Charlene was sixteen, Q.J., Jr. twelve, and Sharon, ten.

As a baby and a young child, she was a delight to all of us. Of course, she was too young to be involved in their games and activities; so she was always delighted when Quinton came home for the evening meal. One summer day, she skipped out to meet him as he came down the sidewalk. He took her hand and led her into the house. She climbed on his lap and picked up a little bunch of something, but I went out to the kitchen to finish supper. Everything was too quiet.

163

Then the doorbell rang. I hurried to answer. I knew Quinton was tired and enjoying his little girl. Perhaps she was about four years old. He started to get up but saw me coming; so he stayed seated with Cynthia on his lap. My mouth fell open when I saw what she had done to him. She had gotten into her sister's curlers and had his whole head of hair wrapped in curlers. Well, I hurried to the door. I greeted a strange lady who said, "I'm from Wisconsin and needed to go through your city. I've often heard your husband speak on radio and wished so much to see him."

"*Oh, please come in. He's here, but our little Cynthia has him all tied up in her sister's curlers. I must tell you, as you've no doubt seen in pictures of him, that he has curly hair of his own.*" She laughed heartily. I'm sure she enjoyed telling her family and friends about that. They had a nice short visit before she left.

* * * * *

Another very warm day Cynthia had been playing outside. Quinton was already at home. She ran in and jumped on his lap, hugging him and saying, "*Daddy, I love you. May I have an ice cream cone?*" This was said with a kiss. So Daddy gave her a nickel, and out of the house she went letting the screen door slam behind her. The Lamont Drug Store was just around the corner.

At age six she started taking piano lessons, too. Charlene gave her a few lessons, but soon she was taking lessons from the same teacher our other children had.

* * * * *

Is it a normal thing to have a wedding in the average home any time of the day, any day of the week? Of course not. But in our parsonage at that time it was normal. Some wished to have large weddings in the church. Most couples in those days liked it simple with a few bouquets from our garden with the bride and groom standing in front of the fireplace. Since Daddy was on the radio and if they had no pastor, it was natural for them to call him to perform the ceremony. However, he required they first meet with him at the church for counseling. A number of times he refused to marry a couple.

Once Quinton forgot to tell me of a wedding. He was in overalls planting trees at the church. Charlene and Sharon were washing the noon dishes. I stood in the doorway and was about to say, *"After you girls are through with the dishes, I'll scrub the kitchen floor. Then our cleaning will be finished."* It was Saturday and almost one o'clock.

But as I opened my mouth, I gasped as I saw a girl in a beautiful wedding gown walk past the living room window (on the porch) and reach for the doorbell.

"Charlene," I yelled, *"run over to the church and tell Dad a bride and groom is here."*

I greeted the couple and their guests. I explained the situation, apologized and excused myself to go upstairs. I changed my clothes and brushed my hair.

Quinton ran home through the alley. He had

to walk past them to get to the stairway after a quick greeting.

Every parsonage should have a rear stairway, I thought.

* * * * *

On a Sunday morning as I walked in to the church, I passed a friend of mine who didn't respond to my greeting or smile. I was about to ask her what was troubling her, but she finally said, *"Why didn't you come to our house yesterday? The chicken dinner got cold. We had homemade ice cream and pie."* I was dumbfounded!

"I certainly did not know anything about that or we would have been there." Why she didn't call us to inquire, I don't know. Quinton and I certainly did our best to apologize. She probably gave him the invitation at the church door the previous Sunday while he was shaking hands with his parishioners. Anyway, I started helping with the schedules for both of us.

* * * * *

An anxious voice on the phone said, *"My brother shot himself and is in the hospital. Will you go pray with him?"* Quinton went. The next day another call. *"Will you preach at his funeral?"*

* * * * *

"Think our house is a laundry?"
"No, mother's just washing for the janitor's sick wife and a missionary and daughter who have been traveling."

* * * * *

166

Cynthia born, Sept. 7, 1947...

"Why is our car stuffed full of used clothing?"
"Oh, Mother and some other women are gathering up and packing clothes for Korea."
"How many barrels?"
"Twenty-three."
Another day, "What's all the paints and cardboard for?"
"Oh, Mother is using this to decorate her Sunday School department."

* * * * *

Years later when the three older children were married and Cynthia was in Azusa Pacific College in California, Quinton and I made a trip to the islands of the Caribbean and Brazil. We visited and ministered in each of our churches. Near one jungle church, twenty coffee farmer's little houses stood in a row. These were plantation workers. The winter before we were there, it was so cold the children ran to the missionaries' house to keep warm. The missionary opened the barrels they had brought from the United States filled with warm clothing and blankets. She wrapped several children in one blanket to keep them warm. They slept on the floor. When she told me that, it nearly broke my heart.

So I went home to the United States churches and told this at every church where I was asked to speak at women's meetings. Jean Granitz, the missionary, told me, *"Don't gather up a few blankets to send. That would never work. Each home needs a blanket."* So I would tell the women at home that we must have twenty.

167

The day came when I had twenty beautiful blankets packed in the back seat of my car. One young lady had just been married and gave me two blankets. She was showered with blankets. Other women whose children were now gone from home were generous to give some.

Our son came home from college that day and said, *"Mother, what in the world are all those blankets doing in your car? You are still gathering things up?"* So I told him all about it.

Now the problem was, I did not know how to find the barrels, nor how to pack and send them, if I did.

I had one more speaking engagement where I told my dilemma. A lady said, *"I just packed and sent off barrels to Nigeria. I'll be glad to buy the barrels, pack them and send them to Brazil."* Oh, was I grateful!

* * * * *

When the children were in college or married, I often traveled with Quinton. I was often invited to accompany him and prayed as he preached. However, many times there were responsibilities to care for; so many times I was alone.

Quinton was scheduled to begin a meeting on Thursday night at Elizabethtown, North Carolina. It was to continue through the following week. On Wednesday morning, he awoke feeling sick. All day we prayed and tried to get him started. We packed his clothes, and he laid on the davenport until evening. He should have been traveling all that day. Finally, he said he felt good enough if he wasn't so weak.

A sudden idea struck me. *"Give me fifteen minutes to pack my suitcase, cover you up on the back seat of the car, and I'll drive."* It was now 8:15 in the evening. *"We'll go as far as the Ohio line, sleep a few hours in a motel, then get up early in the morning and continue. You'll miss the first night, but we'll make it for Friday night. We'll call them in the morning and let them know we are on our way."*

Maybe it took me twenty minutes, but we were soon on our way. However, we stopped at the edge of the city to fill up the gas tank.

We drove until we were near the Ohio line, probably a half-mile past a filling station, when suddenly the car stopped. I managed to stop off the side of the traffic lane. It was pitch dark. I had been so willing and brave but now felt deflated.

"And how long do you think we'll have to wait for help at this hour on Route 80? Pray." Yes, we prayed. In five minutes, we heard a sheriff's car screaming towards us. How kind he was! He took us in his car back to the filling station where there was also a garage.

While we waited there, our car was towed in and tested for a long time. They could find nothing wrong. They pushed the car up to the pump, and the young fellow there said, *"The cap is off the tank. Because of the gas running over the hot pipes, it could have exploded."* He found a cap for us. After spending two and a half hours there, we were on our way again. We drove until we found a motel open. It was 2:00 a.m. We slept just a few hours.

After a bite of breakfast, we changed off driving. Quinton was feeling better. We arrived at the church in Elizabethtown just in time for the evening service. The director of music had preached the previous night in Quinton's absence. They were glad to see us, and we were so thankful to the Lord for His protection and mercy.

Was the delay because Quinton did not feel well? Or was it because of the careless attendant who failed to put the cap on the tank? Perhaps God had detained us for another reason. Could be that He protected us from something.

* * * * *

There were many guests periodically at our house. There were two or three revivals each year, a youth convention, missionary convention, and a Music Week. Each of these was one or two weeks in length.

In Zion at Elkhart, there was a six-week revival that could not be stopped. The power of God was evident in the services and also during the day and night hours. People would call for Quinton to come to pray for them. They had listened to the Word of God preached on radio or in the church, which brought such strong conviction upon them that they said they couldn't eat or sleep. They needed the Savior. After that meeting, one Sunday morning, a line of people from the south wall to the north wall became members of Zion Missionary Church. Beside that, many other churches benefited by that revival. WTRC Elkhart radio station had sold us time from 7:30 to 9:00 air time.

Because of all these meetings, we entertained many well-known, godly and interesting people. What a benefit this was to our children, from babyhood until their marriage.

Even while they were in high school, they would hurry home to rest an hour, then study so they could go to church at night.

After church, we'd gather around the table with our guests. I would ask each of them what they wanted to eat. While I prepared soup, sandwiches, large malted milks, the guests would tell experiences, stories, jokes, and give praise to the Lord for the many souls won. And also stories of great protection from tragedies were told. It was very rewarding.

Sometimes we had almost more than we could handle, especially when they brought more of their family than we knew were coming. But we wanted them to feel welcome. I loved the new experiences but often had to pray that the Lord would give me extra strength. He did. I always had extra things for which to praise Him.

Before the annual Missionary Conventions, we invited all the denominational missionaries who were home on furlough to attend. We paid their traveling fare and housed them in our homes. Before the main speaker, one of our own missionaries gave a short account of the most rewarding happenings of their last term. Our own missionaries were thrilled to be with us, to learn of how God was working in other parts of the world. Otherwise, they would never have heard about these events.

At these conventions, offerings were taken and pledges made for the coming year. We always had reason to greatly praise God for continual increase in giving each year.

* * * * *

For one Missionary Convention, we had a speaker, "the Monk that lived again," from Argentina. He said to us, *"Every day God shows me new things. I feel like a small ant in your presence. I am a young man in this, but what God has put in my heart I want to share with you. This is a surprise trip, and I'm trusting in Christ for what I should say. In the first minutes when I set my feet on your soil, I felt the presence of the Lord.*

"God took me out from a religion which was only conversation. On October 31, 1961, in a small town in the Andes mountains, not even on the map, but God knew where I was for ten years. I had had an encounter with God. I wanted to serve Him. On the road I was taking, I could not. I tried to quench this thirst. But I could not. I sought Him in my personal devotions shut up in the cloisters. I studied in the best seminaries in Italy. I had a very privileged place in the seminary because of my name. I often saw the difference with which the other students were treated. I objected in my heart. These things hurt my weak heart. I asked to transfer into a stricter convent, an isolated one. I wanted to be a regular clergy so my life could be better for God. A great storm was in my soul. I used to consider I was the only one struggling like this. I thought the others had arrived at peace. The most important university I entered in 1949, I

received the robes. I became very sick. They would not let me go to a hospital. I fled away and was twenty-seven days in a hospital. The nuns gave me injections of morphine. The nuns were told to let me die, not to let me escape. A doctor marveled that I was still living with such infection coming close to my heart. God was having mercy on me. The doctor operated that day and said if the superiors would not treat me better, he would protect me.

"But when I was released, I went back to the university, for I yet thought to find peace. I went from church to church. Some did not care about God and peace. They took their religion very lightly. But I wanted to meet God. In 1958, my parents had to pay thousands of dollars so that I might have a high position. But I wanted a place in the heart of God. My sick father that year could have no connection with the outside world. He died without them allowing me to see him. Then I read Psalms 51.

"When a fellow student died, they prayed many times but would not tell us who it was, not even his parents or relatives. A great revolution took place in my heart. When my father died, I wanted to be side of my mother.

"In two months, the election took place, and we were permitted to go home for three days to vote.

"I was ordained into the priesthood. The day before, I confessed. I wanted to put my sins on a man. I cried aloud to give me peace in my soul! Give me peace in my soul! I cried out to my bishop, 'Give me peace!' He said he had peace, but I said, 'Then give me peace.' But he looked at the ground.

"I spent vacations in France with Pope Paul. He was very close. He cried out to the Evangelical

churches to pray for him. He had no peace when he was dying.

"Now we know the One who gives us peace. We know Christ.

"In the southern part of Argentina, they wanted to establish churches. They said, 'Maybe if you go to the mission field, you might find the answer to your spiritual problems.' I was made director of a school there and worked in a mission across the Andes mountains. I climbed on a mountaintop where there was a small chapel. In moments of soul torments, I'd climb up there to the feet of images. One day as I came down, I met an Indian man who asked me why I climbed up there.

"I go up to seek peace.

"He answered, 'If you raise your eyes up.'

"Up to what?

"The Indian said, 'Up to Christ above all these things. Come over to our little church tonight.'

"I've never been to an evangelical church. I have persecuted children who went to Sunday School in church.

"I spoke to my companions about going. They said, 'You can go, but be very careful.'

"Praise God. I wasn't careful.

"It was snowing. I gathered my robes about me and looked around to see if anyone was watching then ran into the small church. They were praying. I looked in my prayer book for their prayers but could not find it. I had prepared to argue with them. After prayer, they gathered round and told me they were praying for me. I said, 'Why for me. I am sinful.'

"Afterwards my companions asked me what happened at the church.

Cynthia born, Sept. 7, 1947...

"For months I had one foot in one place and the other foot in another. The Bible says, 'You cannot serve two masters.'

"Because of my personal ego and pocketbook, I went back to my church. The devil redoubled his efforts, but God had mercy. October 31st, I left my church forever. Nobody advised me. Only God put it in my heart.

"I went back to the Indian chapel but did not sit in the last seat in the back, as I usually did. God reached me. I went up to the front. All the brethren watched me as I came in. For many months they had prayed for me, and there is no limit to the power of prayer. That same Indian man brought the message and for the first time, I realized I was a wayward son of God. He cleansed me from all my sin.

"After having searched for Him in twelve countries, I looked up to the heavens and knew I met God. I did not leave my priest's service, but I felt now I was a real priest, a true priest. I used to offer sacrifice. Now I gave myself to Him. I was then baptized with water. People from the other church had documents to send me back to Italy. They stoned me. They would not sell to me in the stores. When the evangelicals saw the Romans persecute me, they were afraid. I was alone. God spoke to me.

"I went to a very small town and had my first home under a tree. God had paid a price for me. The rocks around me were the benches of my church. My mother was afraid. They in Rome wrote me threatening letters. By now many were getting saved where I was. The Word 'not by might nor by power but by my Spirit.' I prayed for many days. Then wrote a long letter to my mother. Mother wrote, 'Now I know

*God has met you. The peace that you feel I am feel-
ing, too, and if I were younger, I would come to help
you preach the Gospel.'*

"*I decided I would follow the Lord no matter what
happened. A year later, I had a wife. I let the Holy
Spirit take over my life. People ask, 'Why do you stay
in a small town?' Jesus began in Nazareth. I'm good
for this workshop where I can learn from Him. I
know others will learn God from me.*

"*I'm anxiously awaiting the moment when God
will lead me out. I want God to send me back to Italy
to be a missionary in the Vatican as a missionary
from Argentina.*"

* * * * *

Other missionary speakers were the Erneys
from Korea; Peter Deyneka; Clyde Taylor; Paul
Freed; Alex Leonovich; Mrs. Darlene Rose; Roy
Adams; Charles Elkjer; Mitsuo Fuchida, who
was converted after leading the Japanese
Armada to bomb Pearl Harbor.

Many evangelists helped greatly in drawing
the unsaved to hear the gospel of Jesus Christ at
our Gospel Center. Some of these were William
Allen, Torrey Johnson, Jimmy Lentz, the Sutera
Twins, Jimmy Gibson, James DeWeerd, Hugh
Ferguson, Thomas Mosley, Samuel Kamalesan,
Dr. John Church. On one weekend, we had
medical doctors from Canada and the U. S.,
including Dr. Walter Wilson. What soul winners
they were!

During the Music Week each year, we had a
choir of 75-100 voices and a different outstanding soloist or quartet each night with a music

director for the entire week. Usually the director was Orville Butcher or Derric Johnson from California.

We often had one thousand and several times 1400 in attendance. What a blessing came upon us as Rev. Orville Butcher would lean on the pulpit and with his beautiful voice and pleading tone sing, *"Don't Go Away Without Jesus"* as the benediction ceased.

Chapter Twelve

*Quinton's world missionary tour
and Cairo's riots.*

By late 1949, both the church and college were
operating well. Quinton's responsibilities were
scheduled so that he could answer some of the
invitations coming from our foreign missionaries to be the speaker in conventions. His second
extensive tour took him around the world.
Starting in Nigeria, West Africa, there was a
northern and southern convention of missionaries.

One of our pastors from California informed
Quinton of his increasing desire to go with him
on this tour. He also told him he would pay all
of his own expenses. I was thrilled that Quinton
was not going alone. Roscoe Burk was a pleasant, spirit-filled companion. He was also very
humorous.

A travel agent prepared his flight, times and
accommodations for the entire trip, leaving from
New York, going to Nigeria, Egypt, India, Israel,
Japan and Hawaii. Quinton had the office personnel type many copies for relatives, congregation and radio listeners so that much prayer
would be constantly brought before God for the
work of ministry, for their protection and health.

While they were ministering in various

My family — 1949 - Quinton, Sr., Sharon, Cynthia, Quinton, Jr., Mae, Charlene

places, Quinton would produce tapes for the "Sunrise Meditations" broadcast program. Then he would mail them home. Once he made one in Westminster Abbey in London. These were his plans so that the radio ministry could be carried on in his absence.

His last day before leaving was a Sunday. He delivered his morning and evening messages. The baggage was in the car at the church.

The music ceased, and the evening benediction was given. The people filed out of the church.

To one who might have been a visitor, there appeared to be much ado as the crowd hurriedly made their way to their cars. Those who had arrived on foot were invited to ride with others.

In the study at the rear of the church, the pastor, Quinton, eager, too, to get on his way, busied himself with last minute details—with papers,

cameras and briefcase. Then giving his desk a
swift tidying up, he turned to me smiling. We
had not spoken, but I was observing him close-
ly, praying he would not forget something
important. With a great swell of thankfulness in
my heart, I suddenly exclaimed, *"Quinton, the
Lord gave me a wonderful promise for your safety as
you go on your world tour."*

Quickly he snatched my hand and waited
saying, *"What is it?"*

I said, *"It's from Psalm 91. 'For He shall give His
angels charge over thee, to keep thee in all thy ways.'"*

"Good," he said. *"That's an excellent one. And
He has given me a special promise, too. 'Commit thy
way unto the Lord; trust also in Him, and He shall
bring it to pass.'"*

With that, we said no more but gathered the
baggage and hurried out the side exit where the
children were waiting in the car.

The ride to the airport was uneventful. A few
exchanges of thoughts concerning business and
family affairs were given, but our hearts were
prayerful as we rode through the city. We had
never been separated for such a long time and
for so many thousands of miles.

Kisses, hugs, and good-byes and a *"God bless
you"* were given to me, Charlene, Dale, her hus-
band-to-be, Quinton, Jr., Sharon, down to little
Cynthia who was lifted up into her Daddy's
arms. Quinton then made his way to his father
and mother. Comforting them, too, with smiles
and kisses, he backed away from the crowd,
waving and turning toward the airplane. Here
the newspaper photographers stopped him to

take pictures while the congregation sang, *"Bless him, Lord, and make him a blessing."* This was not to be a sightseeing trip. As president of the United Missionary Society, he was to visit the various mission fields, getting first-hand information and speaking many times in several conventions.

When the two men landed at Lagos, Nigeria, Russell Sloat was there to meet them.

Russell then took them to Ilorin where our seminary is located. Quinton spoke to the students and preached to the people in the church.

Then they traveled on to Igbetti where the first convention was held.

Quinton was there as president of all our foreign mission work to inspire, encourage, and counsel; also, to witness the saving, sanctifying power of Christ, effectively working in those who for all their lives had lived in heathen darkness. It was a great joy for him.

They were able to visit all the main stations and a few others.

Igbetti was a small church and was about to be closed. While Quinton was still in the States, he notified all the pastors in the U.S. and Canada to immediately summon their congregations to fast and pray for a mighty revival. In a short time, the power of the Gospel changed the hearts and minds of so many people that hundreds of people were saved.

They built a new church. The attendance grew to 1600 natives. What rejoicing there was both in that congregation and those here at home.

The building was paid for by the Igbetti people. When we consider that the average laboring wage was forty cents per day, we recognize their spirit of love and sacrifice

* * * * *

Our women in the U.S. and Canada raised enough money to build a large hospital at T.M.

Quinton and Roscoe visited this busy place and watched Dr. Bell perform surgery. People came many miles, walking and on muleback to be cared for because the doctors and nurses were very kind. They had devotions every day with the patients. Many found Christ.

* * * * *

After the convention, they went on to Salka for another gathering of the missionaries farther north. Quinton was there to speak, encourage and help them with their problems.

One day Russell Sloat took Quinton to an area where the people had never heard the name of Jesus.

When they heard the sound of the car's engine, they crowded around them. Russell raised his hands toward the sky and tried to tell them about the true God. Quinton took a movie of those people. I can never forget the expression on their faces.

One morning after a night of native fetish, Eileen Lageer asked Quinton and Roscoe to go with her to the marketplace. Quinton was so tired that he had slept soundly. But Roscoe had not slept much. He was awake most of the night listening to the beating of drums and yelling of the people. As the three of them walked down the street, they saw that all the pagan natives had placed blood over the threshold of their houses and down both sides of the door. Feathers were stuck on the blood. They had killed many chickens in the night for this blood. This was their way of running out the devil.

Eileen stopped at a little hut and called a leper to come out of his hut. They waited awhile because he had only a sitting position. He waddled out while Eileen smiled and told him who Quinton was. Eileen interpreted for the men. The leper said to tell Quinton, *"Thank you for sending the missionaries. I now have eternal life, and after this life on earth, God will give me a new body."* He was so happy!

Before the men left Nigeria, Hilda Brenneman gave Quinton a haircut. He never lets her forget it. He had thick, wavy hair.

Quinton had known these seventy missionaries before they went to Nigeria. They are our dear friends.

* * * * *

Before Quinton and Roscoe left, their travel agent had informed me that the men would be traveling VIP so that I need feel no alarm as to their safety. Indeed, I had no feeling of fear as they took off but only one of separation. After twenty-four years of close, happy communion, it made me feel as if part of me had been drawn away.

The travel agent again informed me Mr. Everest would be well taken care of and was traveling on the best planes obtainable. At that time they were all prop planes. The service and hotels he had booked were the best, and there was nothing to worry about.

Up to that time, I had felt absolutely no fear; so I wondered if the agent was actually allaying his own fears or at least knew something of critical foreign affairs that I did not.

Then just a trickle of news about trouble in Cairo, Egypt came through by radio. Not much was given. They were the very days our traveling party was to be in Cairo.

At mealtime, as I was preparing food, suddenly I felt a blanket of fear sweep over me. It felt so heavy. So, stopping my work, I said, *"Lord, the men are in trouble."* And as swiftly came the words, *"Can't I trust you with precious things?"* *"Oh, yes, Lord,"* I said. From that moment, the fear was gone. But I continued in prayer without telling the children of my experience.

At midnight, I still felt the need of constant prayer for them. I was afraid I would fall off to sleep, so I asked Him to lay the burden of prayer on other people. The responsibilities of my Sunday School Department and preparations for my family were necessary.

On Sunday morning before the visiting speaker, Rev. S. I. Emery, greeted the people, he told them that the Lord awakened him in the night to pray for Quinton and Rev. Burk. He felt they were in trouble. And so before he started to preach, he said, *"Let us pray."* As soon as the dismissal was given, and I had not taken one step away from the pew, an elderly lady stood before me and said, *"I was awakened at midnight. The Lord said, 'Pray for Quinton.' I got down on my knees to pray for fear of going back to sleep."* How many people of the radio audience felt the same urgency, I don't know. But praise God for His faithfulness!

We, the children and I, went home for dinner. The phone soon rang. I ran to pick it up.

"Mrs. Everest?" "Yes," I replied. *"This is Western Union. We have a telegram for you from Egypt. We will bring it to you immediately. But we were sure you would want to know the message right away. This message came from Heliopolis, which is a suburb of Cairo. It says, 'All is well with us. Quinton.' "* It was a short but definite statement.

However, here is the story as it was told to me by Quinton and some quotes from newspapers from Chicago, New York, Fowler, Colorado, The South Bend Tribune and others.

The incident actually began for them on January 25, 1952, as he and Burk were flying from Tripoli to Cairo. At Bengasi, a small coastal town, all the other passengers left the plane. Whether they had been forewarned of the approaching riot, Quinton never learned.

They were scheduled to stay at the famous old Shepherd's Hotel. They were required to leave their visas at the desk for its protection. In the morning, after a few hours of sightseeing, our men, along with a missionary friend, Ethel Young, had lunch together in the hotel. They noticed a large crowd gathering in the street. They had plans with their tour guide to do more sightseeing after lunch. However, that never developed.

After lunch, the three returned to the spacious lobby just as the mob broke a large window. Not knowing which way to turn, they went up to their room on the third floor where they knelt to pray. Within a matter of minutes, fires were being started by lighting the long drapes with torches.

The three hurriedly left their room, carrying very little with them. Smoke was becoming almost unbearable. They all crawled on their hands and knees to a stairway. Mr. Burk was pushing an empty suitcase as he crawled along. It was Quinton's, and it was empty. Only saving their lives was on their minds now. Quinton only had the clothes on his back.

When the guide had brought them back for lunch, he left them off at a side door because he was aware of the great disturbance that was about to take place. Had they not known of this side entrance, they would probably have perished in the flames and smoke, as did so many others in this hotel.

Outside the building was a garden where a few people were hoping for safety. But they still saw no way of escape. There were buildings burning on three sides of them, and in front of them was the street filled with rioters yelling, throwing furniture out of the windows, smashing new cars in showrooms and burning all of these in large bonfires in the streets. They threw a man into the bonfire a couple of blocks from the Shepherd's Hotel. Quinton saw a man tie bed sheets together and jump from an upper window rather than lose his life by burning.

While our loved ones were forced to spend three hours in the garden watching and hearing terrible things, Quinton repeated over and over the promise God had given him and the promise God had given me. He also reminded God of his assurance of salvation, of his love for Christ, his commitments to the work around the world of winning souls and of his love and responsibility for the children and me.

Finally, a hotel employee, whom he had seen and recognized, came to the garden and said, *"There is a taxi coming in the street nearby. If you want to run for it, you'd better do it now."*

Rev. Burk, Miss Young, and Quinton agreed that the lady with two children close by them should be first. In about half an hour, another taxi stopped. The three ran to it. As soon as they got in, the driver said to my husband, *"Take that hat off your head. That is what they are shooting at today. Where do you want to go?"*

"We do not know."

It was dark by now.

The driver, with much difficulty, dodging huge fires in the streets and going through the enraged mobs that were overturning other cars, succeeded in getting them to the police station.

"Here we again discovered that a number of the police were involved in the turmoil. Who could we trust, and what could we do? We certainly recognized that we could not trust any man. There was only one way out, and that was UP. We trusted God.

"After talking to the Chief of Police, telling him

that we were Americans, not British with whom they had their squabble, he allowed us to remain in a small back room in the police station for five and a half hours until God sent us another deliverer.

"While in the police station, we were at various times flat on the floor in order to be safe from the shooting that was going on outside. Sometimes we took turns lying under the table."

It was in the police station that God sent a guardian angel in the form of an Egyptian air force officer to rescue them.

After hours on the floor with other Americans, like Steels of the New York Tribune, and Christine Carroll, a French opera singer who lost her voice, suddenly our missionary Ethel Young screamed as she got on her feet and ran to the door. Thinking she was overwrought, they watched as she threw open her arms and met the newcomer in a glad embrace. *"Oh, Waheeb Tawfik! How did you find us?"*

Mr. Tawfik was Egyptian's highest ranking air force officer. He was also the son of the pastor for whom Ethel was working as a teacher in his school.

He related that as the fires grew in Cairo and as her favorite hotel, The Alexandria, was in flames, and knowing she had come to Cairo to meet some ministers from The United States that very day, he knew he must search for her. He went to the Shepherd's Hotel, but it was also burned down. He cried as he told her of seeking God's direction. Finally, the police station came to his thinking.

He was dressed in his Air Force uniform.

"And now," he said, after he introduced himself to her visitors, *"stay right here until I come back with a taxi to take us to Heliopolis."*

In ten minutes, he was back again and took them out to the taxi. *"Stay very close to me,"* he said, as the people around saluted him.

Arriving at the hotel there, he suggested they lay on the beds with their clothes on. The English had tanks all around, and things became quiet. The next day he sent his brother to take them sightseeing.

As soon as their air force officer was at liberty to take them to the American Embassy, he did. The huge gate was closed. He talked to the guards regarding his mission, and they saluted him as they opened the gate. Soldiers were standing in line from the gate down the long driveway to the Embassy.

When he stated their business, they were graciously assisted, but not before the Ambassador asked them, *"How in the world could you get into this building? No one was to let anyone inside this building."* Quinton pointed at Whaeeb. And he replied, *"Only he could have gotten you in."*

They could not get a flight out of Cairo until Thursday. Some of that time was spent going to other embassies to get visas for countries for the remainder of the trip. Their visas had been burned at the desk in the hotel.

It is interesting to note the prices for the famous Shepherd Hotel rooms and tours during their stay in Cairo in 1952. The cost per person, per day, for the hotel was $23.80, which included all meals, tips and tax. Two half-day sightseeing trips, including the Sphinx, the Pyramids, the Museum and Old Cairo was $9.90 per person, which included guides, chauffeur, entrance fees and tips.

From Cairo, they flew to Jerusalem for a three-day schedule of tours.

The first day they visited the Tomb of the Virgins, The Garden of Gethsemane, and Bethlehem.

The second day, they visited the Mount of Olives, the Dead Sea, Jericho, Allenby Bridge, and River Jordan. Then they went to Amman and stayed overnight.

At Beirut they were at leisure for two days.

They arrived at Calcutta, India for a week of speaking in the churches and at the school at Raghunathpur with staff members and students of the mission school, and churches.

Quinton and Mr. Burk, his traveling friend, slept in a tent. In the morning after they were dressed, they went outside where a basin of water was prepared for them. A mirror hung nearby on a pole. While they washed and shaved, many people came up close to them. Mothers carrying children wanted to observe these Americans, too. So the men put on a real "act" for them, slinging their washcloths at each other as if to be washing each other's faces. In the movies taken of this episode, it looked as if they were having a real scrap. When they quit, the mothers wanted them to hold their babies. One of the babies looked into the face of my husband and set up a howl. Quinton just laughed. Then the people all went back home.

Quinton was asked to baptize some of the new converts. A group of preachers accompanied him to the lake.

After Quinton returned home, we received word that a young couple, who was baptized, had a new baby boy whom they named Quinton. John Blosser, one of Quinton's young converts from Goshen, Indiana, was the missionary who took good care of our travelers. Quinton was his pastor when John was in High School. It was a great joy to see him developing in the ministry to which he was so definitely called in his teen years.

* * * * *

Our own missionary, Bessie Cordell, who had spent years in China, was commanded by the communists to leave the country. She loved the Chinese so much that she felt she could not go back to America. Instead, she followed the refugees to Formosa. She pled with Quinton to stop at Formosa on his world trip. He did.

One Sunday morning they were called to the YMCA where a group of five hundred people were waiting to hear Quinton speak. The room was packed with comparatively young, well-educated people. Many had fled for their very lives from mainland China when it fell to the communists. Many had started their careers and were now anxiously seeking whatever they could get. Therefore, they were responsive to the message of Christ. However, the majority of this congregation was Christian.

To hear their heart-rending stories of what

happened on the mainland and their hazardous escape and of fear was difficult to forget.

Quinton and Rev. Burk were taken to Generalissimo Chiang Kaishek's headquarters. There are very few leaders in the world who spend the time with the Bible and in prayer, looking to God for guidance and direction as these did. How they rejoiced to be taken to the prayer rooms of these national leaders and see how in a regular manner they have seasons of prayer with various groups of their own people!

Also, they visited Madame Chiang Kaishek's headquarters where many women were making garments and beautiful vases, large and small, as only the Chinese can make. Quinton brought home small ones for each of the children and myself.

* * * * *

One more hop, over to Japan. Their own mistakes, sins and crimes of war have come back to them with vivid reality.

For a while it looked as if there was going to be a mass turning to Christ, but too few churches and missionaries responded to General Montgomery's call for Christian workers.

"For quite sometime one afternoon, I stood in the shadows by the altar of the most noted Shinto shrine in Japan. Here I witnessed university professors, students, businessmen, and people from ordinary walks of life coming to place their money in a prepared altar, clapping their hands and bowing before this altar, which, according to their thinking, contains the spirits of the soldiers and people who died in the recent

192

war. The Japanese people are returning to their Shinto and Buddha shrines and temples.

"Knowing the true God and Savior, Jesus Christ, we have great responsibility to bring them the knowledge of salvation, which saves from sin and fear, replacing the heart with joy and peace."

* * * * *

On one occasion as they proceeded on their journey by air, they looked out of the window of the plane and saw what appeared to be one of the four motors on fire. It was of such a nature and in such a position that the crew was unaware of the situation. After discussing the matter for a second or two with his traveling companion, Quinton informed the steward of the matter. He rushed back to the cockpit, and the captain came to where they were seated to make a personal observation. He rushed back to the cockpit and turned off the motor. Then he came back to them, stating that they were only ten minutes from an island, which had an airport where they could safely land. After landing, he informed them that the situation was indeed extremely perilous. This island was Okinawa, one place they were not to land because of world tension.

He was a seasoned pilot and declared that in all of his experience, he had never seen or heard of such motor difficulty without tragedy. Their entire trip was made by propeller planes. We recognized God's protection over our men again.

Quinton told the captain that they appreciated him as good captain, but that there was another captain in whom they trusted, the Lord Jesus Christ. He appreciated their trust in Christ and said he was glad to have them as his passengers.

* * * * *

Quinton and Rev. Burk were glad to leave Tokyo, for now they were on their way home. They talked to each other about their experiences and impressions of missionary work as they had seen it. They made ready their messages to bring to the churches back home. By God's help, they would strive to bring a greater vision to the Christian people.

They stopped in Hawaii for a couple of hours and were met by a pastor whom they had known in earlier years. He drove them around Honolulu, which pleased them.

* * * * *

Two men of our church and I met Quinton and Mr. Burk at Chicago O'Hare airport. How happy I was to see Quinton, although I could have passed him by. He looked so haggard and older. There was a box hanging on his back containing a fine china tea set. It was tied around his shoulders. The men with me quickly took it off so that we could greet each other with hugs and kisses. They had been on the trip home for fourteen hours. Quinton had one suitcase filled with gifts for the children, his parents and me. The only clothes he had were on his back. Everything else was burned in the hotel at Cairo.

Each evening he would wash all his clothes and put them back on in the morning.

We hurried to the car and drove the ninety miles to South Bend where twelve hundred people were gathered already when we arrived.

What a greeting for the men! They told of the missionary conferences and the needs of our mission stations and, of course, how God had preserved them through "Cairo's fiery furnace," as the newspaper called it.

During that six-week tour, Quinton had taken many reels of movies. As soon as they were developed, churches began calling for him to come to show the pictures and preach on missions. Sometimes I went along to help him. This was over a period of several months. Altogether, we showed them to fifty congregations in the U.S. and Canada.

As time went on, he became under more stress, for he maintained all his work without an assistant. On Sunday, he preached two sermons and taught a Bible class. During the week, Monday through Friday at 6:15 in the mornings, he broadcasted "Sunrise Meditations." Then the half-hour broadcast "Your Worship Hour" was made with the choir and male quartet on Monday nights. This one was taped and sent out to stations all over the world.

Finally, one evening on his way home, he felt very strange. He stopped at the grocery store and then home, which was just a block and a half. He stopped in front of the house, opened the car door and sat hanging half way out of it.

Why I happened to be near the open door, I

don't know. But seeing his condition, I hurried out and supported him up to the porch and onto the porch swing. I told him to relax. I quickly called Dr. Zeiger only half a block away where he happened to be in his office at the clinic. The doctor quickly ran through the alley. He quickly examined him.

Because we had no health insurance at that time, the doctor agreed not to hospitalize him. I placed a rollaway bed in the front room near a telephone (this was Quinton's suggestion). It was fatigue, not a heart attack, the doctor said. But he stayed in bed for two weeks. In his twenty-two years of pastoring in South Bend, I think the one Sunday during his recovery was the only time he missed his preaching appointment. He was in contact with his secretaries, which lightened his load.

When Dr. Zeiger called on Quinton to find out his progress, he asked him when he took his vacations. He replied, *"I don't."*

"Well, if you don't start taking them, you'll have a permanent one."

From then on, we took the children out of school each year and drove to Florida. A doctor in our congregation always gave us a ham for Christmas. After New Year's Day, we packed the car with children, clothes, baked ham and other foods and started for Florida.

In the mornings in our car, we each ate an individual box of cereal with milk and a banana. At noon we had our main meal of the day in a restaurant. At night after finding a motel or tourist cabin, as they called them then, we sliced some ham, heated a can of vegetables and ate some fruit.

During the day the children played games in the car. Cynthia was not old enough for kindergarten, but the older children took it upon themselves to teach her a few things. Someone said, *"Let's teach her the parts of speech!"*

"Oh, how can we do that?"

"Well, let's try nouns first."

So they did. It was fun. Verbs were not difficult for her to find in a simple sentence. But she favored adjectives.

"I see a brown cow in the field." She found that adjective right away. And on and on they went until we were all laughing and someone said, *"I think little children could learn much more than they are taught in school if we would use their vocabulary."*

The first year we traveled on the east and west coasts of Florida, enjoying everything we could in two weeks. After that for the next forty-two years, we settled on Fort Myers Beach. We loved the Gulf water and breezes. We liked fishing very much. A man, who was the son of a popular fisherman and often took Henry Ford and Thomas Edison fishing with their families, was usually our captain. He and his wife took us out for $18.00 a day, from eight o'clock in the morning to five o'clock in the evening. We were allowed to keep all the fish.

One year when the three oldest children were grown and did not go with us anymore, our good friends, Dr. Bob Thompson and his wife Marjory, were with Quinton, Cynthia and me.

One day's catch was 110 Spanish mackerel and a few other kinds. Cynthia caught twenty. The next day we read about it in the Ft. Myers newspaper.

Quinton showing off our catch

Those were the times we went south in April and stayed three weeks.

Quinton always was called upon to preach at a Missionary Alliance Church and sometimes at the Avon Park Camp Meeting and others. One year he was the Bible Conference speaker at Shell Point. We made many friends as a result.

One Sunday morning, Quinton was scheduled to preach at the Alliance church in the city. He went around to the side entrance of the church to meet the pastor in his study. I, of course, made my way to the sanctuary. I sat a bit farther than half way to the front. Sunday School classes were just dismissing; so I was almost alone in the room. I decided to move toward the middle of the pew so people were free to come in on either side of me.

Soon a couple came and sat beside me.

Immediately she spoke to me. *"Good morning.*

I believe you are a newcomer. I'm Mrs. Gurgle. I'm so glad you came this morning because we have a special speaker. We just moved here from Buffalo, New York, and we listened for years to this man by radio. The name of the broadcast is 'Your Worship Hour.' I'm so glad you came."

I said, *"So am I. I'm just a visitor."*

She handed me a songbook. And then she said excitedly, *"Oh, there he is with the pastor."*

I said, *"Yes, that's my husband."*

"It is?" she said and laughed heartedly while she pulled on her husbandís arm saying, *"This is Mrs. Everest. This is Mrs. Everest."*

The result of meeting Mrs. Gurgle was very important to us for six years. She was a real estate agent and had just sold the largest house on the beach to a rancher and his wife from the West, Mr. Otto and Mrs. Marlene Zerbe.

So Mrs. Gurgle asked the Zerbes, *"If you have bought that house to provide a vacation place for missionaries, ministers, congressmen and people like Charles Colson, please give the Everests the privilege of vacationing there, too."*

After a day or two passed, we received a telephone call from the Zerbes to spend two weeks in their Fellowship House on the Gulf beach. They wanted no rent from us. We always tried to show our appreciation in some way. One year I stitched a unique picture for her.

Marlene is the granddaughter of Abraham Vereide, who started the Good Will Industries, President's Breakfast, and Christian Business Men's organization, started in Seattle.

They also have a Fellowship House in

Washington, D. C. where on Monday, congress-men gather for Bible study and prayer. That is where Chuck Colson first went to declare his conversion.

* * * * *

We loved Ft. Myers Beach and never searched for a different place for vacation.

We played ball with the family after making a circle out in the water. We swam, walked the beach, built sandcastles, fished, had Bible stud-ies. We also played table games. After dark, the children worked on their assignments the teach-ers had given them. The children always were caught up with their classmates when they returned to school. One year they presented each teacher with a good coconut.

After the first three children were married, we rented a cottage on Ft. Myers Beach for their families, one at a time.

The spring Q.J.'s family was there, I bought a big rubber water duck for Paul, age four, to play with at the edge of the water.

His father, mother, and I were standing near him while he was playing. We did not notice that the tide was going out and he with it.

Suddenly I didn't see Paul. But as I raised my head up, I saw him a great distance from us. I looked at Q. J., and he sadly shook his head. He could not swim that far.

We all yelled with all of our might for Quinton who was in our cottage nearby. He came run-ning, took off his shoes, saying nothing.

Paul was smiling while his grandpa was saying, "Come to Grandpa, but don't get off the duck." Quinton pulled the duck to shore.

Quinton said he couldn't swim that far. I believe the Lord or an angel gave him the strength he needed.

We were all hurting so much, but Paul was still having a good time with his grandpa.

I wish I had not bought the duck. It was a bad decision!

* * * * *

Our Bible study and prayer time turned out to be a very enriching experience. It was there that Quinton and I planned the first Music Week for our Gospel Center Church in South Bend, which was repeated for many years.

* * * * *

All six of us went to our Missionary Church family camp in Alberta one year. Several times part of us accompanied Quinton there. It was such fun and very rewarding for the children to see Yellowstone, the Grand Canyon, Black Hills, Rocky Mountains, Garden of the Gods, Banff, Lake Louise, and Jasper Glacier Park on the way.

But the family camp where Daddy was the night evangelist, the youth meetings and childrenís meetings were great experiences for our children. Many were the trips to Ontario, too.

* * * * *

When the three older children were married, it became a threesome—Quinton, Cynthia, and me. We traveled to every state except Alaska. We had no seat belts then; so now Cynthia was alone with her doll, books and toys in the back seat. There she took her nap, too. Sometimes she rode in front with us. Quinton had more invitations for evangelistic crusades than he could accept even after he retired from the pastorate.

* * * * *

At age twelve Cynthia was alone with her parents. She needed a puppy for a pal. So we watched the newspaper ads for one. Finally we saw one about a litter of puppies, pedigreed cocker spaniels. We hurriedly ate our supper and drove to Lakeville. As soon as we saw them, we knew we all wanted the same one. They were so cute and partly trained. The owner gave us some good instructions for its care. I had never seen a more beautiful cocker spaniel. Cynthia intended to take good care of her. The first night the poor thing whined and whined. The second night we placed a Big Ben clock side of her head. The ticking comforted her so that she slept soundly.

By and by it became my dog, for she followed me everywhere I went. If I was working in the kitchen, she laid down in the doorway. We never allowed her in the kitchen. Or if I was sitting or lying on the davenport, she was right there. I petted and talked to her until Cynthia came home from school. She was tied to the old clothesline in the back yard a few hours every decent day. We kept her until Quinton resigned as pastor of Gospel Center Church. Cynthia was nearly ready for college. Taffy was her name, and we thought she was the nicest dog in the world. We sold her to a dentist's wife who begged for her. We were traveling in crusades, conventions and radio rallies. There was no more time for pets. But I missed Taffy for years.

* * * * *

Throughout the winter months, we were often without a daddy. But we understood he was doing the King's business.

Quinton once held a revival meeting on the island of Grand Manan off the coast of New Brunswick. The twenty-mile long island had several churches that united in this effort. He appreciated the cooperation and fellowship of the people. They loved him, too, and the women's missionary society sent handmade gifts to take home—knitted place mats, several dishes, salt and pepper shakers, and a plate with lobsters imbedded in pink and green. Also, he was presented with a wonderful cookbook of recipes for seafood.

While there, he became acquainted with a man who owned an island some distance away, where he and his wife retired, for a month of rest. He wanted Quinton to see it. So by boat they went.

Quinton said it was small with nowhere to go and nothing to do but just enjoy the quietness and sounds of nature.

The man spent his time by reading Quinton's sermon books and others. He had many shelves of them. And he read them over and over. It was amazing to Quinton.

After the meeting was over, a small plane took him back to Fredrickton, New Brunswick, where he was to change to a large commercial plane.

As Quinton was about to leave the small island of Grand Monan, a man came running to him with a large box and shoved it toward him. It rattled.

"What is this?" Quinton asked.

"Lobsters, six of them. As soon as you get home, ask your wife to fill a large kettle with water, heat the water to the boiling point and put the live lobsters in. When the water begins to boil again, simmer them for so many minutes. Cool them to the point where you can shell them. Then freeze in appropriate-sized packages. Enjoy!"

But Quinton said, "Will the plane take them?"

"Sure," he replied.

Quinton thanked him and went aboard.

Men had taken him out on the ocean lobster fishing while he was with them during his stay; and so he wasn't surprised about their giving him these lobsters but was surprised that the plane would accept them.

So that night at 6:00, the doorbell rang. I hurried from the kitchen where Cynthia and I were getting supper. Quickly hugs and kisses were exchanged, the kettle was put on, supper eaten, and Quinton said, "Excuse me. I've a board meeting at seven o'clock."

Cynthia and I did something we never did before or since – prepare live lobsters! But they were certainly delicious!

And now Dad was back with us for a while again.

Chapter Thirteen

Our children are now in Bethel College
and Asbury Seminary.

Charlene got married just before her senior
year in college. She married Dale Sherry, who
was and is a beautiful singer. After graduation
from Bethel College, he accepted a call to preach
at Pleasant Hill, Michigan. After several years,
they went to Wilmore, Kentucky, where she
taught school and he attended and graduated
from Asbury Seminary.

Dale then pastored again for many years. The
last twelve years the two of them traveled in
many states performing Bible dramas and music
concerts.

* * * * *

Quinton James, who we always called Q.J.,
also graduated from Bethel College and later
Asbury Seminary. He married Shirley Metzler,
who taught school. He pastored for many years,
most of the time in Pennsylvania. These later
years he is greatly involved in music and conducting, singing in a large choral group and on
the board of Delaware River Symphony. He and
Shirley are beautiful singers.

* * * * *

Soon after Q. J. graduated from seminary, his father needed to go back to Nigeria, West Africa again. He asked Q. J. if he wanted to go with him, he would see that his way was paid. Q. J. consented, thinking this would be good experience for him since he was interested in missionary work since his boyhood.

A former missionary, Bessie Cordell, who was working for Quinton answering mail in our radio office, heard about this need and prayed, along with the others, for Q. J.'s need to be supplied. Miss Cordell had written a book called "Blossoms From The Flowery Kingdom" about her work in China. She said if Quinton would tell the radio audience of this matter and if they would send an offering toward his trip, they would receive this Chinese storybook. The response was great, and what was left over they used for broadcasting airtime.

They sailed on the U.S.S. ship to London and then flew to Nigeria. They were both asked to preach on the ship.

A union meeting was held at Ilorin, and they visited many of the missionary churches. A few revivals were held also. The weather was so hot it was almost unbearable. Quinton landed in the hospital for a couple of days. Q. J. preached in his stead.

Then they flew to Egypt and Jerusalem. In Cairo, they met Waheeb Tawfik, the Air Force officer. He took them from a cheap hotel and put them in a lovely room in the new Shepherd's Hotel by the river. For two or three days, they rested here and were much refreshed. Then they

Our children are now in Bethel College...

flew to Jerusalem.

* * * * *

After Q. J. had been in the pastorate, he often took the early morning broadcast, "Sunrise Meditation" for his father. He did so well that people often said they didn't know which one they were listening to because their voices were so similar. Then they would sign off, Quinton J. Everest, or Q. J. Everest, Jr.

* * * * *

Sharon attended Bethel College for one year. Then it was suggested she study at another college for a year, then come back and finish at Bethel. Her major was music and the professor of piano was Raymond Weaver whom she had studied under since she was eight years old.

So she decided on entering Houghton College in New York.

During that winter, we were planning for a great banquet to celebrate the 35th year of broadcasting. Highlighting the evening was to be the message by Dr. Paul Freed of Trans World Radio. We were good friends, and he would have a tremendous message that would enlighten us as to what was being accomplished around the world by radio. It was the beginning of a great thrust of the Gospel of Christ into many communist countries.

Sharon very much wanted to come from Houghton to this banquet. She would have to return immediately.

A bad snowstorm hit the eastern states.

College friends drove her to Buffalo. The storm slowed them, and as they came into the airport, she was told the plane had taxied to the other end, waited a few minutes for her and then took off.

"But wait," said a man. "I'll tell them to come back." He did. And she boarded the plane.

As soon as she walked down the aisle of the plane, two men conversed about her.

"Do you think she's a queen from somewhere? She must be a special person."

She laughed.

Special. Sure she was special, to God and the lifetime ministry she would have to perform for Christ.

Sharon came back to graduate at Bethel. However, she did study piano at the American School of Music in Chicago.

* * * * *

After Professor Raymond Weaver had been the pianist for "Your Worship Hour" broadcast for twenty years, he wanted to resign. At the banquet that was given in his honor, he made a speech. In it he declared he had trained Sharon to take his place. This was news to her. But she faithfully played the piano for many years, as did Charlene at the organ.

* * * * *

One day when she rode in a taxi, the driver was very grumpy but talkative. He spilled his troubles on Sharon. Finally she said, "Well, I never have to worry about such things. Money doesn't bother me. My father is very wealthy. He is very good to me." "Who is your father? What business is he in?"

"He owns a thousand cattle"—

"Oh, I know what you are talking about."

He suddenly brightened up.

Sharon was always like that.

She was married to Gary Fry and taught music subjects and piano in Bethel College for a few years but stopped to raise her family. Gary was a schoolteacher and later a high school principal. After his death, she taught piano in her home. Usually she had sixty students.

* * * * *

Cynthia married Michael McKee, whom she met at Azusa Pacific College in Azusa, California. She, too, was a music major, taking one year at Bethel. She fell in love with a senior who would go on to seminary the following year. She came home for the summer. He soon followed her to discuss marriage. The distance was too great. So they were married in August. That summer, she worked for her father in the radio office and learned some cooking techniques at home.

Mike was youth director of a large church in Pomona.

When Mike came to be married in South Bend, he had already rented an apartment. The young people said they would supply the furniture and fix it up to be ready for the bride and groom.

After the beautiful wedding, they had to fly

immediately to their honeymoon spot in San Francisco, California and Lake Tahoe.

I always told Cynthia I certainly don't blame her for marrying Michael, but he lives so far away!

Michael went to seminary. Cynthia was secretary to a music professor.

Later Michael left the ministry and obtained his law degree at UCLA. He worked for a large Los Angeles law firm for fourteen years and now is the Chief Financial Officer for The Irvine Co. in Orange County, California.

Cynthia took two years of court reporting school in Los Angeles from 1974 to 1976 and obtained her license. She worked through an agency for attorneys as a deposition reporter for fifteen years.

* * * * *

It was near the time when Quinton resigned the Gospel Center Church to give full time to crusades, conventions, radio rallies and camp meetings. So many, many calls came in that he often was impressed to make still greater efforts to win more souls for Christ. After much prayer and planning, he resigned the pastorate.

I remember the last Sunday evening so well. Quinton had all our family come to the platform and sing, in parts, "This World Is Not My Home, I'm Just A'passin' Through." Sharon remembers us around the piano at home singing this song among others.

But one thing bothered him. He finally said to me one day, "Mae, you know as many years as we have been married, we should live together. I want you to travel with me as much as you can."

That was the beginning of my eighteen years of traveling into many countries and islands, all for the sake of God's Kingdom. What a joy to be together and knowing we were in the center of God's will.

Many times we were rescued from danger, and I'm sure God kept us from knowing all of them.

* * * * *

So often we'd arrive home, I'd open the suitcases right in the family room, take out the soiled clothes and wash them, fold them and lay them right back in the suitcases again.

After a few days, we'd be leaving home either by car or plane.

But there were trips that I did not make with him. I had some responsibilities, or the place he would be staying would not be right for me. Such was the case when he would be entertained in a home with children. I never wanted to be a burden. If a pastor's wife urged me to come along with Quinton, I would usually do so. I then tried to be a help to her. Sometimes I'd iron, mend or wash dishes.

During the services, I would pray while Quinton preached. A table was placed in the back of the sanctuary or hallway on which were placed his sermon books. These were given to anyone who contributed to "Your Worship Hour" broadcasts. I met and talked with many listeners. People would also tell me of how they were saved as a result of them. Some places the sanctuaries were filled; so during the singing, someone would take us to the lower Sunday School department floor to introduce us to the overflow crowd. They were able to hear Quinton preach upstairs, but the pastor had promised they could see him, too.

* * * * *

Once in a while, I would keep my grandchildren while Sharon, our daughter who lived close to us, would take care of something urgent.

One morning, as I was finishing the breakfast dishes, the doorbell rang.

"Hi, Grandma," said Gary, as I opened the door. He was in a hurry to come in.

"Isn't Mother coming in, too," I asked?

"No. She's in a hurry. Going to do some shopping or something."

"Well, I'm so glad to have you come. You haven't been here for awhile."

"I know, I know," he said, and hugged me as far up as he could reach.

Then he left me and hurried down the hall. I tiptoed after him with a smile, for I knew where he was going—to the pink playroom. It was a combination of playroom and my workroom. In this room I had my desk, my ironing board and my sewing machine. On the walls were pictures of other countries that Quinton would bring me. And there was hanging a framed letter from Pat Nixon, wife of our President. We had met in the White House one day, and when she asked who I was, she lifted her hands and said, "Oh, I know who your husband is. I've heard him on the radio."

She must have heard him on the Long Beach, California, station when her husband was governor of the state. I was so pleased that I asked a guide to give her a hardback copy of Quinton's book, "Prescriptions For Today," which is a devotional book for every day of the year. As a result, she wrote me a letter of thanks, which said that she and her husband read it every day. I cherished that and prayed for them that the Holy Spirit would use the scriptures and messages of the little orange book.

To adults, these things are interesting, but to Gary there was only one thing in the room he was interested. His Grandpa Quinton had made a large walnut buffet in high school. Now after many years, it was filled with toys. Gary quickly opened the doors of it and pulled open the drawers. He turned his head this way and that way until he looked over everything. Then he selected what he wanted to play with first.

There were many little railroad cars, games, a long soft snake, a soft cuddly white kitten, blocks of different kinds, many colored rings to stack, dolls of all sizes, wooden puzzles, and stacks of storybooks. He sat down on the floor to play. So I went out of the room to do my morning's work. After making the beds and doing a few other things, I went to peek and see how Gary was getting along.

As I went to the door and started to speak to him, I was surprised to find no little boy there.

"Gary, Gary," I softly called. He didn't answer. So I looked in the bathroom, in

Quinton's study room, the living room, and dining room. Finally I saw him sitting at the kitchen table with folded hands, quietly waiting for me to find him.

Maybe his mother had told him not to ask for things or bother Grandma too much. Anyway, he was silent.

"Oh, Gary, I couldn't imagine where you were! Are you hungry, or you just want something to eat?"

He looked up with a smile and nodded.

"Do you want some crackers or cookies and milk?"

He nodded again. And I said, "It's a pleasure! I think we'll both have some, a morning snack." Then we prayed, ate and laughed, talking of many things.

It made me think of the many times I had gone to the pink room alone with my Heavenly Father and waited for Him to feed me on the Word of God. We, like Gary, should know what to do when we are spiritually hungry, even if we don't know exactly what we want. He, too, likes to have us come quietly to Him and enjoy His presence.

* * * * *

When I stayed at home alone, I often asked the Lord to make me a help and a blessing to someone that day. I kept in touch with my family, but I determined to keep busy.

One morning in my devotions, I asked God to allow me an opportunity that day to be a special witness for Him. Something that would glorify Him.

About ten o'clock that morning, a car drove

into the driveway. Who could that be? I did not recognize the car or the man behind the wheel. A woman and a beautiful baby were with him, too.

All at once, I noticed the color of his skin. That he should be here in South Bend was a surprise. He was one of my Sunday School Junior Highs years ago. His teacher stopped at an orphanage to bring him to Sunday School and church every Sunday morning. I always took an interest in him, not because I was Superintendent, but also because he was a troubled boy.

I opened the door before they could ring the doorbell. We had a jolly good reunion. Then he introduced his fair-skinned wife to me. She smiled and said, "We are in trouble. We've been driving all night, and the baby's formula is all used. We've had no breakfast either."

There wasn't much time to ask why. I invited them inside and took them to the kitchen.

"Sit here at the table. I'll warm some milk for the baby's bottle and then fix bacon, eggs and toast for you."

While I was busy, he told me his troubles of last night. They were put out of their apartment, and they fled without taking anything.

When their breakfast was ready, I prayed for another miracle, a job for the man, and that they would start a Christian life for their sakes and for the sake of their child. Then I thanked God for the food He provided.

He claimed he wanted a job. I prayed quietly to the Lord, "Help me." I immediately thought of the Good Will Industries.

I looked up the number, asked for the manager and told him our problems. I kept nothing from him.

"Surely," he said. "If he is willing to work, I'll use him until he can get a more profitable job. Have him come tomorrow morning."

I went to the kitchen. He seemed amazed but said he'd do it.

Next, his wife said, "I need to wash my hair and bathe the baby." So I found a sack of curlers our married daughters had left in the bathroom.

In the meantime, he was walking through the house. "You have plenty of room for us here. Could you keep us for awhile?"

"Well, there wouldn't be room when the children and grandchildren come. We must find an apartment for you."

About that time, Quinton came home from a distant revival meeting.

He went directly to the classified section of the South Bend Tribune and located an apartment in a desirable part of Mishawaka. Quinton called the party, asked the rental price, which was moderate. He paid a week's rent for them. It was a furnished apartment. However, these friends had no bedding or towels and washcloths. We supplied them with some, plus a few other things.

We did not see them on Sunday; so we called Good Will Industries to find out if all was well.

"No," the manager said. "He would not attend the 10:00 a.m. break for the chapel service; so he could not work here, for that is a requirement of this establishment. Sorry, but he wasn't very dependable."

I was saddened but was still glad I did try to help them.

I never feel I really fail if things don't turn out right because I was obedient to the Lord. I have never heard from them since.

* * * * *

One day I had a call from Hilda Brenneman, a former missionary to Nigeria and a pastor's wife. She invited me to go with her to a Women's Bible Study Fellowship in Elkhart. I had never heard of this international group before.

She explained. It was started by an American missionary to China. When the communists took over, Miss Johnson was house-arrested but finally allowed to go back to California. Because she had been a Bible professor at a seminary in China, she was restless without her teaching position. Neighbors begged her to start a Bible study course for her community. Thus, this intensive, inspirational Bible course developed into nationwide opportunities for women of all denominations. Finally it spread to England and Australia. We have hundreds of them in the United States.

I visited a few times and learned from the lecturer that there were too many women coming from South Bend, Mishawaka, LaPorte and Niles. They could not take us in.

"Pray and ask God to help you start one in South Bend," she said.

She asked me if I would have a "tea" for

women who have not known or attended one of these meetings. I said, "I will if you'll come and explain the course."

I entertained twenty-six women, many of whom I did not know. The first meeting all came but one. There were several hundred that day. It has grown and many unsaved women have become staunch Christians. That was about twenty-five years ago, and it's still operating.

It is a five-year course. Each year is spent in a different book of the Bible. The years I attended we studied Genesis, John, Acts, Minor prophets and Romans, I believe. Each week we took home study sheets, plus two sheets of questions. Thank God for those five years!

Chapter Fourteen

A trip to Bonaire for Trans World Radio.

The first trip overseas on which I accompanied Quinton was to Bonaire, one of the ABC Islands. These islands are owned by the Netherlands.

Trans World Radio had selected this island to erect transmitters for the purpose of broadcasting the gospel. This island is sixty miles off the coast of Venezuela.

Dr. Paul Freed invited my husband to be one of the speakers on the dedication day. Princess Beatrice, who is now Queen of the Netherlands, was to speak on behalf of her government, giving permission (with gratitude) for their great venture. The only thing she asked was that this radio station would give time for the Dutch news, both morning and evening. Dr. Berterman of the Lutheran Hour and Rev. Andrews, speaker of the Wesleyan "Light and Life" broadcasts, were also to speak.

When Quinton asked me to go, I was thrilled. I hurried to the River Park Library to find books describing the island.

We sat in the family room to read and discuss all we found printed about this new 500,000-watt transmitter on Bonaire, the most powerful AM standard broadcast transmitter in the

Western Hemisphere. With this addition of the new Bonaire station, Trans World Radio would be operating with more than one million watts of transmitter power, making it one of the world's most extensive.

We traveled alone to Kennedy Airport in New York. After waiting more than an hour, our plane was announced. We soon found ourselves in a line with people, when suddenly we saw Dr. and Mrs. Paul Freed among them.

What a cheerful group of people, and we were to join them. They were board members and their wives from several states. However, Trans World Radio Headquarters was located at Chatham, New Jersey.

Our first stop was the island of Curacao. We boarded a bus to Willemstad probably fourteen miles from the airport. The bus was filled with our group, except for six or eight New York people who were on vacation.

Suddenly Ruby, one of the board member's wives, started lustily singing "Blessed Assurance, Jesus Is Mine." Instantly we all joined in. Hymn after hymn was sung, one after another. How refreshing it was! There was perhaps nothing else that could have identified us or introduced us to each other more quickly.

We checked in at a Holiday Inn for dinner and overnight. After we ate, we strolled around. As we went to our room, I asked someone nearby where Ruby was. I had not seen her since we left the dining room.

"Oh, she's in the bar."

"Ruby," I exclaimed!

A trip to Bonaire for Trans World Radio.

"Yes, just step over here. Look in. There she is sitting between two men. She's probably drinking 7UP or Coca-Cola. She is also inquiring what they know about Jesus. She will tell them all about Him and His love for them. She witnesses every day."

I learned to know her quite well, not only in Bonaire but also in Monte Carlo and for the many years we attended the National Radio Broadcasters Conventions in Washington, D.C.

Early the next morning, we flew to Bonaire. As we left the plane, we saw a large group of people waving, smiling and yelling, "Welcome to Bonaire." These were the many office workers, engineers and others who could leave their work to welcome us. We were royally entertained. They had heard our broadcast "Your Worship Hour" for many years but had never met the speaker. So they showered us with much love.

Between services, one of the missionaries, Dan Harvey, was so pleased to have us there that he took Dr. Berterman, Quinton and me to the beach to show us where the beautiful flamingo gather at that time of the year. Hundreds of them, so graceful and colorful! There were also small stone slave huts. Black people were brought here from other parts of the world to be sold. There were also billows of salt that would roll onto the beach.

Interesting, too, was the little Volkswagen we rode in. A large hole in the top, the back glass was broken out, and we wondered why he must ride in a thing like that. Two weeks previous to our coming, he loaned this car to one of their reputable national workers for the day. He had an accident in which it rolled over a couple of times. It was almost a total wreck. My husband felt so sorry for him, that he gave him a little money for a down payment on another one.

When we left the beach, Dr. Berterman found a large flamingo egg and wanted Quinton to take one, too. They found they were rotten and could hardly clear their hands of the awful smell! That was a fun afternoon getting acquainted with two very fine Christian men.

* * * * *

We learned much in those few days about Trans World Radio and the Freed family. They were godly, passionate men, making way for the spreading of the Gospel to the whole world. They wanted our program, in the beginning days, to represent the Gospel preached in English. "Your Worship Hour," they said, brought them more mail than any other broadcast in English at that time. When Ralph Freed, Paul's father, first met Quinton, he hugged him and said, "I love you, my brother. I always hoped I could take time out to write a book on Revelation, but after reading yours, I won't try. We believe alike." Ralph, Paul, and Quinton had wonderful fellowship in the Lord until both men died.

* * * * *

We received much mail from South America and islands as a result of being on that station. For example, here is an excerpt from French Guyana.

A trip to Bonaire for Trans World Radio.

"A group of thirty sat beside a radio only a few hours ago. To our delight, the Worship Hour came on with Pastor Everest. We were deeply impressed, so much so that we have resolved to secure a copy of your sermon book."

Another from Argentina:

"The broadcast was like water on thirsty ground. It has been a tremendous blessing to me and many other workers who, like myself, still have needs of their own to be met. Thank you for your help."

A missionary in Colombia was overworked and needed more help from home. Finally his brother felt the Lord calling him to go down to Colombia and help in the ministry there. He was preparing to go when suddenly he was killed in an auto accident. What a shock, burden and loss to this dear missionary. Again he prayed for help, and God called another member of his family. This person also died before they got to Colombia.

One night he walked the floor. He simply couldn't sleep. He turned on his radio. He sat down and listened to a sermon entitled "Don't quit." This was what he was contemplating. The only thing he thought he could do was to go back home and let the nationals carry on the best they could.

But somehow he struggled back to bed and again tried to sleep, but no sleep came and no rest.

He got up again after a few hours, turned on the radio, turned from station to station, when suddenly he heard that same voice preaching "Don't quit. Don't quit."

At the end of the program, the announcer said, "You have just heard Pastor Quinton J. Everest of 'Your Worship Hour' broadcast coming to you from South Bend, Indiana"

The first time he heard it on HCJB Equador and the second time on the Bonaire station. Thank God he took courage and stayed. Letters like this blessed Quinton, too, in the battle for souls.

* * * * *

A letter from Trinidad:

"Your broadcast has continually been a spiritual uplift and blessing to me. I could not be disobedient any longer, and I went down on my knees and made things right with God. Your literature has been a great help."

Barbados:

"Pastor Everest, your sermon material means very much to me. Time and again I refer to this material. Not only the congregation has been spiritually helped, but I can testify that I have been closer drawn to the Savior as a result of your ministry of the Word."

Letters even from California said they hear our broadcast from Bonaire.

"It sounds like you are talking to us in our home, it is so clear."

* * * * *

Quinton had me stand with him on the platform at Gospel Center Church the next Sunday night, and we related the great experiences we had at Bonaire. How thrilled we were that we

A trip to Bonaire for Trans World Radio.

were given this great opportunity to preach the "Good News."

Back home our hearts and minds were drawn to our family and to the church and broadcasts. Again Quinton was working twelve or more hours each day. He never complained about it or seemed frustrated. Everything he did he loved to do. His interests were in the family and people. Always there were new experiences, no matter now old he became. That is why we needed to pray about everything and still do.

One day a young man came to his office to talk to him. Of course Quinton naturally talked to him about his need of the Savior. He could see that the fellow needed help. So he finally allowed Quinton to pray for him. The unique thing about it was that he pleaded for money. He finally said he just got out of Sing-Sing prison on a certain recent day. He also gave Quinton his prison number. Quinton gave him a good tract and five dollars. As soon as he was gone, Quinton called Sing-Sing, told the official the man's name and story, plus his number. Quinton was asked to wait, that he would find out for him. After the investigation, the official told Quinton they had no one there like that. It was a fraud.

* * * * *

Quinton often met families that never went to church. After visiting in their home, he sometimes told them he would come to their house on Sunday morning and take them to church. Many families were brought in this way. Many other people did the same thing. Soon they would come regularly by themselves; then he would bring others. Always they came to Sunday School and church. If it rained or was very cold, he would arrange to take the families early so that he could pick up his own family. It was very interesting how many, many families were won for Christ in this way.

A certain lady became a Christian and was quite faithful, but her husband was an alcoholic. This gave her much trouble. He was a fairly good man when he was sober, but too much of the time he was unable to work.

Finally he became under such a strong conviction that he came to church and to the altar for prayer. Sometimes he came to Quinton's study room at church to talk and pray. Always he felt better when he left. But he never stayed away for any length of time from his old tavern. Many months of effort to believe God would deliver him went by, and we became encouraged. All seemed to be going well at home, too.

However, one afternoon, one of our churchmen rapped loudly at Quinton's door. It was Saturday. He was very busy. The man said, "I was downtown across the street from the tavern and was shocked to see our new convert going into that place. Just thought you'd want to know."

Quinton was so saddened that he got up from his chair, got into his car, and hurried downtown. He parked, leaving the motor running, went into the tavern, and walked down the long aisle. Looking from side to side into every booth, he couldnít find his man. The bartender

A trip to Bonaire for Trans World Radio.

was staring at Quinton. But he was determined. It was in the very last booth that he found him.

Quinton said emphatically, "Come with me. You do not belong in this place."

When he saw who it was, he replied, "Oh, I'm not worthy to walk out of here with you."

"Come take my arm. We are going out."

With some help, he got on his feet, passed the astonished bartender and got into the car. This was one of those cases that seemed impossible. But we know all things are possible with God. He died at an early age in this condition. It shows youth that the decisions they make at an early age are very important. Christ called him, others beside Quinton prayed often for him, but he never made his decisions for eternity.

Chapter Fifteen

The Crusade in Jamaica.

An invitation came from Pastor Hewitt to Quinton for a crusade in Mandeville, Jamaica.

We flew into the Montego Bay airport late afternoon. The Missionary Church there had asked for a one-night meeting before going to Kingston and Mandeville.

It was a very rainy day. Dinner was served at the parsonage. It was raining very hard yet as we ran to the church nearby. Only a few young people came to the service. Most people had to walk, and one man told us they would have had to wade in water to their knees.

Anyway, Quinton spoke as to a crowd. They were glad they came.

Back at the parsonage, Rev. Minton, the pastor, made phone calls canceling our night flight to Kingston. That airport is quite a distance from the city. The road around the mountain was closed because of a landslide. Others tried going to Kingston by boat but had great difficulty because of the torrential rain. So we escaped all of that.

In the forenoon of the next day, we arrived at Kingston. The bad stories we heard were many, and we were so thankful to the Lord that He provided for us. What a welcome we received when we arrived at Rev. David Clark's home. The family was glad to have us for a week.

The next day was Sunday. Quinton preached at this church next door in the morning.

After lunch, they suggested we take a good rest because Rev. Spencer would take us to his church downtown, the First Missionary Church, for an evening service.

So we climbed on the bed to take our naps, but suddenly I groaned, "There is something on my side of the bed. Get it quickly."

"It's a lizard," he said, as he grabbed it. But he had only pulled off its tail!

"Oh, well," he said, "it will grow another tail."

"Where is the rest of it?"

"It won't hurt you. Missionaries like to have them in the house. They eat bugs and flies, etc. They even call them by pet names."

When we were taken to the downtown church that evening, it seemed so dark in the city and around the church. Inside, too, electric power is not as strong there as we are used to.

The ushers greeted us warmly. The church was filled with people. The sanctuary was very long and narrow. Hoping I would not have to sit on the platform, I followed the usher to one empty place kept for me on the front row.

The organist, pianist and song director were all male. What great singing!

After prayer, Rev. Spencer, the young pastor, who is today a strong leader of the island church and theological school, introduced us to the congregation.

"How many of you listen to 'Your Worship Hour' ?"

It looked as if everyone did, I thought, as I turned around and saw hundreds of white palms of their hands turned toward us. I suddenly felt I was among friends. They clapped and were so happy to see us.

Monday morning Quinton prepared broadcasting messages, dictating them over at the church.

Then off to the Seminary to take some movie pictures at the dismissal of their faculty meeting.

We took the Clarks out for dinner this day and would leave money with them when we left. Whoever keeps us for a period of time must be remunerated, for these are missionaries.

The sun was shining brightly; all four doors were open. They had no screens. There was a doorbell, but few used it. The maid would soon come so she would not allow me to wash dishes. Black Hazel would stay all day until 7:00 p.m. In this city, the middle and upper class homes can hardly be seen from the streets except for the gate and narrow driveway. The flowers and bushes, plus trees, make it look like one great garden.

The extremes are very noticeable, the clean and filthy, the barren and foliage, the vile and the pure, the sad and the joyful.

The Christian faces are so different than the unsaved ones.

The pastors say even if the Christian families live in just a room or two, their bodies and clothes are clean.

In the countryside, the water was scarce. It was on at breakfast time, always turned off at

9:00 a.m. I washed my clothes in the bathtub, scrubbed it, and refilled the tub, teakettle, pans and bottles. On Wednesday water trucks went through the countryside to fill the barrels that were set at the end of the lanes.

* * * * *

The next Friday, a high school teacher, Deta Clacken, from Kingston took us in her Volkswagen to Mandeville where she lived with her sister, Valerie, and in the town where we were to have a two-week evangelistic meeting.

We went by way of Spanish Town, which was quite an experience.

The Clacken sisters lived across the street from the parsonage. They served dinner that night to us and the pastor who lived alone.

Their maid looked wide-eyed at us as she opened the door. I wondered why she stared at us. Later, when we were acquainted, she said she thought we were such large people, she wondered if she had cooked enough food. And I had wondered why our plates were so full. It certainly was a delicious meal!

The Clacken sisters were mixed blood, Jewish and British, highly educated and spiritual. The island people loved them. Valerie was youth director of all our twenty-eight churches. She had 128 young people in her Sunday School class.

Many years later, we had a surprise visit from one of them who had come to the States to visit a relative in North Carolina. What a blessing to see her in our own home!

We stayed for two weeks with Rev. George Hewitt in the church parsonage.

At noon we ate lunch sometimes at Mrs. Graham's house around the corner from the parsonage. She had a boarding house for three elderly widows of different nationalities. They were always ready to tell us stories of their lives.

Mrs. Graham had a maid who served us so that she could entertain us at the table. She was a dear person. In her younger years, she had been the nanny of Col. Eddie Rickenbacker's son, Jimmie.

Once Eddie stayed in the sun too long and got a blistered nose. He asked Jimmie if he didn't sympathize with him. Jimmie said, "No, there is only one person I sympathize with, and that's Nanny."

Once she found him lying on her bed when his parents had gone to New York, and he said, "No one in this whole world loves me like you do."

* * * * *

The pastor had a lizard for a house pet called James who lived in his study room. In my presence, George would often stop and say, "Now, James, as long as Mrs. Everest is here, don't ever leave this room. Never go into her room," which was next door to the study. "James, you listen to me."

This pastor was a dear father to the people and especially to the youth. Besides preaching, he told them how to live the Christian life. They loved him.

Some people would pretend to be poorer than they were so that they could receive free clothing from the States. I heard him say to one woman at the church door, "Don't come to church again dressed like this. It is disrespectful to the Lord. I saw you downtown yesterday all dressed up."

He described to her what she had on. "Never do that again," he said.

One Sunday morning, he announced that no man should wear a suitcoat tonight because many men who are coming to these meetings do not have a full suit. So for one night, the pastor and all the men showed brotherly kindness.

The Holy Spirit was present to save souls. It was a great meeting with much conviction of sin. The radio preacher had come to Mandeville; so many came to see him and told us they had listened for many years to "Your Worship Hour."

Another interesting thing was that the choir loft was full every night. There is much interracial marriage in Jamaica; so the choir was of mixed colors. There was the Chinese Jamaican girl, a German Jamaican with brown freckles, etc., and cute children with red hair.

* * * * *

On the first Sunday morning, there were 800 in Sunday School. The church service about the same. Pastor Hewitt wanted me to come to the platform. I wasnít told what to say or do.

After the music was over, the pastor informed them that this was a very special day. He called out the name of a little girl. She was so sweet. She climbed the steps to the platform carrying a basket of forty beautiful roses. The pastor brought her to us, and she looked up smiling while Rev Hewitt presented the basket to us for our fortieth anniversary. He had pinned an orchid corsage on me as I left the house that morning.

Then we found out it was also the pastor's birthday; so he was presented with a large, lovely cake.

What a nice surprise while being away from our family, that the family of God remembered us.

* * * * *

Being entertained in Mrs. Howard Smith's (Dr. Oswald Smith's sister-in-law) home after Quinton talked in the Chapel of the Jamaican Seminary was a special blessing.

We had high tea at the Brown's up in the mountains at 4:30 one afternoon. Most of the elders and their wives were there, the Clacken sisters, Pastor Hewitt, and us; about twenty.

They began with prayer by Mr. Johnson, a paint contractor. A great variety of food was covering two long tables through two rooms. There was much talking, hearty laughter, and finally telling stories of robbers.

Before we left, there was a great seriousness that came upon the group as prayer requests were made known. What a volume of prayer! We felt so close to those people.

Pastor Hewitt made the remark as we traveled down the mountain that he was never invited to a high tea before. He believed it was because Quinton brought me with him to

Jamaica. It was amazing to hear the people say that we looked alike, Quinton and I.

Jamaica had the Gospel preached to her many years ago but became a backslidden island. There were twenty-eight Missionary Churches at the time we were there.

Before we left Mandeville, the Clacken sisters wanted to tell us about their Jewish mother who had come from England to visit them the year before we arrived. She was a very sophisticated, elite lady in her country. One day she got very sick. Valerie finally got hysterical and thought her mother was going to die without God and be lost. Deta hushed her and said, "Where is your faith?"

But she too cried hard many hours to the Lord. Light finally broke into her mother's blinded eyes and was gloriously saved.

A fashionable friend came to visit her one day. (All this happened at the girl's home just across the street from the church and parsonage.)

The friend said, "I heard you were better. We won't believe you are better until we see you smoke again." Until then, their mother couldn't even take a bath without having a cigarette in her mouth.

But she said, "When God comes into your heart, there is no room for cigarettes. They are no more."

Deta overheard her mother go on and on to her friend about Christ, and Deta said, "Lord, am I hearing a testimony from my own mother who lived in sin for seventy years?" And Deta praised God and wept.

Chapter Sixteen

Haiti, Puerto Rico and
islands of the Caribbean.

In two years, we planned for a six-week trip.

Five years ago, a radio listener, whom we had never met living two thousand miles from South Bend, sent five hundred dollars with the request that Quinton visit Haiti and Puerto Rico. His purpose was that Quinton investigate the HVEH and WIVV stations as to the value and outreach in giving out the Gospel. He had been supporting these stations for some time. Furthermore, he was fully supporting our Missionary Church Bible Bookstore in a prominent city of Brazil that Quinton was aware of.

Quinton had put off going until he had resigned from his pastorate at Gospel Center Church, South Bend.

We started praying about this, desiring that the time be right.

On a certain day, our Brazilian missionaries had gathered together to plan and pray for the coming Spiritual Life Conference. It coincided with our trip to Haiti and Puerto Rico. They were on their knees praying when someone brought a letter from the post office. Thinking it might be of importance, it was given to the chairman who immediately read it. He stopped the prayers and said, "Our answer is here in this letter. Rev. Quinton Everest could be our speaker."

It was really an answer to us, too. God was opening and approving this trip.

So after many days of making future radio programs and but little time for getting together the clothes and supplies that would be needed for six weeks, we took our leave of the house. We were now living on Swanson Drive, having moved out of the parsonage in which we lived for twenty-two years.

Two things we knew we should have done before locking the front door. One was to pick up and take along the flashlight that one of us had laid on the kitchen counter the night before, and the other was to hide the box of Christmas toys I had purchased a few days before and meant to wrap. This box was in the entrance just inside the door. But we were desperate for time.

I also knew that when our son and his family would come up for Thanksgiving that they would use our home as a base to see the rest of the family and friends. I anticipated much excitement as they viewed this open box of Christmas toys. But nevertheless, it was past time to be on our way to the airport.

Then our wait began. (I could have hidden those toys!) The man at the desk told us the plane became iced over on the run down from Detroit.

This made us late at O'Hare in Chicago. We ran most of the length of O'Hare, had two minutes until takeoff.

The flights were delightful, and we began to

relax. I have never been a very brave person, but I thoroughly enjoy flying.

We left home November 2nd, stopping a week in Jamaica. Rev. Clark and family entertained us again before we made our way up to Mandeville for another two-week revival. The annual conference followed those meetings. Quinton had devotions in the mornings before the sessions began, then preached at night for the open meetings.

Then back to Kingston by train to take a flight to Haiti.

In Haiti at 10:00 p.m., we were met by Eldon Turnidge, the first president of Men For Missions of the Oriental Missionary Society. He took us by truck through the center of Port Au Prince to view the horrible condition of the people sleeping on the sidewalks in the rain. They were covered with newspapers and rags.

Back at the airport, the first thing we saw and heard was fifty young people blowing their horns in a downpour. I was impressed with these young people, welcoming a man, hoping whoever he was would sincerely appreciate the gesture of good will.

The Hotel Plaza was some distance from the downtown and market area where Mr. Turnidge wanted us to observe the sight of the city at night. The air was stifling, but the ground or sidewalks were wet. I couldn't find words to express my sadness; so I said very little as we traveled back to the other side of the city.

We checked into the hotel. In the open lobby we were introduced to a young missionary nurse and a mother missionary with a baby in her arms. Our man had brought these women from the other side of the island to take the baby to the doctor. The child was two years old, but she looked no more than one year. It was so hot that she was wearing only panties. Her ribs and stomach protruded. Her little head was limp and dropped on her shoulder.

What a night! Our room was almost unbearably hot but had a very small fan. So after a couple of hours of sweat, prayer and thinking of that sick little baby, I fell off to sleep.

The next afternoon, I was thoroughly ashamed to learn that the rooms in which the others stayed had no screens or fans. I was embarrassed to know that they had reserved the best corner room for us.

The baby had a case of worms, which was common, for the children want to go barefooted. They need to wear anklets and shoes, but they love to go barefooted and often take off their shoes when their mothers are not looking. Worms enter their body through their feet. After some time, these children will cough and often have choking spells. They become restless, irritable and lose their appetite. This baby got strong and well again. Many people in the United States' churches prayed for her.

* * * * *

The following morning we ate breakfast in an open dining room. We were constantly bothered by men trying to sell us their beautifully carved mahogany dishes and trinkets.

We told our friends to tell them that we were going to Cape Haitian today and did not want to be bothered with extra baggage. We could buy on our return. That just made them more eager to sell now. I suppose they were afraid we would make our purchases over there because they seemed frantic to sell.

How fortunate we were to have Mr. Turnidge there to take us over the mountains to Cape Haitian, for he had just arrived from the States the day before. Otherwise, it would have taken us fourteen to eighteen hours by bus or truck and very roughgoing.

As soon as we were seated in the one-engine plane, the nurse who had come with the woman and sick child turned to me and said, *"If you get nauseated on the flight, here is a bag to use."* I thanked her.

I didn't tell her, but I had often flown in commercial flights and never felt sick. Nor on a ship. But it wasn't long until I was holding her bag while she threw up!

About five miles out from Cape Haitian, we found the compound of 4VEH compound. There are at least seventeen buildings, some very new, some very old.

For each meal, we'd go to a different home of missionaries. We made the rounds and then did it again. We always had beans and rice with meat broth no matter what else we'd have. Two families had five children. We slept in the only house trailer, which belonged to Mr. and Mrs. Turnidge. They flew on to San Juan to buy supplies for the missionaries and would be back the

240

day we needed to leave. He would fly us back to the airport at Port Au Prince.

Again we saw how God fit all things together so very smoothly.

Each morning, Quinton had a devotional period with the radio staff and missionaries. In the evening, he preached in the church, which was located on the edge of the compound. He had an interpreter by the name of Napoleon. In all of our travels, anywhere in the world, he never had a man with such great ability. Even to hear him one night was a great privilege, but to hear him night after night brought tears to my eyes. Anyone who ever heard my husband speak with great burden would have been blessed to hear the two men working together. Mr. Napoleon was a forceful, quick speaker. It seemed he took the thoughts and words out of Quinton's mouth before he stopped talking. It was a blessing to be there with these thankful people, drinking the truth of God.

* * * * *

These people dressed in clean, white clothes.

During the daytime, we were taken to the large market in town. It was horrible to get away from those who wished to sell you their wares. Sometimes the missionaries liked to play tricks on us ignorant newcomers. They'd slip away from us and let us at the mercy of a crowd of natives pushing their wares at us. I thought they'd smother us. Then we would look around for the missionaries. They would be about twenty feet away laughing and giggling. What fun they had at our expense!

On Monday morning when I went out the door with my washed clothes to hang them on the line, I noticed the "yard boy" was caring for the plants. But as soon as he saw me, he straightened up. He started talking. I figured the way he was motioning that he wanted my trash to burn. I only had a little each day, but I let him do it. However, my hands were full, so I motioned to him that I would be right back. I walked across the front yard and around the house to the clotheslines. I turned around to hang the first garment, and there he was so close he could have breathed down my neck.

I let on as if I wasn't startled, but I was very much surprised as he shoved out both his white-palmed hands and "jabbered."

He wanted me to let him hang the clothes. I just smiled big and said, *"No, thank you,"* shaking my head. So he backed off from me, about four feet, and watched me hang every piece of clothing, even six unmentionables, plus everything else.

"Now," I said, *"I'll get you the wastebasket and matches."* I did, and he smiled. Soon he was back with the empty wastebasket and matches. Quinton came just then and took them with a smile.

Later that afternoon when I was in the yard, a boy about ten years of age rushed up to me and said, *"Hello,"* stuck out his hand, *"a dime?"*

"No," I said.

He asked again. I was glad I had no money with me.

242

The school bell was ringing, so I asked, *"Do you go to our school over there?"*

He said, *"Yes."* But he wouldn't leave me.

I asked if he worked for anyone as a house-boy.

Then his eyes opened wide, and he said, *"Oh, no, Madam!"*

Maybe he thought I meant did anyone send him out to beg. Anyway, that closed the subject. Missionaries in almost any country we visited told us not to give money to beggars. If we would, there would very suddenly be many more.

When Quinton and I discussed the afternoon activities, he thought our houseboy, who was seventy years old, wanted me to let him hang my wash on the line. He always carried a machete, which had alarmed me. But I got used to him always wanting to do another job for me. Perhaps he followed Mrs. Turnidge around the house, too, when she was home. He was a kind man.

The office girls and missionaries have Haitian girls do all their cooking and laundry. They are clean and very well trained cooks. We never ate anything served that was not cooked. Almost all the island people served us beans and rice. Many places we had huge platters of fried plantain, which were very tasty. I was always glad to see them being served. Baked things were delicious, but we dare not think of milk. We missed drinking milk.

The compound was a large, beautiful grassy area perhaps as large as three square blocks.

There were paths worn to each house and building. In the middle of the day, we appreciated the many large trees, especially in the middle of the day. As soon as we got into the shade, it was delightful, with a light breeze.

4VEH was buying hundreds of little radios. They set them so that people only heard their station with the Gospel. They gave these or charged eight dollars to those who had money.

While I was in the office one day, one of the national staff young men came into the office looking so serious and started talking in Creole about a problem. Marilyn rushed up to him and said, *"What's the matter?"*

He answered, *"My wife is in pain. She's going to have the baby! What can I do about getting her to the hospital?"* I guess he thought he dared not leave his work.

Marilyn said, *"Go on! Go on! Take her to the hospital."*

He was gone for awhile and then returned.

One of the new girls congratulated him on his new baby girl. Boy, did he turn around and look at her! She was just kidding him because it wasn't even born yet, and he wanted a boy so very much. Then he showed a mouth full of white teeth as he laughed with her. That night he had a boy!

* * * * *

I was out at the road gate this morning watching the people on donkeys go by. Everyone walking held out their hands for money before they'd let Quinton take their picture. So he waited until they were past and then took pictures.

A big boy sitting at the gate talked to me in English and interpreted for others who wished to converse with me. He asked me if I would like to be a missionary.

"Oh, yes," I said, *"but I have four children and seven grandchildren."*

He jerked his head and said, *"Oh, no. You a grandmother!"* He said he asked me because he thought I loved the people.

On Sunday morning, Quinton preached to the Sunday School classes and church combined. The front wall of the church was decorated with large plants.

In the evening, Rev. Picazo and Mr. Graffenberger took the O.M.S. famous Haitian choir and us to Cap Haitian's First Baptist Church. That choir had previously toured the U.S. (and I believe sang in the White House).

Rev. Picazo said there were perhaps 2,500 people there. They were packed in like sardines, with crowded balcony and steps, people sitting in all the windows, doors and aisles. The platform was filled with their own choir plus the choir we brought. Children and young people sat on the platform floor, hanging their feet.

I was sitting on the front seat wearing a veil, as all the women did. I could hardly breathe; it was so stifling hot, without air able to come in.

The music was beautiful. Quinton preached, again with Rev. Napoleon interpreting. In spite of the discomfort, the Holy Spirit took charge. A service I will never forget.

Going back to the compound was only five

miles, but it took twenty-five minutes to drive it. The road into the city was very poor. It was so rugged that the men had to get out of the bus and use shovels to fill up holes so that we could pass through.

Saturday morning, Quinton and visitors were to go up into the mountains about twenty-five miles to see the Citadel which was built by Henri Christopher, the conqueror in the early 1800's. It is 3,000 feet high. In the building of it, 20,000 men were killed. However, it rained in the night, so they couldn't go. They were to ride up as far as they could go and then walk for two hours or ride on donkeys. They said it was very steep and the mud was so bad that your legs were mud to the knees. But that could also happen when you just walked out to the country churches.

We appreciated the staff considering our health, as this was but the beginning of our six-week trip. Much travel and work was ahead of us.

On the way back to Port Au Prince from the compound, Eldon Turnidge flew round and round the Citadel. We got some interesting movies of the place. This was a stronghold built to defend the island from her enemies.

Now it is 4VEH who is, with the Word of God, the true and all-powerful defender of the island. I pray God will open their hearts to this truth. God bless those who daily toil for their Lord in this destitute land.

* * * * *

246

On the day of our leaving, after having devotions with the staff, I went back to the trailer to clean it so that it would look well cared for. After a while, I heard the Turnidge plane come twice over the compound, buzzed us and flew back to the airfield. Immediately, Rev. Picazo got into the station wagon and away he went to pick them up. Now we were to find out if he would fly us back to Port Au Prince that afternoon or tomorrow. It was nice that day, but it might have been rainy and heavy with clouds tomorrow. Mr. Turnidge had the only plane on the island.

Suddenly, the old lawn boy appeared when the plane buzzed.

He came and swept the long enclosed porch (although we had done it), wiped all the screens with a cloth (and it must have been 35 feet long), dusted the furniture, wiped the windows inside and out. He either is happy to see them, wants his eighty cents per day, or knows what she required of him when she was at home. Maybe he just wanted to keep his job.

God had been good to me for allowing me to come along on this trip. To see the need is not enough. To pray and plead with God for these dear families would be my task. 4VEH is reaching the Caribbean islands who speak English, Creole, Spanish and French. The translators are doing a fine job. "Your Worship Hour" went out from this station.

Wednesday morning we were flown back to Port Au Prince where we met two missionaries who allowed us to rest in their rooms at the

Plaza Hotel while they went sightseeing. Afterwards they took us to a restaurant for a cheeseburger and shake before taking us to the Pan American plane. We had to wait for many hours.

Before we left home in South Bend, I had finished reading the "Ugly American." On this flight, we saw a perfect example of this book.

Before boarding the plane, we observed an American who produced a bottle of whiskey and attracted a group of Haitians while gulping it down. Then he unwrapped another and offered it to a Haitian. He drank it, or so the American said. We could not see too well for the crowd was getting larger.

The American boastfully asked, *"Who will drink two bottles?"* He acted as if he were an auctioneer. I was very disgusted with him. All this time, his wife was standing side of him with a nonchalant look as if she knew her husband well enough that she could not stop him from making a fool of himself. Finally Plane No. 435 was called, and she gathered up their luggage and led him to the plane. On the way, he stopped another couple to talk and make a further fool of himself. Then he tried to get on the plane at the wrong end.

The next time I saw him we were filing past on the way off the plane at San Juan, Puerto Rico. There he was, slumped down in his seat. It looked as if all the liquor he had drunk had come up and out all over his nice white suit from his chin to his belt, all over his large sub-division. His wife was side of him, embarrassed and expressionless, waiting until all onlookers were off the plane. After all of us had alighted, we saw a stewardess helping him down the steps. He didn't even know where he was.

We had stopped at the Dominican Republic and then flew on to San Juan, arriving at midnight. Rev. Don Luttrell was there to meet us.

It was a wild ride (on the left side of the road) when we passed through the city and up the mountain to his home and radio station.

He was the reason for our being there. He had been very anxious that we come to the Caribbean and meet our radio listeners of the various islands.

The Luttrell home was formerly owned by a doctor; the furniture was formerly owned by the governor of St. Thomas. After breakfast, we visited their radio office, met their workers. Mrs. Luttrell explained much about their work. Quinton called his home head secretary, and then we packed for our Caribbean cruise.

Mr. Luttrell had a one-engine plane that cruised at 150 miles per hour. Before we left San Juan, he flew over and buzzed some of his friends' homes. This was a new experience for me. I had always flown in large commercial planes. This tilting made me feel uneasy. He observed this in his rearview mirror, and he teased me, but told me to bend with the plane and I'd feel better. He took along his radio station manager, too.

Sometime in the afternoon, we landed at St. Thomas. They needed a few supplies. Don asked me if I had a straw hat for the cruise. I didn't. So he said, *"We'll all go with Mrs. Everest to buy her a hat."* Well, I never had so much help buying a hat in all my life. The five of us going into the store and my trying on one and then another. It was fun to get their reactions. Finally, I put one on with a rim, to Don's satisfaction, a two-inch ribbon around it with a black, cute doll fastened in the back. Thanks. It cost three dollars. I have it yet. It served me well, and I wouldn' t give it up yet. With our purchases we went to Yacht Haven and the Shellback.

We were not going on a large ship. This was a sailboat 45 feet long. It belonged to Frank and Pat Van Lohn. Mr. Luttrell introduced us properly to the Van Lohns, and they took us to every part of the boat. It was great. They had been sailing for twelve years and happily married for

The boat's crew, as we traveled from island to island visiting with our radio listeners.

Our home for 5 days and 4 nights.

twenty-three years. Frank is properly licensed by the U. S. Coast Guard, and Pat is a thoroughly experienced first mate and cook. The Shellback is the full-time home for the Van Lohns. It accommodates four guests comfortably. We lived on the Shellback for 5 days and 4 nights.

The first evening we sat together and watched the beautiful sunset, which was the most gorgeous one I have ever seen. As we sat there, we shared scripture and prayer. The Lohns are wonderful Christians with many stories to tell you of witnessing and converting some of their guests. They often have honeymooners or people celebrating an anniversary.

The next morning, the men took a short swim in the beautiful Caribbean water, staying quite close to the boat because of the sharks.

I had a restful night. But it was unusual to sleep in a hammock, which keeps gently swinging back and forth. Then I thought, this must be what it felt like when my mother rocked me as a child. So I closed my eyes and pretended I was being rocked. I soon fell asleep.

How refreshed we were after sleeping in the fresh air. For breakfast it was scrambled eggs, link sausage, a half grapefruit, fresh cinnamon rolls and coffee. At lunchtime it was ham and cheese sandwiches, pickles and a fruit drink. At night our dinner consisted of lamb chops, eggplant, rice, salad and after-dinner mints. Meals are about 7-7:30 a.m., 1:00-2:00, and 7:00-8:00 p.m. On the deck, there was a large bunch of apple-bananas to munch on. They also gave us dried fruit periodically with drinks – 7UP, Wink, and Coca-Cola.

"Today the temperature, 83 degrees, winds ten miles per hour, gusts to twenty." We sailed until we arrived at a mountain island called Jost Van Dyke. Mr. Lohn anchored out a little from the island. Mr. Luttrell climbed down the ladder of the ship into the dinghy, which took him to the shore.

He introduced himself to the officer, and the officer gave him an English flag to take back to the Shellback to hoist it there. The island is governed by the British. There is no church on the island, however, a minister from England went there twice each year to preach and teach for a month.

They do have a school for the children.

When Mr. Luttrell came back to the Shellback, he said we had permission to visit all three hundred homes on the island. Our plan was to go from house to house covering the whole island. Don would introduce Quinton and myself and ask them if they listened to "Your Worship Hour" broadcast. We had gone to find out if indeed it was being heard and to leave with them some Bible lesson and get information about how they were receiving it. Broadcasting was very expensive. This place, as with many other places, was important to evangelize.

So Quinton and I followed Frank down the ship's ladder into the dinghy to the shore.

It was indeed thrilling to be so far from home and to be introduced by Mr. Luttrell at these homes. The people were so surprised to see us.

One lady got so excited that she walked out the door, looked up to the heavens, and with her arms raised up said, *"Oh, Father, I didn't think I'd ever see them until I got to Heaven."* Then she came back into the house, invited us in, smiling all the time. Later in the week, we had a service in her home.

There were no cars or taxis on this island. We saw only one donkey that a young man had to ride. So it was slow going for us. There were no roads, only paths. But the scenery was wonderful. There were no stores on the island either. Most of their food came from their lush gardens. I never saw such large vegetables and flowers.

One man told us he was offered one million dollars for his piece of land. He flatly refused it, not because he didn't need the money but because it would have changed their island into a beautiful vacation place for wealthy people, and most of the islanders would then have lost their homes.

The people had little in their small houses – a stove, table, chairs, beds, sewing machine and a little black box, a RADIO! That's what we wanted to see. Every home on the island said they listen to "Your Worship Hour" over WIVV, except one.

Well, I didn't get very far around the island until I told Quinton it was too hot and the climbing was wearing me out. So Frank said, *"I'll take her back to the Shellback. Then I'll be back and catch up with you"*

How glad I was to be on the boat again.

The men anchored in three different harbors that day to get around the mountain island.

The men had interesting reports when they got back. They were happy but very tired.

The Bible lessons had blank marks on the pages, which they were to fill out by the next day when the three men would come back again and see how they got along. The men told the parents that if they could not read or write, to have their children help them. Most of them did it as families. Those who were unsaved were told the way of salvation and were prayed with, knowing God is faithful. Some very definitely accepted Christ.

Frank helped a man and his wife who got stuck on a sand bar just at an opening between islands looking out to the big ocean swells. Frank and some natives were unsuccessful; so from our boat, the Coast Guard was called. When they had almost arrived, the men got them loose. It was interesting to watch. The woman was scared and nervous.

I enjoyed the sailing, got my sea legs and didn't get sick by the rocking of the boat. The breeze was delightful, and I often rested on the six-foot long sponge pillows topside (cabin roof) and under the canvas top.

The next day, we sailed to Caneel Bay at St. Johns Island. We were planning to sail to Tortula and other islands, but because the weather in the States was bad, the ocean became rough just beyond the islands. As we sailed in the Caribbean, we could see between the islands, as we passed by, and the great swells of the ocean. Therefore, we sailed to St. Johns.

This is where the elite go for rest. Important business people, presidents, and politicians vacation here.

But we were most interested in the natives, the hired help, servants and young people. Mr. Luttrell was acquainted with many of them and had Bible study groups among them.

One Sunday Quinton preached twice in a Baptist church. Sunday evening the pastor told Quinton his people always came late to church. Now he knows the reason. "Your Worship Hour" broadcast always signed off at seven o'clock and that was when church started. *"That's why many came running to church,"* he laughed.

So many said, *"I hear your voices but wish to see your faces."*

One man said, as many people did, *"I should correspond with you, and I plan but don't do it."*

Another said, *"I've been praying God would give me friends."* And, *"Oh, He sent me Christian friends."*

Another said, *"When I listen, the Spirit speaks to me, and Jesus' name is the sweetest name I know."*

"Great manna for the soul because He leads us to everlasting life. I am proud to see your faces." "We listen carefully."

When people gather around, as they did, to express their true feelings to us, we indeed were blessed. And we often praised God for leading us into this worldwide missionary work. Many Bibles were distributed there.

The next day, we were taken on a trip up into the mountains, and at one place we stopped, got out of the car to take movie pictures.

We were on a very high cliff looking down on Caneel Bay where our boat, the Shellback, was anchored. What a beautiful sight!

* * * * *

Ruth Luttrell had told her husband to come home by way of Vieques, a very small island. "Your Worship Hour" broadcast was on this station, too.

Chapter Seventeen

*On to Brazil for a Convention
with our missionaries.*

Then we sailed back to St. Thomas. We
thanked the captain and wife of the sailboat
Shellback and said *"Goodbye."* They were so gracious and kind to us. It was difficult to think we
would never see them again in this world.

* * * * *

We packed our things in Don's little plane and
returned to San Juan. After spending a night at
the Luttrell home, we packed all our luggage for
the big trip to Brazil. It was quite a privilege to
meet so many people who seemed to know us
by radio. We thanked God many times for the
work of reaching so many people with the
Gospel.

Before reaching Brazil, we had a four-hour
stop in Trinidad airport. We didn't know what
we could do there, only sit.

But as soon as we arrived, we went to the desk
to ask about our flight to Rio. The clerk said it
would be on time.

Just then a man, strange to us, appeared at
Quinton's side and asked, *"Are you the Everests?"*
We replied, *"We are."*

He said his name and explained that a banker,

Mr. Robertson, from Kingston, Jamaica, called to tell him that we would be on this plane coming in at this time. He informed me that we would have a wait of four hours.

"Well, I'm"—he gave his name—*"a 'Team missionary' up in the mountains. We have many youth there and a staff of missionaries waiting for you. They have cooked a big dinner for you. We all listen to your broadcast. I've come down to get you. Please come."*

Now, all this time, the man at the desk kept shaking his head at Quinton saying, *"No! No! No!"* I began to think the man could be a hoax. But Quinton smiled and said, *"We'd be happy to go with him."*

Then the man at the desk talked very sternly to the missionary. He told him he was taking a great responsibility to take us away from the airport. Twice he made him promise to have us back at 9:30. Our plane was to depart at 10 o'clock p.m.

It turned out that we had a very enjoyable, profitable time, plus a delicious meal. They explained to Quinton their desires to have a radio station in Trinidad.

Our night flight from Trinidad to Rio, Brazil was uneventful except for the fact that the stewardess saw our height and kindly asked us to take the lounge chairs in the First Class section. It was much more comfortable for a night flight. I guess the Lord knew we were tired and provided this for us.

We arrived approximately at 4:30 a.m. San Juan time. As we approached the airport, we heard our names called and looked high up to see Rev. Paul Mast at the upper railing.

After much waiting in line, we came to the customs officers. Not one or two, not three or four, but five to question us and look through our baggage. We decided each of them didn't trust the other. And the last one was a woman!

Paul Mast had business in the city; so he got us settled in a hotel for a few hours sleep.

The next morning we got up at 4:30 and flew to Sao Paulo, then to Campinas; then a ten-hour drive to Maringa.

The missionaries had a very full schedule for us. It looked like a good variety of meetings. We were to travel into the jungle churches as well as to the city churches.

The first night we had the evening meal in the dining room of Maringa Bible School. After that we gathered with the staff members, the missionaries from all areas where we had churches, and church people who wanted to be at the first graduation. This was a great occasion for all of us.

With great joy, we assembled in the open air on the tennis court, a place prepared with chairs and a few lights. Quinton was asked to give the address.

We were given a room on campus in the children's home, a large house which was home to all of the missionaries' children, except those living nearby, for eight or nine months of school. They had a schoolhouse for them, too, on the Maringa campus called Green Acre School.

Mr. and Mrs. Knapp were their houseparents.

It was interesting to eat with the children and see how well trained they were. She had a little fellow to sit side of me, to pull my chair out and to help me in any way he could. How cute he was!

* * * * *

The next morning at seven o'clock, we were awakened by music, loud and clear. Each morning it was the same old hymn, "Only Trust Him" translated "Christo Salvo," sung in two languages. It was a beautiful parrot singing under our window. How delightful to be awakened by a bird!

We went with the children each morning to school. Quinton spoke to them for a half hour before they started class. There were classes from grades one through six.

One morning, five children wept and prayed for Jesus to save them. One morning after Quinton spoke, he asked them it they'd like a little gift from the States. Oh, they did! So we gave them packages of M&M's we had stuffed in our suitcases. They had not had any for years. They giggled and thanked us as if it was something expensive.

We were surprised, though, when the teachers asked if we had enough for them, too. They were as eager as the kids were. *"Sure,"* I said, *"help yourselves."*

They all called us Grandma and Grandpa Everest.

After speaking to the children, we went across campus where Quinton spoke each morning.

260

From 9:45 to 11:00 he spoke to the missionaries; at 1:30 and again at 3:15.

One night four United Missionary Churches came together for services.

Perhaps a letter we received after we got home explains.

"We look back on your visit to us here in Brazil as a highlight—the personal interest you took in us and our children. Also, the wonderful challenge and practical thoughts given by Bro. Everest. Yes, and the good heart-to-heart ladies' group we had with you, Mae."

I knelt in prayer one night, and these words came to me. *"Thank you, Lord, for helping me to speak this morning. All the nice things the women said to me afterwards really belong to You because you helped me. If I kept the Glory to myself, I could not see it anyway. With you wearing the Glory, I can see it on You and it becomes You, not me."*

"We are so thankful that you could both come. Thank you again for everything and for your continued prayer interest in our behalf. We shall be remembering 'Your Worship Hour' in prayer."

* * * * *

We had pleasant fellowship in the journeys from one place to another. Eating homemade ice cream at one place. Each of us turned the freezer on a hot afternoon.

Something I will never forget was the great effort our professors and missionaries were doing on Sunday. Several were starting new churches in the city. Some of the women, too, were doing all they could to reach people for

Christ.

Mrs. Knapp, the children's housemother, found her own unique way to reach the city's children.

After her husband and the children were ready for church on Sunday mornings, she would pack her car with flannelgraph and easel, Bible and whatever she needed for outdoor Sunday School classes.

She would drive a short distance, park her car, set up the easel on the street corner and start singing. I think, if I remember correctly, that she had an instrument of some kind.

Soon children would come running to hear her stories. She was a good storyteller and loved children.

From neighborhood to neighborhood, she would do the same thing. Her aim was to locate unreached children. She would have many new experiences each Sunday to tell her family at the dinner table.

When six or more classes were over, she made her way back home to prepare dinner for the missionaries' children, plus her own family.

I greatly admired this woman. With eighteen or twenty children in one group and changing locations six or eight times each Sunday morning, it gave her a combined number of over one hundred each Sunday. She told me the children ran to her classes, and when she stopped, they begged her to stay. Mrs. Knapp had a great burden for these dear children from non-Christian homes.

* * * * *

On to Brazil...

One day Mrs. Paul Fretz (Merriam) took us to the Bible Book Store in Maringa and explained the progress of the business. On one day they sold forty Bibles. We gave a good report on our return home to the man who sent us to Haiti, Jamaica and the Brazilian Book Store. He fully supported that Bible Book Store for ten years.

We were to visit and preach in each of the Missionary Churches in Brazil at least once, even those in the newly-built towns in the jungle.

I remember the day they put us on a one-engine plane to fly out over the jungle. Quinton had been there a number of years ago, and as they flew out over it then, he asked the pilot what would happen if he had engine trouble and crashed. Would anyone search for you? The pilot said no one would make that effort. There are too many animals. You wouldn't last long.

I remembered Quinton's telling us that when he got back home. He did not know this pilot.

Jackie Ummel had told us the pilot would take us to Umerama and gave us a note that she wrote to show anyone who wanted to know who we were and what we were there for. She signed it. The Ummels were to follow us through the jungle in their jeep.

They had a breakdown; so they were delayed three hours. It was a good thing we carried that note, for we could only speak English. There was no airport; so we sat on a little grassy knoll and waited. A small building was nearby, but it looked like a bar. The weather was hot. I was quite comfortable, though. At least the Ummels and God knew where we were! And I was glad to be on the ground again. The pilot came in too fast and had to go up and try again for a smooth landing!

The Ummels finally arrived. It was about 3:00 p.m. They took us in the jeep to our Missionary Church in the town. Behind the sanctuary there were two rooms where the carekeepers lived. The man was not at home when we came, but the wife wanted to fix us something to eat. We were hungry and tired.

The woman went out to catch a chicken to kill for supper. It took some time for her to catch it and then kill it and scald it. After defeathering it, she washed and cut it up. She cooked it up on a very small stove in the corner of the room. This room was their living room, kitchen and dining room.

While Jackie and this gracious little lady were holding a conversation in Portuguese, I was sitting on a hard chair by the wall. Jackie turned around and looked at me and then asked the woman something. Jackie came over to me and said, *"You may go into the bedroom and lie on her bed until supper is ready."*

"Oh, that is so kind of her, and I think I will."

When I laid down on that crude, hard bed in that tiny room, I felt as if she had given me a great gift and I thanked God for that place to lie down. I fell asleep almost instantly. I was so refreshed after the rest and the good meal. It was the most tiresome day, I believe, on the trip in Brazil.

We had a call to make in that town, a church service, and then more traveling through the jungle to Xambre. How glad we were to be in Dick Ummel's home in spite of the heat. In the daytime, the temperature was 112 to 120 degrees in the shade. That night I fanned myself with a piece of paper until I dropped off to sleep.

In one town, Ribeirao Preto, where Mervin and Lucille Traub were missionaries, Quinton held a service that was the beginning of a great revival in one family.

A girl by the name of Eugenia, and known to Lucille, persuaded her strong Catholic parents to go with her to church to hear the speaker from the United States. She told them he would be only one night at the church. They came, and I remember how earnestly they responded to the message. They knelt at their seats and called upon God to save them. They were so happy that their daughter begged them to come.

From their testimony and changed lives, her own husband was saved soon after this.

The grandmother was so very sick that the doctor said she would die at any time. Her daughter, Eugenia's aunt, told her about Jesus' power to forgive her sins and also heal her. After two years, we were told by Mrs. Traub, the pastor's wife, that the grandmother was saved, strong and well.

It was amazing how their influence continued. Two aunts with eight children each and an uncle, all strong Catholics, were also converted at an Easter service.

Quinton and I felt strongly that God had sent

us to encourage our missionaries in prayer and evangelism.

Missionary Paul Fretz took me one day to a board meeting of different missionary societies to discuss and to vote on the "Glint" Sunday School material. Since I had used this material in our Primary (nine classes) and Junior High (six classes) for twenty-two years, Paul persuaded me to tell them of the value of "Gospel Light" called "Glint" in Brazil. I was pleased to do it. Henrietta Mears is the author of this material, and I think of her as being my mentor, having heard her speak at National Sunday School Conventions. There were ten board members in attendance that day from nine denominations. Paul Fretz later went to Europe to attempt to get this wonderful material translated into different languages. India also has it translated in different languages.

Another day after having breakfast with the Masts, we hurriedly drove two hours to Longrine. On the way, we bought gas, eight bottles of Coke, mineral water, and Guanana. It was pleasant going, but returning it was very hot, the temperature being over 100 degrees.

Rev. Elkjer met us as we drove into the parking lot of the Bible School (OMS). He greeted us warmly, for he had once been our speaker in a missionary convention in our home church. We were taken to his apartment and served a cold drink.

I met his wife for the first time.

We soon went next door to the chapel where Quinton spoke to the missionary staff on "A

Happy Heart." After he spoke, they continued to discuss it and to visit for a little while.

We were then taken to their radio studio and control room, which was air-conditioned! The only one we had experienced in Brazil.

Mrs. Elkjer served us a lovely dinner with the help of her maid and the Bible School cook. We had beef, chicken, mashed potatoes, apricot jello salad, green beans, rolls, ice cream and brownies.

It was a rewarding day.

* * * * *

One Sunday, we had services at the coffee farm church where the workers attended, a church built for them.

There was a row of twelve houses built near the church for the workers and their families. The "fazenda" church, they called it.

Rev. Don and Jean Granitz and Rev. Norman and Betty Charles were the missionaries here.

The Granitz family was home on furlough. Rev. and Mrs. Charles were in charge of the work.

Just before it was time for us to leave the parsonage for church on Sunday morning, a little girl came to the door and asked for Mrs. Charles. I could not understand what she was saying, but she was excited and crying. Mrs. Charles hurriedly went to the cupboard, pulled out a bottle and said to me, *"Her mother sent her to get me because their baby has a high fever."* Mrs. Charles doctored the people the best she could, for there was no other help for a very great distance.

* * * * *

Back to the city of Maringa. Our clothes, like my dress and Quinton's shirts, were washed nightly because the dirt was red or purple. The dust colored our clothes. After washing them, I'd hang them on hangers. They would be dry in the morning; so we'd wear them again the next day.

Jackie Ummel whispered to me on the way back, *"I'm going to take you to a Japanese hair shop. We'll have our hair and nails done for a dollar. These girls are very clean and artistic."*

We had a great time. The girls were so jolly, laughing as they worked on me because I was from the United States. They made a great fuss. One knelt down in front of me and asked Jackie many questions about me.

This shop was on the second floor of a building downtown. They had girls bring buckets of water up the stairs and warm it. Then one would stand by the operator and pour water over my head as the operator asked her to do. It certainly was an unusual experience, but we were satisfied with our appearance after they were through. And all for one dollar!

Six weeks had gone by very fast. This was the longest I had ever been away from home. Except for my husband being with me, I would have grown homesick.

* * * * *

But one very important thing was yet to be. The missionaries' children were to put on a Christmas program before we could leave.

On to Brazil...

* * * * *

We were fascinated with those farm people. They sang so heartily and seemed full of joy as they fellowshipped together. Quinton preached and asked if there was anyone there who wanted to be a Christian. There was a sweet spirit in the service. Many came to the altar.

Mrs. Charles came to me and said, *"Go, pray with that woman over there. She's sobbing."*

I said, *"I will, but she won't understand my prayer at all."*

"But God will, and she'll be blessed to have you praying for her."

I went and knelt down at her side. When I prayed in English, she cried the more and prayed aloud in Portuguese.

Mrs. Charles told me afterward that she was the mother of the sick child.

After the service, Quinton had the congregation all come outside so that he could take pictures of them. After the pictures were taken, a lady came over to me holding her hand out with a lovely fan for me. It was beautiful, and for years I kept it in my purse, often using it in camp meetings and in hot weather elsewhere.

Another woman also brought me a gift. It was a long scarf made of coarse, white material. The lace was made with ordinary cord. But, oh, how I appreciated it, for I knew she gave me her best. Another woman gave me a handful of flower seeds. Then all the people sang, "God Be With You Till We Meet Again."

How far we traveled to get to that church I have forgotten. But it was a great distance.

269

Amal was the name of the story they played out. And very effective and well done, we thought.

At the end of the program, the program director gave a very impressive speech about certain people. He didn't give any names but elaborated on their work. I thought he must have been talking about the principal of the school and his teachers. When he was through talking, he paused. The people clapped, and I did, too.

Then he said, *"Rev. Everest and Mae, will you please come forward?"*

Oh, I felt as small as a mouse! I was so embarrassed. We went forward to receive a large, beautiful copper picture plaque. It has on it a ship with sails protruding with heavy waves reminding us of the Caribbean sailboat we lived on for nearly a week. Tears ran down my face as I smiled, and Quinton gave them our thanks. This was his reward for coming to Brazil for the New Life Convention. The Lord had provided the funds, and great blessings were provided for all of us.

* * * * *

Back to Campinas with Jim, Jean Coalter and their children again. They found the city water was very low and was turned off many hours of the day. But we had a wonderful evening with the family.

In the morning, we got our bags ready. Two of the boys were going with us to the airport. On the way I heard the boys whispering. I caught one sentence, *"Let's throw out their luggage so they won't go home."*

On to Brazil...

When we arrived at the airport, we met a Rev. Earl and Gladys Mosteller and daughter, Virginia, age seventeen. Her parents had asked if we would accompany her as far as Miami. Then she would have a wait of four hours after we would leave for Chicago at 11:00 p.m. She was going to a Nazarene College in Idaho.

All went well on our 9:30 a.m. flight to Miami. We ate and visited much of the time. Virginia was a bright spiritual girl. I felt the Lord would truly use this young, tall, six-foot, one-inch girl in His work somewhere. She was raised in Brazil where her father was superintendent of the Nazarene Missionary Society.

When we were all settled comfortably in the Miami airport, Virginia soon became very sleepy. Scooting down in her chair made her legs and feet go far out from the chair.

"Virginia," I said, looking right into her face, *"I wish we had something you could rest your feet on, but we haven't. Why not let me sit up as tall as I can. You lay your head on my shoulder and go to sleep."*

"I'd like that," she smiled, *"but you may get too tired to stay in one position or need to go to the restroom."*

"Never mind. I'll let you know if I do."

We turned and twisted until we were both comfortable. She fell asleep almost instantly. I felt I was taking the place of her mother because I had seen them say their good-byes with hugs and kisses, not knowing when they would see each other again. She slept that way for probably two hours, when I needed to get ready for our 11:00 p.m. flight to Chicago. We said a hearty goodbye. I dreaded leaving her alone.

When Quinton and I reached Chicago, the last plane to South Bend had already left; so we checked into a hotel for a few hours of sleep.

For Virginia back in Miami, things didn't go as well. She waited until 3:00 a.m. when they called her flight number. She got on the plane and settled down. The plane was ready to take off, when everyone was ordered back to the building while the FBI checked all the baggage. A bomb had been reported, but finally they decided it was only a scare, and the plane took off. She was used to flying; so it didn't upset her much, and she said the Lord really helped her.

When she got to Boise, Idaho, the plane had to circle an hour because of fog and was practically out of gas when it did come down. So she had some excitement all the way.

Her mother wrote to tell me all about it. *"Virginia is very happy and doing well in school."*

* * * * *

What a wonderful Christmas we had. To see our family again was one great present itself. In years to come we would be separated many times for longer periods of time.

These were always times of catching up on news, seeing how the children had developed in their schoolwork or business and how the grandchildren were doing. I loved being a grandmother. What I liked to do was to watch them play together as cousins and listen to what they said.

Our entire family loves to sing. Our oldest daughter, Charlene, had us all in the family room to sing carols with Sharon at the piano and she directing. After the carols, she told us each what part we were to sing in "Twelve Days of Christmas." What fun!

With five of us supplying food, we had a scrumptious meal! *"God bless our family, and get the most possible glory from their lives for Your name,"* I often prayed.

Chapter Eighteen

The annual trip to Washington, D.C.
and second trip to Bonaire.

Besides all the foreign trips we took, there
were the annual
trips we made to
Washington, D.C.
for the National
R e l i g i o u s
B r o a d c a s t e r s
Conventions.

Ready to broadcast.

Quinton was a
board member for
over thirty years.
After our children
were married, he
took me with him.
For at least twenty
years, I was privi-
leged to experience many unusual things.

The sessions opened on Monday morning, but
we would arrive on Friday for the board meetings, which were held on Saturday. On Sunday,
each one could attend church anywhere in the
Capitol. However, there would be a service in
the hotel for anyone who preferred to stay in the
hotel. Quinton was chosen one time to preach
there.

On Saturdays, I was on my own. I always had

stitchery and a good book with which to spend my time.

One year, before we left home, I learned that the son of my first cousin was a judge in D.C. His name is Ronnie Yoder. I found his phone number and called him. He answered. I gave him my name, told him where I was and why I was in Washington. Then he asked in what hotel we have the convention. When I told him, he laughed.

"You won't believe this," he said, *"but you are just across the street from my office and the judges' chambers. Do you have time to come over? I'll show you around. I'll be glad to see you. I seldom ever see anyone from Indiana where the rest of my family lives."*

Well, I was very pleased. We had a wonderful time but too short, he said.

Later he called and said he and Shirley, his wife, made plans for our Sunday. He and his family would pick us up, take us to his church, the Peter Marshall church, for Sunday School and the church service. He is a beautiful light opera singer; also, he sang in his church choir.

After church, they entertained us at their home in Alexandria. They have one boy and two girls, a delightful, interesting group that could hold a conversation about most any important thing. Over the years, we often spent time with them.

My first cousin, Ronnie's father, was Ray Yoder, an artist who taught art at the University of Virginia and wrote books on art for public schools.

Another time in D. C. I received a telephone call from my niece, Susan Rensberger, on Saturday morning. She said, *"Aunt Mae, what do you want to do this morning? The Vice President is out of town, and I'm not busy this morning, I'd like to take you to the oval office, Vice President Mondale's office, and mine."* Susan was a scriptwriter for him.

When I saw her name plate on a door just across from the Vice President's, I said, *"Little girl, how did you ever get here?"*

She just laughed. She unlocked his room, and we stood talking a little. She showed me the small closet where she made his coffee. She had me sit down at his desk.

I had been at the Oval office before, but she took me anyway. She thought she could take me into it, but a guard standing in the doorway said, *"No farther."* She said to me, *"No farther today."* So we left and went back to the hotel.

Some periods of the day had open sessions. I loved to be in on all of them. I learned so much and heard some of the greatest godly and knowledgeable men to be heard anywhere.

Usually on Tuesday night, the President of the United States was the speaker. This was very exciting. The board sat on the platform, which included Quinton. Seats on the front row had the names of the board members' wives on them. Mine was Malinda Everest. The other ladies always wondered about Malinda. That is my first name.

When President Ford was to speak, they had a beautiful, little singer render a song just before he spoke. Instead of going to the podium, she walked to where he was sitting and took his hand and said, *"Come with me."* He smiled and followed her to the podium. She again held his hand, looked up into his eyes and sang so beautifully and powerfully, *"Jesus loves you, this I know, For the Bible tells me so."* She sang every verse holding his hand and looking into his eyes. He responded by smiling all through it and then thanked her heartily. The people clapped for sometime. It was so unexpected and touching!

President Nixon, Carter, Reagan, Bush, all I heard speak.

We heard President Nixon once in person, Ford twice, Carter three times, Reagan four times, and Bush five times.

At night the convention was open to the public, and in the later years that I attended, there were over four thousand people present.

Each year they would move to a larger hotel until it was finally held in the largest one in the city of Washington, D. C.

Always on Tuesday mornings the Congressional Breakfast was held. A thousand and more attended this, usually one hundred Congressmen. We always went in as early as possible to get a table as near the front as possible. Always there were interesting people to chat with. We were introduced to many people we never dreamed we would be able to meet.

* * * * *

The FCC sent a speaker each year. I always

appreciated their informative speeches. They were the ones who helped the religious broadcasters. Usually they gave good personal testimonies also.

There were European broadcasters who came to be encouraged and to report of their struggles in communist countries.

One Bishop who sat at dinner with us told Quinton and me that he would be arrested if he kept up broadcasting the Gospel. He told his wife he was so busy that she would have to take his place in prison. He said he was too busy to go. Then he laughed and said, *"No, I quit broadcasting on land. We purchased a yacht, took our equipment out from land far beyond their jurisdiction and carried on."* He was not a young man, was highly educated and had a vision of lost souls in his country. *"If God is for us, who can be against us?"*

We have many tapes of great speakers of these conventions.

I got a bit acquainted with a 55-year-old beautiful singer one year. Miss Josephine Carpenter was her name. She became very depressed and suffered greatly from dental surgery. Jerome Hines, another great singer, led her to the Lord. They had known each other in Europe. She sang in all the European languages. As a result of the surgery, one side of her face became paralyzed and a tumor developed on the other.

But after her conversion, she prayed and began vocalizing, working very hard to see if God would restore her.

I had a mixture of feelings when I heard her

sing. She must have been a very beautiful lady one day. She sings only sacred numbers, has still a beautiful voice and says her only agent is the Holy Spirit, for she never writes or phones for any appointments. She has a full schedule. She is also treasurer of Farms, Inc., New York. It seems to be a place for unfortunate boys. I could listen to her for hours!

Monday through Wednesday our authentic guide for the board members' wives had always arranged many trips. Early Monday morning, I, with a few women I knew, would go to a designated place, look over all the days of activities and buy tickets for the places we wanted to go for all the three days. That way I could schedule my time for the NRB sessions that I wanted to hear.

Some of the places I accepted were:

- A reception in the home of Rev. Elsner, chaplain of the Senate;

- A reception in the home of the ambassador of Ecuador;

- A reception in the home of the ambassador of Taiwan;

- A reception in the home of the ambassador of Switzerland;

- A reception in the home of the ambassador of Liberia;

- A reception in the embassy of Israel;

- A reception in the home of the ambassador of Egypt; etc.

Mrs. Richard Nixon (Pat) invited us one time. She asked that the doors would be closed to tourists for two hours so that she could be hostess to us for that time. She greeted each of us. We were asked to tell her our name and the name of our husband and his broadcast. When I told her the name of our broadcast "Your Worship Hour," Mrs. Nixon threw up her hands and said, *"I know that broadcast."* They must have listened to it when he was Governor of California because we were never on a station in Washington, D. C. They no doubt heard it on Long Beach, California. She seemed so interested that I said to the guide, *"I would like to give Pat a book my husband had written entitled, 'Prescription for Today.' It is a hardback book of devotions for every day of the year."*

"That is no problem," he replied. *"I am going back to the White House tomorrow morning and will take it to her."*

A few days after I got home, I received a letter from her saying that she and her husband used it daily. They were then feeling the weight of Watergate. I sincerely prayed for the family. I framed the letter and hung it in my workroom.

Pat was very gracious to us, not only because of the delicious food she served and the fact she allowed us certain rooms to browse in, but her questions, remarks and attitudes were friendly and sincere.

As Pat was greeting other women, the ones I was with moved around the room a bit. Soon I turned around to see what was decorating the wall behind me. To my surprise, I found I was standing in front of the fireplace. I was amazed to see this carving in the mantle:

> *"I pray Heaven to Bestow,*
> *The best of blessings on*
> *This House;*
> *And all that shall hereafter inhabit it,*
> *May none but Honest and Wise men overrule*
> *under This Roof."*

(From a letter of John Adams)

In the paper that night, it said that Pat remarked that the NRB group of ladies was the nicest group she had received. I told her my husband and I were praying for them at this crucial time. I suppose others said the same.

* * * * *

The following year, Julie Nixon Eisenhower came to a room in the hotel and spoke to us. She said she was asked last year to receive us, but she was so bitter at that time, she simply could not. But she went on to say that after she accepted Christ into her heart, all the bitterness was gone, and she wanted to receive us now. The entire time she spoke to us, it was of Christ, her concerns, and that she wanted to grow spiritually.

I talked to her personally, and I knew she was very sincere. Someone took our picture together and gave it to me afterward. I then talked to the lady who was the leader of the women's Bible study group in which she was saved. The woman said Julie is growing, but she needs her husband David to also accept Christ.

An article in the newspaper that night said

"Jesus Christ Keeps Julie from Malice." It is a beautiful article I have kept.

There are many Bible study and prayer groups among the wives of our congressmen.

* * * * *

One year we were taken on a tour of the Blair House, which was interesting, and then to the home of Vice President Agnew. Mrs. Agnew was a very gracious lady. I learned in my conversation with her that her grandfather was a Methodist preacher.

She stood just inside the living room door to greet each one of us after disposing of our coats. Our guide had told us before entering the house that we should never allow our hostess to stand alone while we conversed among ourselves. So as some were seated, others would stand near her to ask questions or make remarks. We also casually went into the dining room to be served tea by her secretary. Then we would take our cups and return to the living room.

As we were all drinking tea, I suddenly felt it strange to be drinking tea and Mrs. Agnew standing all the time without having refreshments, too.

So I went again to the dining room to ask her secretary if it would be out of place if I would serve Mrs. Agnew tea.

"Oh, I'm sure she would appreciate that." And I did. That gave me another chance to talk with her as she thanked me.

When we had first entered the Blair House, as the door opened and we filed in, there suddenly was an attractive middle-aged lady beside me whom I had never seen before.

She touched my arm and said, *"I'm sorry, but I just had to crash this party. You see, I did not buy a ticket."* She laughed but did not say who she was, and I did not ask her.

On the tour, we were told of the many elite and royal guests who had stayed for periods of time at the Blair House.

When we returned to the hotel, we gathered for a meeting with all of the NRB board members' wives. Who was the speaker? The lady I met at the Blair House. She was Gloria Vanderbilt who came to give her life story and conversion to Jesus Christ during the Billy Graham Crusade in New York some years ago. She told of her love, marriage, which had many difficulties, and which followed with divorce after she was saved.

Her life was wholly given over to the will of God. With the love and peace of God, she faced life with great purpose.

The last night of the convention was always a banquet with very special speakers. Quinton and I were led to a table where someone was patting a chair, motioning for me to sit down side of her. Yes, it was Gloria. Christians can make quick friendships.

Sometimes a Senator would invite us board members' wives in to talk with him and to allow us to ask any questions we wanted to ask. The Senator would usually have a large semi-circle of chairs and sit himself in the middle of our group. Usually he'd smile, slap his knee and say, *"What do you want to talk about for one hour?"* They could be funny, serious, or very informative. We usually felt good about our visits.

Once one of the ladies smiled and said, *"Yes, but you know, he knew who he was talking with, and he is an elective servant!"*

* * * * *

I learned to know quite a few of the board members' wives, but I had one woman who was so friendly to me from the beginning who continued year after year to endear herself to me. Her husband, likewise, became a dear friend of Quinton's. Rev. Alex and Barbara Leonovich of New Jersey. It all came about because of our broadcasts of "Your Worship Hour" and the confidence they had in Quinton.

Alex, a native of Byelorussia, Russia, had escaped Stalin's reign of terror as a boy of seven, immigrating to the United States. He was saved early and was called to preach.

For forty-six years, Alex broadcast Christian radio programs, often jammed, back to his homeland.

He knew many of the Russian people who were persecuted and tortured for their faith.

He is one of the "old guard" of warriors who have prayed for more than half a century that change might come to his homeland.

Alex Leonovich, together with a group of men from the United States, consisting of pastors, businessmen, mission executives, educators, television and radio broadcasters, etc., were invited to go to Russia as guests of the President, to be interviewed with questions of faith, morals, and many discussions about Russia's spiritual crises.

Alex and these men met with General Stolyarov, Vice-Chairman of the KGB, in KGB headquarters, Alex sitting next to him translating for him what was being said.

We had been friends for many years before this. Quinton had invited him and his wife Barbara to our Gospel Center Church in South Bend and also to speak on a Sunday afternoon on Mission Day at our camp. Over 2,000 people listened to a great message that day.

* * * * *

We often sat together at the banquet the final nights, and "Babs" and I toured together sometimes.

We both tried to befriend the newcomers. That brought some new experiences to me.

One afternoon, our group of ladies was at the entrance on the first floor waiting for our bus to go on one of these guided tours. We were all chatting and exchanging experiences, when suddenly I noticed a lady standing by herself.

I thought to myself, she looks like I felt the first time I came here with Quinton years ago. I wondered if she was one of the NRB group or not.

I left the group and walked over to ask her if she had come for the NRB Convention. She said she came with her husband, Dr. James Kennedy. I told her that I was Mae Everest and that my husband is Quinton Everest, speaker on "Your

Worship Hour." Then she said, *"My name is Ann."*

We were both glad to meet. Then I led her to the group and introduced her to them. She was accepted at once, of course. Soon she was seated on the bus between two strangers but not strangers for long.

* * * * *

Several years after that meeting of Ann, I was not able to go to the convention. A week before Christmas, I was hospitalized. The doctors found I had cancer. I was not sick or suffering. But I did have much suffering as I went through the process of getting rid of it. The following year, I returned to the NRB Convention with my husband.

The first day I saw Ann Kennedy, I asked her if she was here last year. She said, *"No, I had cancer."* I was amazed. When I asked her about her condition and the procedures she went through, they were the same as mine. How strange. And as we exchanged reports of how good the Lord· was to us, as He comforted us with songs, scripture and prayers of family, friends and the church, it seemed like a bond between us. When I see Dr. Kennedy's program on television, I always watch to see if Ann is still in the choir. *"Oh, there she is."* And twenty years have rolled by since our cancer experiences! How good God is to all of us who put our trust in Him.

* * * * *

It was a surprise when the gynecologist came into my hospital room that evening and said,

"Mae, I have bad news. You have cancer. Now the good news is that there is not a large amount of cancer cells and that it is in the safest place to be cured."

"You must have eighteen radiation treatments, an implant, and then surgery."

I had no previous thought of cancer.

The first words that tumbled from my lips were, *"Well, I'm no better than anyone else. Jesus will be with me tomorrow just as He was today and as He was yesterday. We'll take it a day at a time."*

I was to be an outpatient while having my radiation treatments. So all of a sudden the doctor said, *"Nurse, get her robe; then wrap her in blankets. Take her in a wheelchair down to the emergency door. I'll check her out and have my car running to warm it."*

There was a blizzard that day. The doctor wanted to take me home and break the news to my husband himself.

This was five miles in the opposite direction in which the doctor lives. After telling Quinton about it, he left to go home.

This stunned Quinton. He said little for a few minutes. But again it seemed the Lord put words in my mouth. *"Quinton, if this would be terminal, I'd just get to see Jesus first before you folks do, and my mother and father and all the wonderful Bible characters and people we love."*

"But I want to go the scriptural way. Call Pastor Murphy. Ask him to come to anoint me, and then both of you pray for my healing."

In the morning, I looked to the Word of God for support. Almost immediately I began reading I Peter 5:6 through 11. It would have been easy, perhaps, to choose verse 7 and let it go at that. However, that never occurred to me at that time. I read and reread the whole portion. I studied it verse by verse, phrase by phrase. I prayed over it and asked the Lord what He wanted to do to me and through me. I felt wholly abandoned to His will. I found later that many times and in many ways I was humbled. I didn't care. Even the suffering didn't really matter. I felt so close to Jesus. I felt wrapped in His love.

At the beginning of this experience, I awakened singing a hymn. It was such an encouragement. Each day thereafter or during the night hours God gave me a different song. It is still happening.

Oh, the richness of the old hymns of the church is such a blessing to me.

One of the special cancer doctors had said, *"Trust us."* They knew what they were doing. I earnestly thanked him for what they were doing, but I said, *"Doctors can cut out the bad, they can shrivel and burn the bad, but only God can heal. All the glory and thanks goes to Him for my healing."*

Previously I did not know I was sick. I did not feel badly. But, of course, the radiation treatments caused side effects. And as I was seated in the waiting room each morning until they called my name over the loud speaker, I visited with other patients who were so much worse off than myself, although I was suffering, too.

Sometimes I felt guilty to have such love surrounding me. So many of them seemed forsaken and helpless. Some, however, were very encouraging to others, and I tried to let them know God loved them very much. Suffering people often listen for hope in a conversation.

Quinton always went with me. He cancelled almost three months of meetings.

The day of the last radiation treatment I was checked into the hospital for the implant. In the morning, this was done under anesthesia, and in the afternoon, the physicist came into my private room to insert the radium.

I laid in a certain position for forty hours. A quarantine sign was put on my door and closed. No visitors allowed. I had many nurses waiting on me during that time because no one nurse could be near me more than a few minutes.

I used to tease them and say, *"You can hurry out, but I have to stay with it for forty-eight hours."* Before it was over, I was suffering greatly.

The 1978 blizzard was on at that time. Cynthia, our youngest daughter, came from Pasadena, California, to stay with her father while I was in the hospital. The day before the blizzard struck, she bought a lot of groceries, thinking she would make casseroles to freeze for my homecoming. Also, she bought some stitchery to do while waiting for me to come home. People were arrested who were out on the street. The snow was so deep at our house that Quinton and Cynthia had to stand up to see out the window. Doctors and nurses were stranded at home or at the hospital. One of the nurses told me she hid some clean sheets for me because they were running out of them.

My family doctor would come in early in the morning, slump down in a chair and ask, *"Mae, how are you this morning?"*

And I said, *"Doctor, I think I'm more rested than you. How do you get by with so little sleep?"*

Then he asked, *"What are they feeding you these days?"*

I was on a diet that he selected for me. I answered, *"How about bologna sandwiches?"* He didn't like that one bit. He said, "I know food is low."

Some of the pregnant mothers were brought to the hospital by snowmobiles.

I was so glad Cynthia had come to be with her dad and cook for him. They could not go to the store these stormy days; so they ate the food that she was going to prepare and freeze for my return.

* * * * *

The doctor waited nearly four weeks before I could have the surgery. I was anxious for that to take place. Now that was all they could do for me. The radiation treatments, implant and surgery were over.

In a few weeks, they examined me again. When the great cancer doctor looked at me and said, *"Mrs. Everest, you are dismissed,"* the tears wanted to flow. The doctor immediately left the room while I was trying to thank him for all he did for me, but he was out of the door so fast, I'm sure he did not hear me. I thought he must be in a hurry to help someone else who needed him more than I did.

Peace and trust in the Lord sustained me. Otherwise, I would have lived in fear. I had none. *"He holds me in His hands and binds my feet to the path."* Praise God! Psalm 66:9, Living Bible.

* * * * *

In April, Quinton and I vacationed in Florida. That was twenty years ago!

Now that I was well again, we continued to enter the open doors that God had given us.

We were on our way again to Bonair where we had been a number of years ago at the dedication of Trans World's radio station. We had reservations for a room in the Holiday Inn on Curacao.

We arrived at the small airport. We had been here once before, but we were in the hands of Trans World Radio's personnel, and all had gone fine at that time.

Tonight we were alone. So we went to the desk at the airport to ask if we could check with our hotel in town to confirm our registration which Quinton was holding in his hand.

We soon learned that they had no room for us. Quinton declared that they certainly did. He had their reservation in his hand. All the reply he could get was, *"We have no room reserved for you."* Well, we were now convinced we had been "bumped" by someone who gave them more money or a large party had come in.

The lady at the desk heard our predicament. She suggested she could perhaps find another place for us. She called several places without success.

In the meantime, we felt very weary having traveled from South Bend to New York, then after waiting a few hours flying to Curacao. It was now dark. I looked around but saw nothing comfortable on which to spend the night. No lounge chairs. Just slat, wooden benches. We had no supper; so we were also hungry.

Finally the lady tried one more little hotel. They had one room. After talking awhile we said we had better take it.

She called a taxi, whose driver seemed to understand where he was to take us. But he went across the drawbridge into Willemsted, a completely different part of the island than we had seen before when we were there.

It was very dark now, and he was driving through alleys and ominous-looking places, telling us that he was *"taking a shortcut."* I suddenly wondered, *"a shortcut to where?"* It wasn't like a taxi we were used to at home.

Suddenly we entered a well-lighted street with small business buildings on each side. He stopped suddenly, and we stepped onto the sidewalk as he set our baggage down on the sidewalk. Quinton paid him, and away he went.

We entered the small hotel to approach the desk. The woman clerk could not speak English; so she called her husband. Quinton told him we had no evening meal.

He took us into the next room, which looked like an ordinary country dining room. The man handed us a menu which we, of course, could not read.

I asked, *"Do you have some kind of cooked cereal or porridge?"*
"Yes," he said.
I don't know exactly what it was, but it was well cooked. I was confident we would sleep well on it.
"Now," he explained, *"here is your room."*
I turned around. Right there was a door. There was one step up into the room.
"Here is the toilet," he said. So we stepped down into the dining room again, walked several steps and stepped up one step into the small restroom. To say the least, everything was handy!

Now, while this was going on, a number of burly-looking men in work clothes were coming in saying something to the manager, then going upstairs to bedrooms above us.

Our bedroom consisted of two narrow cots, one at one wall, and the other at another wall. Near Quinton's cot was a small, round lavatory about the size of a cantaloupe.

We prayed, said goodnight, and crawled onto our cots.

After a few quiet moments, I said, *"No one in this world knows where we are tonight! Anyone could cut out this screen beside me and step inside. We could be mugged, robbed and never be heard from again."* I could hear every footstep on the public sidewalk going just outside our room. I felt we were in circumstances we were not supposed to be in. So I thought.

After a pause, Quinton replied, *"God knows where we are."* We both fell asleep even though it was hot.

In all of our travels, I was seldom afraid. I had a very good traveling companion, and we were on mission trips because of our love for God.

The next morning we flew on to the island of Bonaire where many of the staff was waving as we descended from the plane. They greeted us as old friends. Of course, they were used to listening to Quinton's messages by radio every Sunday.

Each morning, Quinton had a special time of devotions with the whole staff. It was a very spiritual uplift to all. How precious those people were to us.

Some of these people we renewed acquaintances with, three different times in Europe.

* * * * *

It was always so good to be at home again on Swanson Drive in South Bend. By this time, our children were married and living in various places – Charlene in South Bend, Quinton, Jr. near Philadelphia, Pennsylvania, Sharon in Indianapolis, and Cynthia in Laguna Beach, California.

We kept in touch mostly by telephone. For many years, we vacationed for two weeks in the fall in Arizona, then drove to Cynthia's home in California. We traveled to Philadelphia and Indianapolis, too. The children came home regularly, but with more grandchildren the visits became farther apart.

Now the great grandchildren were arriving, which made it more difficult to get together often.   But our telephone bills were large! We would not have had it otherwise. Everyone was busy with ministries, occupations and families. We loved to hear their voices and exchange experiences and questions. Giving our love and learning many happenings from the families gives us thankful hearts for answered prayers. God is so good!

We kept taking invitations for family camps in the summertime, revival meetings in the fall and winter months with conventions in between. Quinton laughed and said, *"I used to have calls for 'Youth for Christ' meetings. Now they call me for Senior Citizens meetings."* However, he kept very busy.

* * * * *

We went to Pennsylvania for a family camp, which was a very interesting ten days.

The one thing I remember now that perhaps I shall never forget is an experience of a small woman that made quite an impression on the community.

The first day at the first meal, I was asked by one of the cooks if I had yet been introduced to the woman who removed a mountain.

"No," I told her. *"I had not heard about that."* She assured me that I would without a doubt. Throughout the camp, not a word did I hear about her.

The last Sunday evening when the service was over, the benediction said, I turned to go out of the tabernacle. The car was nearby, and I started for the car. I had said my good-byes to our new and many friends at supper so that we could leave immediately following the meeting.

As I neared the car, a voice called my name. I turned around. There came hurrying toward me a small woman.

"Oh, Mrs. Everest," she called, *"I did want to talk to you during the camp meeting, but I wasn't able to be here all the time. Do you have time now that I can tell you how God wonderfully answered prayer for me?"*

I told her I just wanted to be near the car so my husband wouldn't have to go hunting for me.

"Well, this is an experience I wanted to tell you about. For as you repeat it to others, they also may tell it."

"The mountain behind my home was becoming quite a severe trial to me. I cried to the Lord about it many times. I don't know what I expected Him to do, but I didn't know who else to turn to with such a great impossible problem."

"Then one day it hit me. I mean the verse of scripture from Matthew 17:20. 'If ye have faith as a grain of mustard seed, ye shall say unto this mountain, it shall remove and nothing shall be impossible unto you.' "

" 'Oh, God,' I cried, 'remove this mountain! Give me faith, more faith to believe you can do it!' "

"So I reminded the Lord again and again of the mountain and my small faith."

"I have not told you why that mountain behind my house was such a sore trial to me."

"You see on the top of that mountain was a street with houses on both sides. And when Friday and

Saturday nights came, there was much drinking and loud noises. It lasted long past midnight. I could hardly bear the noise and the kind of music that was going on, besides losing my much-needed sleep."

"Finally, I asked the Lord if I could help Him remove my trial."

"Then the answer came. Yes, God needs people to work with Him to accomplish things."

"So day after day and some evenings, I made my way to the top of the mountain, rapping on the doors, passing out tracts and talking with the people"

"Gradually they became interested in the Gospel."

"Family after family was won to the Lord Jesus Christ."

"Now the nights are more quiet, children and parents are in Sunday School and church on Sundays. The result was that souls were saved and happy. The people became my dear friends. That awful mountain was removed."

I thanked her for relating this marvelous story to me and assured her I would tell others so that they might be encouraged.

* * * * *

The day we arrived home from a tour, I received a call telling me my Aunt Lynn was very sick in Memorial Hospital in South Bend. She was my father's only sister and was then my only living aunt on either side of my family.

Knowing there were no relatives other than me in South Bend, I ceased my work and drove to the hospital immediately.

As I entered the room, she was calling for Ruth, her daughter, who lived some distance away. The lady sitting in a chair on the other side of the room said to me, *"Oh, I'm so glad you are here."* She has been calling for her daughter all day.

It was now early afternoon.

I hurriedly went to her bed, not inquiring of the nurses what her sickness was. I leaned down close to her face and said, *"Aunt Lynn, this is Mae. I just got home today and heard you were here."*

She became calm and quiet immediately.

I said, *"I love you. I would have been here sooner. I'm going to pray for you."*

I did, at once, that His love would be with her now – and I didn't finish the first sentence until her spirit left her body. I felt it. I opened my eyes. She was gone. It was a beautiful experience for me!

Chapter Nineteen

An Invitation to European Christian Broadcaster's Convention at Monte Carlo.

We received an invitation from Trans World Radio to be guests at the European Christian Broadcaster's Convention at Monte Carlo.

We flew to Chicago, then to Montreal, Canada. We started from there at 8:00 p.m. for a night flight to Nice, France. We each had less than a half-hour of sleep. At least we arrived safely. For some time we waited for someone to meet us. Finally David Carlson made himself known to us. He is a very friendly, gracious man. He and Quinton searched for our baggage, but they were finally told it had not arrived from Chicago. Making arrangements for the baggage to be brought to us, we hurried along the Riviera to Monte Carlo where the office and radio station of the European Trans World Radio are located. Mr. Carlson first took us to our hotel, Alexandria.

We had fifteen minutes to freshen up, then be taken immediately to the mayor's reception, which was to be held in his exotic gardens. He had plants and trees from many countries of the world.

We had no clothes to change into and found no soap in the hotel's bathroom. The nearest thing to soap was Quinton's shaving cream. I tried it but could hardly wash it off my face. We combed and looked the best we could. Poor Quinton had a sick headache.

But we did enjoy the fact of being there among so many of Europe's fine Christian people.

Then back to the hotel. Our hotel had black iron elevators. The convention did not convene until the next day.

* * * * *

The government of Prince Rainer allowed Trans World Radio to use their underground government rooms for the radio convention. They were on the fourth floor down, underground.

As Quinton and I pressed the button, the door opened, and we stepped inside. We continued to talk as a man and his wife on the elevator started smiling at us.

"*Are you Quinton J. Everest?*" he asked.

"*Yes,*" said Quinton.

"*I knew you right away by your voice. We hear 'Your Worship Hour' broadcast every week. We are from Edinburg.*"

That was only the beginning of meeting many friends from many countries.

Each day the sessions were filled with speakers from Germany, Italy, France, Czechoslovakia, Poland, Finland, Russia, Turkey, Armenia, Greece, Romania, Spain, Holland and England and more. Some of these burdened, godly men were forced to live out of their home countries while broadcasting from a free nation over the Trans World Broadcasting

An invitation ...

The Hitler Building, where our broadcasts aired for many years.

station.

Trans World Radio towers were built up in the French mountains above Monte Carlo by Hitler for the broadcasting of communism to the whole world. When Hitler was defeated and this building was put up for sale, Dr. Paul Freed heard about it.

He cried to the Lord to make that station become a Christian station to spread the Gospel of the Lord Jesus Christ. But he had no money for the down payment. The son and new bride of a Mr. Haanes, a Norwegian ship builder, were in Monte Carlo on their honeymoon. They overheard Paul Freed confiding this possibility of buying the Hitler building to someone. They rushed to a telephone, called his father, telling him excitedly about the matter.

Mr. Haanes sent $80,000 immediately to his son to give to Paul Freed for the first payment.

How quickly the Lord sometimes works.

Now what the Devil was going to use for evil is instead blessing the great territory of Europe with the Gospel.

Dr. Freed got in touch with Quinton. He wanted to send out "Your Worship Hour" program over this station.

As the doors opened, Quinton was obedient, not knowing how the expense could be handled. But realizing there would be millions more hearing what they had never heard before – the plan of salvation through Christ – he accepted the challenge.

This European convention was for the purpose of hearing the reports and letters from all the countries.

This was a great encouragement. Tears flowed easily and, oh, the love that bonded us. Several times we were taken up to the Hitler building and through the offices of the high building in Monte Carlo.

One day something went wrong with an elevator. We were standing on the sidewalk when I suddenly heard Paul Freed's father, Ralph, who was now eighty years old, say he needed to be up there in his office. He couldn't wait until it was fixed.

I said, "*Oh, Quinton, he shouldn't climb all those stairs.*"

He turned toward us and said simply, "*I must do my work.*" He climbed the eight flights.

* * * * *

Between sessions, one day, David Carlson

took Quinton and me back along the French Riviera to where the Flagship of the U.S. Sixth Fleet was in port. We had a tour of all but the restricted section. We met the admiral. Trans World employees held Sunday School classes for the officers' families. They had a good relationship with the crew. We were asked if we would like to set up an organization for the benefit of the Navy men when they were there. A building would be provided for this to have services, games, food and a homey place for especially the new sailors. Be a "Mom" and "Pop" to them. It was intriguing but impossible.

* * * * *

During the first sessions, there was much whispering in the audience, and as I looked around, the wives of the broadcasters had their heads lain on their husbands' shoulders and their husbands were interpreting what each speaker was saying. That was helpful for them but disturbing for the rest of us.

The next day, that changed. Evidently the government provided equipment that we each could put on our ears and receive translated messages immediately, each in their own language.

Our two meals a day that were provided for us were delicious. Much of the fruit and vegetables were raised in Israel.

Someone announced the next morning that we were going to the mountains that noon for a catered lunch. We were included. We were delighted.

As we left the city of Monte Carlo by bus on this beautiful August day, we watched our bus driver fighting congested traffic more and more the farther we went. Once outside the city proper, the roads got more narrow and cars almost bumper to bumper.

The Riviera is a popular place for tourists at that time of the year. The drivers stick their heads out of their window as they pass, yelling in French, cursing the other cars and our bus that came too close to them.

I don't remember how far the place of our picnic was from Monte Carlo, but by and by the traffic lessened, when suddenly the bus driver stopped abruptly. The reason – the person who was to direct was missing. He had not been on the bus at all.

Some of the people were very weary. But some were enjoying the scenery. Those sitting across from them could only see on their side the mountain wall that was so high, just outside their window, that their time was taken up by concern that the cars would not push us into it.

The driver stood up and asked, *"Does anyone know where we are going?"*

The driver and many others had gotten off the bus, strolled a bit, not far. It was very noisy. Everyone was buzzing in his own language.

All at once Mr. Bob Stokes raised his arms and loudly cried, *"Yes, I know where we are going!"*

When we arrived, there were many others who had arrived before us. I had the feeling our busman was supposed to follow others and got separated in the wild traffic.

An invitation ...

It was a wonderful day. Many leaders and their spouses were there from many countries. One young couple with three children sang for us. They had been Youth For Christ leaders in Elkhart, Indiana, my husband's hometown. They since were doing evangelistic work among the gypsies in northern Germany. Many hundreds were accepting the Gospel. They even changed the names of their streets to Glory Street, Hallelujah Street, etc. Mrs. Paul Freed sang "The Old Rugged Cross," and some gave thrilling testimonies of what God had done.

We saw Princess Grace one day as we approached the palace. Her chauffeur was taking her out to their yacht. We walked on the street nearby and visited the Cathedral where the Prince and Princess worshiped. The organist was playing as we sauntered down the middle aisle. She stopped playing and greeted us by saying, *"You just missed the Prince. He comes in every morning at nine o'clock for his devotions."*

Chapter Twenty

Our second trip to the European
Broadcaster's Convention.

In six years we were again invited by Trans World Radio and Dr. Paul Freed to attend the European Christian Broadcaster's Convention.

We accepted because we were eager to learn of the importance and far-reaching of our own "Your Worship Hour" broadcast. Not only of ours but also of the many others in communist countries.

We expected, too, that the tremendous fellowship we experienced in the former convention would be very profitable to us again.

Quinton arranged his schedule making many tapes of broadcasts for the time we were to be gone. These included not only the Sunday ones but the daily 6:15 a.m. "Prescription for Today" broadcasts.

We informed our children and grandchildren. We had our shots and bought our tickets. It was less expensive to visit other countries also in Europe; so together with our travel agent, we decided on Holland, Switzerland, Rome, then to the convention, which was to be held in Monte Carlo. After that we were to minister in Yugoslavia with Dr. Joseph Horak, who was the president of Baptist churches in that country.

When we left there, we would fly to London and rest over Sunday before going home.

* * * * *

Now after saying goodbye to our family and the office girls, we made our way to the airport.

We had another night flight, quiet and restful, but we didn't sleep much. In those years we had never been introduced to sleeping pills. I'm sure if I would travel again, I would know how to get a good night's sleep on the plane.

On Monday morning in Amsterdam, we took a bus tour of the city. The population was thirteen million with 700,000 bicycles in the city.

Our guide said, *"You Americans had mental pictures of a Hollander with a tulip in one hand, a herring in the other, and wearing wooden shoes."*

As he was talking, we saw little huts on the airport land. They were "bird scarers." When flocks of birds became an annoyance, a very loud noise came from the hut and scared them away.

Their main crops are flowers, sugar beets and wheat.

When the Hollanders want to *"look after the sun,"* he said they go to Spain or France.

He spoke of how they balance their finance, which was a very interesting method.

One pound of Dutch green beans costs two gilders, which is too much for the Dutch to pay so they sell them to other countries. Butter is five gilders per pound, again too high for the Dutch to eat so they export it for three and a half gilders, all this so they can buy bananas, which they can't raise but like so much.

Water is almost always higher than the land, but the dykes deep it from flooding. Dykes are running through the country everywhere.

We visited the famous Delft dish factory. The room where many kinds of dishes were displayed were only visible through bars.

Houses there are smaller than ours. Flowers were abundant in most windows, the largest African violets, tubular begonias, and the best looking small begonias I have ever seen.

The wealthy have very large homes. The parents used to live on the first floor, children on the second floor and their servants on the third.

The children are broadfaced and pretty.

* * * * *

It takes a few hours to get a homey feeling in a new city, Geneva, Switzerland, new hotel room and different money.

Our room was on the seventh floor, but the elevator went just to the sixth. So we had to climb steps to the next floor, then walk a long way to the back of the building.

But I wasn't alone. I had a good bodyguard. At least my husband was much larger than 99% of the other men. I never went out alone. We walked a lot for everything we wanted. Our hotel was built along the Rhone River, a fast-flowing, beautiful river. We sat on the steps awhile that extended the length of the hotel.

It was very funny to turn on the television set and watch the news trying to make out what was being reported. One station was all French, one was all German, and one Italian. We watched the pictures and learned about a few things that were going on.

We had wonderful tours of Geneva. Our guide spoke three or four languages. One day she had to speak three.

The Japanese men were on board but could not understand anything. They sat at our table when we stopped for tea and cake. We tried to help them, but we all just laughed. It was surprising how we could make out by signs.

Our food there was good but very expensive.

One morning we had hot drinks, hard rolls and porridge. They didn't seem to know it was oatmeal, but it was.

There were so many white-coated waiters buzzing around, they got in each other's way. I hadn't yet seen girl waitresses in Europe.

We had feather covers on our bed. They were almost like a large feather pillow, wide as a blanket and not quite as long. We each had two pillows. One was very large and one square pillow lay on top.

It was chilly in the room; so between tours we got into our beds and pulled the largest pillow over us. We enjoyed that. I read part of the time. The person at the office told us they never turned on the heat until November. That was September.

We were getting our exercise because we walked eleven blocks to the bus station.

In a Park of Living Waters they have Redwood trees brought there from California. There were three hundred different kinds of roses in this park and very large beds of different flowers.

We also stopped to see the statues of the men of the Reformation.

We saw original masterpieces of Picasso in an art museum, Russian church built in 1815 with gold-leaf covering five towers; Cathedral of St. Peter; great Music Center; League of Nations; World Headquarters Health Organization; European Broadcasting Organization; the original Red Cross World Headquarters building; and many other things.

Most interesting to me was the tour into the mountains and many villages. We started early in the morning when the bedroom windows were open, and in almost every window there was a pillow hanging over the windowsill to air. Just below the sills were wooden window boxes filled with red geraniums and other flowers.

It was thrilling to see how the people lived because my ancestors were from Switzerland. I so much wished I could see their farm before coming home, but I forgot to read our family history book until I came home. We were within a few miles of the place.

* * * * *

The next day we flew to Rome. We had four tours in Rome. There was much to see. We heard someone in our hotel (Bernini-Bristol) say, *"My feet don't feel like my own."* This is a very noisy and busy city. You take your life in your hands to walk across the street.

When we came back from one bus trip in the

afternoon, the guide called to some of the passengers getting off at a certain hotel, *"When you cross the street, turn your head the other way, and if they run you over, you say, 'I'll not speak to you again!'"*

This city has many Basilicas and ruins and famous historical places. A teacher recently asked me to speak to her class when they studied a certain country that I've been in.

Of course we were at the Vatican, saw its library museum, Sistine Chapel and many buildings.

Sunday morning we had expected to go on the group tour to St. Peter's but overslept; so we read a section of Psalms 119, had prayer, then left the hotel and stood on the corner to watch for a city bus.

A young couple (who later told us they were on their honeymoon) suddenly stood beside us. Hearing us talking in English, they chimed in and said they were going to St. Peter's, too, on the city bus No. 62. They asked us to follow them. They were glad to help us.

So we went to church across the city with the "faithful."

We stood all the way. Every stop they made the conductor hollered at us to "move back" on the bus. People pushed and shoved and pushed some more. I never was so near strangers, nor smelled so many people's breath at once. I thought once that no one could push me one inch farther, when suddenly a short, fat man who wanted to get off and had to pass us solved his difficulty by pressing hard against my upper back with his hand. Then quickly he pressed against my buttocks so that momentarily I knew what a sardine feels like. And then he was gone!

Can you imagine that we came back to the hotel the same way? We could have returned by taxi, but we didn't. We saved a little (no, I mean a lot) of money and saw how some people go to church every Sunday.

When we arrived at St. Peter's, we were "on our own." Quinton had been there before. I told him I really lived that day in Romans 8:28 because the group we were supposed to be with got caught in the packed crowd (over 30,000, perhaps) in the sun.

We visited the church, watched the people kiss the toe of St. Peter's statue as they entered, saw the mass, and after the processional, edged our way out of the building, way out to the edge of the steps where Quinton wanted to wait until the Pope appeared so he could take more movies.

I took courage to break away and went to a wall in the shade far from where he was. But I stayed exactly in the place I told him I would be so that he could find me afterward. I could see all he could!

After the Pope came out on a balcony, he spoke and blessed the people. Then he prayed, and as he did, some people dropped to their knees.

Dad's estimate of the actual attendance at mass was 1500. I was amazed that the place was not full of benches.

After all I had heard, seen and read these few

days in Rome, I'm thankful I studied theology and Christian doctrine in Ft. Wayne Indiana Bible Institute while I was very young. Many truths came to my remembrance that day. Not so much is made of our Lord Jesus Christ, but much is made of the Pope. However, they admit having had some scoundrels among them. And they can laugh about it – I mean the guides. My eternal hope and trust is in Christ, and I am happy.

* * * * *

Toward noon the next day, we took our baggage downstairs, paid our hotel bill and changed our money back to American. However, Quinton first asked the clerk how much money he should keep for the taxi. So when we arrived at the airport, he paid the cab driver and turned to take out our baggage. Already a uniformed man had grabbed it and was hurrying into the airport. Quinton wished to care for it himself. The distance to the information desk was only about fifteen feet from the door. There was quite a long line of people; so we got in line, but the man hurried toward us and reached out his hand for his pay.

Quinton informed him that he had not asked for his help and that he preferred to do it himself. This angered the man; so Quinton gave him all he had left of his country's money.

"Oh, but that isn't enough," he kept saying. He argued and got closer to Quinton. The man reached into his pocket, drew out a card showing he was licensed. That did not impress

313

Quinton.

"Do you see that policeman standing over there," he asked?

"Sure," Quinton said.

"Well, you could go to jail for this." And away he went for the policeman who was not far away.

We were in a hurry and kept moving with the line of people.

I hunched Quinton and asked him to settle with him. What would I do if he went to jail? But Quinton said they couldn't do that. Anyway, it made me nervous. However, I remembered that he had traveled in foreign countries before with Rev. Dick Reilly, who was General Secretary of our Foreign Missions, and they had some unique stories to tell. Well, here came the policeman with the little angry man.

The policeman told Quinton he'd better do what he wanted; then he walked away.

Quinton finally had a fresh idea.

"You give me back the money I gave you, and I'll give you an American dollar."

He did, and the man was very happy and skipped away. That was less money than he gave him in the first place.

When we got to the end of the line and asked what our gate number was to go to Monaco, they replied, and we hurried to that gate. When we were near the door of the plane, I felt uneasy and asked the woman in front of me where she was going.

"To Amsterdam," she said.

"Oh, Quinton, this is the wrong plane!"

Our second trip ...

A stewardess quickly informed us which way to go. She said that plane is ready to take off. We ran, and she was right. We left immediately.

As we were rushing through the airport, we wondered why everyone was eating hot dogs.

Now, on the plane we were informed by the steward that the stewardesses were on strike. There would be no lunches served, nor drinks, nor water. This frightened many people. One man begged immediately for water so his wife could have her medicine. I don't recall if she got it. Of course, we all suddenly felt very hungry and thought it was a cruel thing to take their gripes out on the people.

We arrived at the Hawthorne Hotel in Monte Carlo mid-afternoon. The dining room was closed. We even went to the kitchen. There was no one to help us. But we saw a man and told him our trouble.

"Do you see the tennis court over there? There is a concession stand there. Maybe you could get a little snack or something to drink."

We thanked him and hurried over there. I don't remember what little snack we had, but unbeknown to us, a fellow went over to the hotel and got us two tea bags. I don't drink tea, but how could I turn down such graciousness.

We found our room and had a long rest. When we came down for dinner, there was no one in the dining room. We looked farther and saw an open, outdoor restaurant close to the water's edge, which was the Mediterranean Sea. The lights were on, a canopy overhead and people crowding the place.

315

We seemed to be latecomers. Surely in this large setting we had some friends, but we couldn't immediately see anyone we knew.

A white-dressed waiter seated us with a good view and handed us a menu. So many words, so many phrases we didn't understand.

When the waiter came back to take our order, it was quite simple. At least it would be nourishing.

We waited and finally were served.

"But this is someone else's order." We assured him there was a mistake.

"No," he kept trying to convince us to eat and enjoy.

But he brought three or four courses. The first was a large fish, head and all, for each of us. Delicious! There was so much we could not eat it all. But as we enjoyed the beautiful scenery, the fresh air and night sky, we were refreshed and thankful that the Lord supplied our needs.

At one point during the meal our eyes met with the smiling eyes of Mr. Haanes, the Norwegian shipbuilder. At once we knew who had ordered our delicious meal. The waiter never brought us our bill. Mr. Haanes was thanked heartily and didn't deny that he ordered and paid for it.

The next morning the convention of European Christian broadcasters began. How thrilling!

How anxious we were to assemble with the several hundred broadcasters and their board members from all countries of Europe. Again Prince Rainier graciously loaned us the fourth floor, underground, of their government headquarters.

Dr. Paul Freed opened the first meeting with much thankfulness to God for His faithfulness in bringing us safely together. Also for the millions of people in many nations who have heard of Jesus our Saviour for the first time.

After prayer, many speakers gave accounts of their broadcasting.

One speaker from Romania, who must live in Paris, to make possible messages of the Gospel to be sent over Trans World Monte Carlo station tearfully said, *"As I stand before you, I cannot hide the emotions of my heart for twenty million people of Romania. I believe and therefore I speak. I give you facts. We have received 5,000 letters in a short time."*

One letter, quoted he, *"I kissed my radio on all four sides and put it to my bosom."*

"One man had a transmitter and thirty people around him. After the message, they knelt right on the street and prayed for the people who sent such good words."

His wife was in Romania at the time of the convention and wrote, *"Do not cut the people of Romania short by giving them only a half hour per week. Can't you do a little more?"*

"The people of our church in Romania are giving thirty per cent of their income that they might have these broadcasts."

Many people write from these countries that they had never seen a preacher, a Bible or heard a sermon before they heard the broadcasts about God and Jesus Christ over Trans World Radio.

Radio goes into many parts of the world where people have no television.

Mr. and Mrs. Semenchuks sang a duet in Russian, "His Name Is Wonderful."

The Russian speakers told us the people in Russia are restless under communism. Many in Siberia are being saved by their radios.

Youth are unafraid to trust Christ.

When some came out of Russia by train, there were three hundred there to say goodbye. They kissed, hugged and then burst out in singing hymns in front of guards.

On a dining car when the young people were served, they stood and blessed God for their food.

A small group of Russian Christian young people showed up at the convention one day. They had permission to go to Germany for a sports affair, but they heard about the convention at Monte Carlo and determined to be in a Christian place. Ralph and Paul Freed helped them with food and bedding. They slept nights on the floor at the office building. They were so joyful. They stood at their seats and sang a hymn for us in Russian. It touched our hearts.

A broadcaster from another country said, "*Of all the centuries put together – this is a brand new day. My life is like types in the scripture, 'darkness upon the face of the deep.' That was my life. 'Let there be light.' That happened to me. The 'call of Abraham out from his country and kindred.' Yes, Lord, I know what that is all about, too. And like John the Baptist said, 'I am a voice.' "*

"Who I am is not important. It is my message. I find myself throwing my hands around, and no one is there when I'm in front of the microphone. I can sit

on my hands. It doesn't make any difference, because
I am just a voice."

One speaker when he first heard the Gospel
on radio cried, "Eureka, I've found it! I've found it!
Jesus! Jesus!" The cry of discovery.

"When Jesus Christ has captured our hearts, we
will go out and proclaim and share the most important person in our lives. That is our message. He
said, 'A house on fire,' and I'd say, 'Oh, if I just had
my camera, I'd sit out on the curb and watch the people through the window around the supper table
while they die?' " No!

We were not far into the convention when at
one point Paul Freed, President of Trans World
Radio, stood to entreat us about awareness of
Christ having the preeminence and glory in all
things; Colossians 3.

"We stand at the crossroads. It's the masses out
there that are waiting to hear the Gospel. I just came
from Spain where we saw people saved. Time is running out. I beg you all to search your hearts. We
must be sold out to God at the beginning of this convention. Don't wait until the last night to become
stirred!"

"What kind of people are we? We are here one in
Christ. The masses out there would welcome you
here. What we hear in this convention is a sign of the
last days."

"Go ahead. Prepare for the conflict, but the
Victory is of God!"

Four hundred thousand letters from one
country. Others gave a great plea for more airtime. It was impressive and very sad.

Another broadcaster, Rev. Thomas Cosmotis,

said he is Greek, born in Turkey. Turks want
European things but no Christianity. Giving the
Gospel to the Muslims is like trying to give a gift
that is most hated by them.

But during these days, God is doing something marvelous through Trans World Radio.

Turks always lived in their own land even if
they were starving. Now they are leaving
because of desperate times. Five million Turks
are in Germany.

We are trying to gather them together for services. Their minds are full of darkness. They are
so sure in what they think. They do not welcome you, but we give them the Light anyway.
They do write letters and ask questions. One
wrote that *"for many nights – six weeks – someone
appears to me and preaches to me. I need much theological knowledge because I have many sins."* This is
typical of the conviction of sins.

A Bulgarian letter from a Turk says, *"You are
our friends who make broadcast. You say Jesus
Christ. Is it only Jesus? We believe in Allah. Don't
leave me down."* (There are twenty Biblical sites
in Turkey.)

We cannot mail answers to Bulgaria, but by
tourists we send them spiritual help. Turks
never had an organized church.

This speaker's wife went to Taylor University
with Jean and Don Granitz.

*"I live with the Turks; I walk with them, but my
wife and I often say there are no real believers among
them. But we believe in these last days God wants to
pour out His Spirit upon these early Bible lands
again. Thank God for Trans World Radio broadcast-*

320

ers *who send them God's truth. They need it even though they don't know they do."*

Day after day and night after night we heard the messages of hope for people who have no other way to be informed of the Truth of the living Savior but by radio.

Some told of copying a page of scripture or of having one Bible in one village or community to learn how to live the Christian life.

Burial services are used as evangelistic services. One man said when his father died there were 3,000 people in attendance. Night after night a man preached from 6:00 to 11:00 o'clock.

Persecution and kidnapping puts much fear in most people, but many Christians are not afraid to die because of their hope of Heaven.

In many countries it is not possible to have open Bible schools or seminaries, but they do train strong Christian young men who in turn train others. Thus new pastors start new house churches, sometimes in basements or even the forest.

These conventions we attended were years ago, and at this time, there is much more freedom. Yet reports say there are more martyrs now than there ever have been before.

* * * * *

Between sessions we had unique things happening.

When we returned from sessions to the Hawthorne Hotel, the lobby was full. People seemed to all be in conversation with new and old friends.

Quinton and I started chatting with another couple. Then I noticed a woman across the room eyeing us rather strangely but suddenly broke into a smile and started toward us. I nudged Quinton, but he paid little attention to it. The woman came to us hurriedly and said loudly, *"You are Quinton J. Everest of South Bend, Indiana!"*

"Yes," Quinton said.

"Lucia Gilbert is my name, and I would know your voice anywhere in this world. You see, I'm a monitor for Trans World Radio from the island of Wight off the southern coast of England."

We were very pleased to meet her.

That noon in the lobby, she told us she worked for T.W.R. and at a certain hour at night after monitoring for a number of hours, Quinton's booming voice comes in loud and clear. Then she told how she appreciated following his sermons and how she had been helped by them.

That evening she was asked to speak before the main speaker gave his message. It was to be her testimony.

As Lucia stood at the podium that evening, she looked so small and unimportant. Then this seventy-year-old servant of the Lord stood straight and declared, *"I've been asked to give my testimony."* She told of her early conversion, of her love for Christ and of a deep longing to spend her life in a special ministry for Him. She wanted nothing but the best for Him, she was so happy.

Years went by. This Scottish girl and her parents lived in England. When she was eighteen years old, she wanted to go to a Bible School to prepare for missionary work. But her father took sick and became a helpless invalid. Her mother needed her. She took care of her father until he died many years later. Then she thought, now Jesus will let me do something for Him.

But her mother took sick, was paralyzed, and she spent many more years caring for her until she died.

She often wondered why she could not serve God as she so much wished, but she was faithful in carrying her cross.

After her mother's death eighteen years ago, Lucia's doctor told her she needed a long rest. He pleaded with her to go south farther for sunshine and sea air, not to work, but to have a long rest. She moved then at fifty-eight years of age to the island of Wight.

During this time, she listened to Trans World Radio many hours each day and sometimes late at night. Many times she prayed that God would heal her that she might serve Him in a special way. Oh, how she loved Him! She didn't have much money, which caused her to move sixteen times in nineteen years. At the time of her speaking, she was living in rented rooms on the fourth floor.

"I felt I was living in Heaven. Languages I did not know," but she said, *"I have strong senses. I wrote to Trans World Radio at Monte Carlo from where these wonderful programs originated. Don't just tell me to pray. I do that day and night."*

They wrote to her concerning her eagerness to be a servant. They told her of the need for a monitor but that it would be night work.

She had no idea what a radio monitor would have to do. So she asked the Post Office what it meant. " *They said 'propagation,' but I didn't know what that meant either,"* she said.

In turn she kept encouraging the broadcasters by letters. She knew hundreds of soldier boys who were allies in many lands, listeners of TWR.

No wonder that she moved once into a cheaper flat so that she could have more money for stamps. She refused payment for her work because of her love for Jesus and to make up for all the years that she had nothing to do for Him.

The work became more complicated through the years. She had most of the daytime to herself so she could do her cooking and washing.

In the course of time, she reported programs for TWR in Bonaire also. *"I live alone with no one to say good-night, but a lovely voice says 'good morning' from the wonderful flamingo island of Bonaire off the coast of Venezuela."* Many are the good evangelists, teachers and music she heard and praised God for them.

Our broadcast "Your Worship Hour" of which Quinton had been director and speaker for over fifty years, was one of them. It aired from both Monte Carlo and Bonaire, Cypress, Swaziland, HCJB, and we received letters from eighty countries.

Paul Freed, president of TWR, was delighted to give her the monitoring. Right in her own home she could listen and fill out the questions each night on the reception of the English programs over the Monte Carlo station.

Every night – actually morning at 1:00 a.m. – she turned on her light and started listening to the programs one after another until daylight.

Lucia walked with us from the hotel to the conference sessions in the government building. So we have had her as a special friend for many years.

Our broadcast was clearly heard on Sunday mornings for many years and in other European countries, too.

Lucia said one of her ears listened for technical things; the other ear for the messages. The music she loved was the Romanian, American, Arabic and Polish.

Like Lucia, there were many, many more dedicated people behind the scenes.

Well, Lucia gave a wonderful, soul-stirring account of her love and work for Christ. But suddenly, Bill Mial, who had charge of the evening session, walked up to her and touching her on the arm said, *"Lucia, I'm sorry, but you must stop now. We have the main speaker yet this evening."*

Oh, how embarrassed she was and apologized greatly. With that, she left the platform!

But the crowd was not finished with her. The people all stood to their feet immediately and clapped heartily.

* * * * *

The next day at noon in the hotel lobby, a young woman stopped me to say she was from

Chicago and wished we could go to a quiet place to talk. We did not have time to go up to our room before dinner would be served. We looked around and saw three steps up to another room. The doorway was wide, and we saw a davenport but could not see the rest of the room. She said, *"Oh, that's the bar. Let's look inside to see if it is empty now."*

It was a large room. We didn't see anyone close; so we stepped inside and sat down.

I fail to remember the girl's name, but she certainly was committed to the work of child evangelism. I felt a Christian love for her immediately.

She told me of the encouragement and challenge to form Child Evangelism classes. She also holds children's evangelistic meetings and has seen many children saved.

But the most striking part of her accomplishments was the method she used to train the many women who came across the lines from communist countries into Austria, the country in which she worked.

These women had permission to sometimes cross the line of countries to shop. Then they would contact her and proceed to go into intense training. Her method was to not only have them memorize the scripture verses for the course but to memorize the class material word for word from the class books. This was so thrilling for her to have this opportunity of teaching and drilling these women that it brought tears to our eyes. We praised God together!

Then they would do their shopping and go back to their homes across the line. Think of all the spiritual food they took back to the children that they secretly gathered together and taught.

They had no Bibles, nor did the children. The next time they came back for more training, they would have many happenings to tell her. Some were of children being saved, and some stories were sad.

Twice during our talk in the hotel bar waiters approached us and asked what we would like to drink. We thanked them but said we just wanted a quiet place to talk. Lunch was now ready.

* * * * *

One lovely afternoon Paul Freed and Betty, his wife, asked Quinton and me to go with a few other couples on a boat ride. We became such good friends. The trip was so refreshing and beautiful. The Riviera from Monte Carlo to Nice, France and back again had many unique and famous places that he pointed out. But the wonderful visit we had was memorable.

Back to the convention for the last session.

We learned that 435 miles northeast of China the radio reception was good. Those people wrote and asked, *"How do you pray? Where do you pray? Where is God?"* It was all so new to them.

Others wrote after listening for some time. *"Oh, you heralds of God! Don't be silent. After you are through, we fall on our knees and pray for you."*

Another said their whole family was enlightened and were saved because of the radio messages.

"I try to obtain a Bible, but I cannot."

A broadcaster said, *"I prayed for twenty-five years to carry the Gospel to the Arabs. In 1960 I was called to Beirut, Lebanon. I met Dr. Paul Freed there after a few days, who asked me if I would preach on radio to many countries. We have received letters from all fifteen nations of Arab people. Many Arabs live in France. Letters from Iraq are asking for tracts and New Testaments. But many cannot read; so they listen every night. Many are like nomads and travel around. But in almost every shack and tent – and I can say on almost every camel back – there is a radio."* These must be the last days when the Gospel is reaching so far into the unknown areas with the Gospel of good news.

Many all throughout Europe found the good music and messages from the Holy Word by just dialing around. It first was very strange to them to hear such words, but as they were enlightened, they were anxious to have this eternal life with Christ.

Some said they were going to kill themselves but now have something to live for.

A wife was going to leave her husband but not now.

How we laughed, cried and praised God for what he was doing. Some Christians in America were and are still unaware of the millions of people saved through radio.

On the first day of the convention, Paul Freed spoke on "To Do Thy Will."

"To my knees or to the ends of the world," this he said in his prayer before he spoke his last message.

Dr. Freed: *"I stand here to magnify Christ. Oh, if we could see Him in all His Glory and majesty! May no man be the climax of this conference. Let it be Christ. Let us see Jesus. Let us not be personal."*

"What does Christ say to you? I am not speaking to you. Let Him speak to you. I am speaking to Paul Freed."

"I thank all my staff and all of God's good people, some of the greatest people on earth."

"But I, Paul Freed, want Christ to speak to me and tell me what to do. I beg of you and plead with Paul Freed. What do you ask of me tonight, Lord?"

"Doesn't it thrill you, what God has done, but do you think we have come to the end?"

"Everywhere countries are asking for more time, they want to hear more. No drummed-up emotion. I want the Holy Spirit to speak. You don't dare walk out of those doors without telling God you will do His will."

"Dear fellow worker, when He speaks, you'd better listen!"

"I remember standing in Warsaw, Poland and saw hands reach out to touch me because they are so grateful for the Gospel over their radios, but I said, no, do not thank me, thank God. If you walk out of here with only a human plan without the plus of God's benediction and leading of the Holy Spirit, it will all be in vain."

"He may want you to move committees or boards. What changes does He want you to make? Are we 'proving God,' as Quinton Everest taught us the other evening? Are we satisfied with the crumbs?"

"There is not much time. There is no more time for some people who slipped into eternity today. Thank God for all these brethren that came out of communist

countries to this convention."

Then Mr. Freed honored his mother and father who were missionaries to the Arabs and talked of his mother's daily prayer life. She consistently prayed two to two and a half hours each day. *"Do you wonder why things have happened?"*

The convention was over except for some singing. All sang in their own languages but the same tune. That was thrilling!

The duets and solos during the convention were such a blessing.

One of the songs sung by the whole congregation was "Give the winds a mighty voice." How appropriate.

The leaders of the different foreign broadcasts were very appreciative of "Your Worship Hour" for their own study of the Word and the encouragement they received from them. We were amazed and thanked God.

We had our last meal in Monte Carlo with all those who had not gone home before the convention closed. It was served on a long outside porch restaurant. Not knowing if this would be the last time we would see each other on earth, it was both a happy and sad occasion. As we were finishing our meal, someone started singing. We all chimed in. Then one by one – rather two by two, for most had brought their spouses along – we started leaving, saying goodbye and waving to all.

When Quinton attempted to pay our hotel bill, the clerk said it had already been paid. We could hardly believe it, but he assured us that it was so.

Chapter Twenty-One

Ministering in Yugoslavia.

Before we left home for this European convention, we had received a strong invitation from Dr. Joseph Horak to come to Yugoslavia before returning to the United States. He is President of the Baptist churches of the entire nation.

We took special precautions, prayed about it, then took our shots. Quinton also inquired of Dr. Paul Freed whether he thought it safe to take me into that communist country. He encouraged us to go for the people who had known of Quinton's messages and books and that it would surely be an encouragement to Dr. Horak.

Dr. Horak comes out of Yugoslavia every six months with a briefcase of twenty-six sermons and taped songs to Trans World Radio to be aired back into Yugoslavia. He told us he knows he is *"sitting on a volcano."* However, he is also a lawyer for the government.

Quinton and I met both Mr. and Mrs. Horak the first time we were in Monte Carlo years before.

We flew from Nice, France non-stop to Zagreb. As we got off the plane, we looked at the crowd on the balcony of the airport and saw

Dr. Horak waving to us. We were so happy to see him, for this was a very strange place for us to be.

He took us immediately to an unfinished hotel, signed us in, and then left, assuring us that he and his wife would come at a certain time after supper. There was to be a church service that first night.

He could not drive; so he had no car. There were very few cars on the streets. We either walked or took a tram (streetcar). We would give him the proper coins before we got onto the tram. After that we would scatter and not talk or pay any attention to them.

Dr. Freed had told us that while in Yugoslavia we should do as Rev. Horak told us to do. That way we'd be safe.

The first evening he had rented a room in an old church with dark purple walls and a small balcony.

The congregation was already singing as we came in. Dr. Horak pointed at the front seat. We sat down.

They were singing "What A Friend We Have In Jesus." It was a shock for me to hear them singing so beautifully and lustily, that tears immediately streamed down my face. Then I smiled and started singing in English.

Dr. Horak had prayer in his language, then introduced Quinton, who proceeded with the sermon "The Blessed Hope" – Titus 2:11, 12, 13. It was to be an encouraging message for the Christian.

It was a new experience for me to have everyone looking me over after the service. I doubted if very many had ever seen anyone from the United States. But the Holy Spirit was with us and we felt a Christian oneness as if we'd seen each other somewhere before. After the service, we all shook hands and smiled.

Back to the hotel on the tram. But the Horaks went to their home.

They had two girls living at home, Nella and Yarma. One was in the Zagreb University. In class one time they were having a debate. A student asked why the government did not just rid the country of all Christians. The professor replied, *"Because as long as people die and don't come back, we don't know if there is a God or not."*

I don't remember how old the other girl was, but they were both dating age. However, they could not go walking or shopping alone. Their mother always had to go with them.

Their place of living was on the fourth floor of a large apartment building. That meant climbing eight flights of stairs. Everyone is told where he or she must live.

There were three rooms. In the dining room two cots were placed on two walls for the girls. It was amazing to me to see a grand piano in their home. A few years before we were there when some friends had to flee out of the country, these friends gave the girls the piano in exchange for their mother's silverware.

The next day they took us shopping, and as we walked down the street, we were not to talk to them if we heard footsteps coming toward us or in back of us. Neither should we ever turn around. We went into a little shop, but there was very little in the glass case. The clerk would go into a back room and bring a little article out for us to see and then go back and bring another. We finally settled for a carved shepherd's cup. They also took us up into a high building to look over the city. But the streets were nearly empty, very few cars.

They also showed us their little church that was being prepared in a downtown 13th Century stone building. The front was being remodeled; so he took us around to a back door.

We entered a very tiny room where an old lady was sitting. This was her home. She looked very lonely but was so glad to see Rev. Horak.

Inside was a small room the government had given them in exchange for a new church they had built with money from the United States Baptist Convention when the Horaks had visited the convention in Miami, Florida.

Because they needed more room, they were building a very small balcony that would be just above the heads of the people around the edge of the room. It was one of the saddest things I had seen.

Dr. Horak wanted to rent a car for Quinton to drive us all up to a more beautiful part of the country. But Quinton refused, feeling that he could be in real trouble if something would happen, even a bump.

Dr. Horak had promised the people of a certain village – I think about fifty miles from Zagreb – to bring us there for a service.

Churches were scarce, but a carpenter in the village had built a new building in his back lawn. It looked like a church inside, for it had a platform and a pump organ. The floor was filled with benches without backs.

Now, before we left the hotel that day, after the noon meal, we were to take a taxi to the large train station and meet Dr. Horak, his brother, and a black man from the university.

We ordered a taxi at the hotel desk and then waited and waited. We were to be at the train station at 1:30. We looked out the windows, then tried to talk to the clerks, but we couldn't understand why they did not respond.

Finally, an old, old taxi appeared. We hurried into it. He smiled and drove us to the station. The three men were at the door, all telling us that the train had just gone. How disappointed they looked. But Dr. Horak already had an idea.

We hurried back to the taxi before he could leave and asked him to drive on the road parallel to the train. When we approached the edge of Zagreb, Dr. Horak encouraged him to drive faster.

I wondered what good it would do if we did catch up with it.

After going about ten miles, we did catch up with the train. The taxi man blew his horn and got the attention of the engineer. Then Dr. Horak waved at him to stop. We all got out and the train slowed up but did not really stop. We had gone a little ways ahead of the train before motioning at it; so as we ran through the grassy field toward it, we all thought the engineer would stop for us.

Dr. Horak was in front. He told me to follow him, then Quinton and the other two men.

Just before we reached the berm of the tracks, there was a wire fence to climb before reaching the train. Dr. Horak climbed the fence. I did, too, although I had thought I couldn't. He put one foot on the step of the train, but suddenly the train pulled away from us.

Quinton said, *"Mae, don't climb the fence again. I'll hold up the lowest wire, and you lie on the ground. Crawl under."* I did, but how embarrassing the whole situation was.

So the men wondered what next. Dr. Horak said that he had promised the villagers that we'd be there that night.

Quinton told him to ask the driver if he would take us on to the next stop if he would pay for it. He drove there faster than the train. The taxi man stopped at a small building, which had two benches. After a while, the train stopped there for us.

As we got on the train, we were told to go to the rear where the first class seats were. As we passed through the first several cars, it was sad and rather frightening to see the condition of the cars and of the working class of people who were returning home from shopping or work.

When we arrived at a certain place, Dr. Horak said to sit wherever we could. Every car was crowded.

The first ten minutes of the ride I felt, because of the terrible vibration, it would be impossible to withstand it. My insides were never treated like that before! I prayed the Lord to help me. Right away I felt ashamed for my timidity in the face of the daily suffering of these people.

Perhaps most of the breadwinners from the villages were on this train. The government allowed each farmer no more than five acres, which made it impossible to make a living on the land.

On the many miles to the village, we saw only one wagon and horse; no cars.

I wish I could remember the name of the village where we stopped for the evening.

A carpenter built a little frame church almost alone on the back of his property. It held perhaps seventy-five of the villagers.

There were perhaps two hundred people of the village who were not saved. Some could not see how they could believe in God when they have suffered so much.

Those young people and children did not need television excitement to fill their minds. This was their background, and they'd had enough.

The carpenter's wife and a few other women helped cook and serve a delicious meal for us out on the back lawn of their home near the church. The table was set along side of a primitive stone oven. I saw one woman take a long pole with what looked like a paddle at the end to pull out several loaves of bread. We found them to taste very good. The table was set with a white cloth, and we sat on benches with no backs. Each held three people. The menu consisted of stewed chicken pieces in broth, together with carrots and egg potpie or rivels. Then they brought deep fried chicken, potato salad, and a salad of green peppers and tomatoes. Dessert was wafers with many layers. All was very good.

After the supper, we were asked if we would consent to walk through the village because Dr. Horak had told the townspeople that he would let everyone see us. He also wanted us to see the people.

We said we would, but we felt strange about it. Just as if no one had ever seen anyone from the United States. People came out of their houses, which were built close to the street. There were no sidewalks or pavement. Some hung out of the upstairs windows. The windows had no screens. I never will forget one lovely couple who greeted us from the upstairs window.

We found everything as it was in America at the turn of the century, very crude, without electricity, bathrooms, and so on.

Before the service, which was about to begin, I told Quinton I must find a restroom or go behind the barn. He told Rev. Horak, who took me to a house nearby. He asked the lady if I could come in her house before the service. She opened the screen door. I walked in while he was telling me that he would wait right there for me. I was shown the place of a toilet upstairs down at the end of the hall. It was patterned after an outside privy, but the sideboards from the seat went straight down to the chicken pen. The chickens were running underneath this newly built toilet. The toilet paper was pages of letters stuck on a nail.

Again I wanted to cry out to God for these dear people.

When I got to the foot of the stairs, there stood Dr. Horak with a pan of hot water, a bar of soap and a cloth. He assured me that the cloth was clean. Bacteria, he seemed to understand.

Dr. Horak also told us that there would always be two communists in each of our services because they had to give a report of what was said and done. Dr. Horak assured Quinton that he could preach a Bible sermon but give no altar call. The communists would call that proselytizing. Sometimes the reporters believed and became followers of Christ. So he was always glad for them to be in the meetings.

As Dr. Horak, Quinton and the other two men and I entered the church, I was amazed to see the place full, and the singers with the instrumentalists were sitting on the edge of the platform with their legs hanging down. People were singing heartily, old tunes with foreign words again. An old lady was playing a pump organ. But Dr. Horak told me after the service that she was younger than I. She had no teeth and worked hard. She was still in her fifties.

The men went on up front. Dr. Horak and Quinton to the platform. I don't know and could not see where the other two men went.

I loitered at the back a bit and really felt there was no place for me. There were few young people there, but suddenly I saw movement on the back seat. A girl at the middle aisle started shoving the people side of her until I could see a little of the wooden bench. She smiled and motioned to me to come and sit down. I sat with just one leg on the bench all evening. She was perhaps twelve years old, blond hair, one long braid, was fair of skin and very friendly.

She shared her hymn book. There were only words in the book, but because most of them were songs that I knew, I tried to read and pronounce the words. She always pointed to each word of each song. I could see that she was enjoying it. I was, too.

Quinton preached with great freedom, and the people listened with joy. Of course they waited until it was interpreted before they responded in any way.

The music with its harmony was inspiring to me. They are great singers.

As the people left the service, the women all stopped at the door where I was standing with Quinton and Dr. Horak. Each one would pat my hands and many wanted to put my face in their hands and look into my eyes. They would all say something to me, but I didn't know what they were saying. Sometimes they would weep, and I couldn't help but weep also. A few times I told Dr. Horak what to tell them quickly before they would pass by, that I loved them. Sometimes tell them I'll see them in Heaven. It was a thrilling time I shall never forget.

We lingered with the musicians and the carpenter for a little while. Then we went to the house where we had eaten our evening meal. They served us some lemonade and cookies or crackers by the light of a lantern. Again we sat on benches without backs.

Finally we made our way back through darkness, to the train stop shed through the grassy path. Many followed us with lanterns and called goodbye as we boarded the train.

It was 11:00 p.m. when we reached the hotel.

* * * * *

Sunday noon we walked home from church. Mrs. Horak wanted me to sit in the kitchen and visit with her while she prepared the food. Without the conveniences we have, it took her much longer. I asked to help her, and she said, *"Maybe later on."*

The one thing I remember we had that noon was strudel. After making the dough, she stretched it out large enough to cover her kitchen table. Then some kind of fruit and other ingredients were poured on it and spread around. She then rolled it up and put it in the oven while she prepared the rest of the dinner.

Quinton came to the kitchen to tell me he had a severe headache.

Mrs. Horak immediately got a pan and poured some green coffee beans into it. She set it on a low burner and gave me a spoon to keep the coffee beans moving around until they got brown. After quite a long time later, she said she would grind and brew it.

I knew it was hard for Quinton to wait so long, but it did help him to drink a cup of coffee. The green coffee beans were from America, a "care package."

Sunday evening the service was in a large very old church with many steps up to a high pulpit. However, Quinton preached from a lower level.

On the way to the service as we walked along, I heard Mrs. Horak ask her husband to please let Mrs. Everest speak to the people before her husband preaches. I quickly prayed that the Lord would put words in my mouth and encourage especially the young people. They had studied English and could understand us very well. I finished by telling them I wanted to see them in Heaven.

We certainly enjoyed our Christian fellowship with the Horaks. When they had traveled to the Baptist World Convention at Miami, Florida, they were amazed at the friendliness and openness of all the people. It was not so in Yugoslavia because they did not know who might be communists. Also, American people were polite. *"Pardon me," "excuse me,"* and *"watch your step"* when getting on and off a bus was new to especially Mrs. Horak.

When the convention was over, they wished to visit or see our country, from the Atlantic to the Pacific. They rode buses every day and had a very thrilling time. If they knew some of the Baptists in a city they were passing through, they would contact them and often stay at their home overnight.

At the time of their visit to the United States, we had never heard of them.

But one afternoon I received a call from Chicago asking for Quinton. They had listened to our broadcast "Your Worship Hour" for years, but they didn't tell me that. They just said they were from Yugoslavia and were here for a convention in Miami.

I had no intention of housing some Yugoslavians that I didn't know. We were threatened by communists but one time; so I was a bit afraid. I declined because Quinton was away in meetings.

When I learned to know the Horaks, I was so ashamed of not giving them a bed and breakfast and "serving angels unaware."

When they traveled as far as Detroit, she was determined to locate the place of her birth. Her parents, both Yugoslavians, came to know the Lord as Saviour in Detroit and with a great burden for the people in that old country, felt the call to be missionaries. Mrs. Horak was five years old at that time and had never been back since. She had their old address in Detroit, located it and talked to an old lady in that neighborhood who said she was the one who cared for her at birth.

What a reunion they had. Furthermore, the lady said no doubt she would still be a United States citizen. She went to the courthouse and found it to be true.

She was so happy to tell me this and cried, too, because she wanted to move back to the United States. Her husband said he could not leave.

* * * * *

Sunday evening we made our way back to the

hotel by tram. The Horaks came with us for this would be the last time we four would be together. We stood in the darkness on the street corner chatting for some time before saying our good-byes. Finally Quinton and I started down the long walkway to the hotel, but I heard her calling after me. She hugged me and cried. I smiled and told her that I loved her. She started back to her husband and we went on. But she repeated this three times. We then hurried on. As we turned to go into the hotel, we all waved.

The next morning we made our way to the airport, went through the checkpoint. Then we stood in line a long time. Quinton and I were conversing in English, of course, when a young man in front of me turned sharply and asked if we were from America. We told him we were.

He told us his reason for being in Yugoslavia was for his company in Connecticut. He said it was good we did not try to leave last night. The group that was to leave then was told the weather somewhere on their trip was too stormy. So the people who had gone through the checkpoint were not allowed to go back into the other part of the airport. Instead they had them go into a room where there were not enough chairs for all of them. The rest had to stand along the wall or sit on the floor.

What color ticket they gave them I've forgotten, but he told us that when they called our plane number, we should run for the plane. Don't hesitate or walk, he said, run for it. We did and were happy he told us to because not everyone could get on.

We were truly sorry for the people, but we had to make that flight.

* * * * *

At Bonaire years before this, we became acquainted with Mr. and Mrs. Herman Schulte. He spoke English. She did not. They wanted us to stop in Wetzler, Germany for a day or two on our way home. We finally consented and were later glad that we did.

We were taken by bus on the highway along side of the French Riviera to Nice where we got our plane to Frankfort, Germany.

At Frankfort we were detained because we could not find our baggage. It seemed no one we could find could speak English. Finally someone told us to go to the Post Office. We both thought that didn't make sense. We stepped outside the building as we continued talking. A well-dressed, kindly looking gentleman asked, *"Are you having trouble? May I help you?"* His English was very clear. We told him our difficulty. He smiled and said he was an official in the airport. We were told to stay inside and he would bring our baggage to us. He did, and we thanked him.

We traveled on the Autobahn. Some were traveling up to one hundred miles per hour.

Mr. Schulte was owner of a large religious printing company. He built a church for his workers, for he himself had a unique encounter with God.

Forced to fight in Hitler's army, he was often in great danger. Battles were fierce around him.

He was shot and left for dead. United States soldiers found him and after examining him, took him to their hospital. He was very seriously wounded, but with much care, he improved enough to send him with our own wounded soldiers back to a United States hospital.

For many months, he was cared for as a German captive. He wondered why all of this was happening to him. Everyone was pleasant and helpful. A minister in the city came to visit him regularly, and he was genuinely converted to Christ. He became strong and anxious to go back home to Germany to do a ministry for the Lord. He also wanted to tell his story to his relatives because he became burdened for their spiritual condition.

When we were in their home, he told us many things and took us to his print shop to meet his sixty workers.

At night he had Quinton preach in the church. How friendly and eager they were, asking many questions after Quinton ended the sermon.

That evening at eight o'clock, Mrs. Schulte served our dinner. I don't remember everything she served, but I do know we had great dishes of mashed potatoes and several bowls and plates of cheeses.

Their grown boy filled his soup plate with piles of potatoes at least three times. It reminded me of boys at home eating large amounts of ice cream.

We talked for some time at the table after we were through eating, as people do in many countries.

Afterward we went to the living room and a pretty little girl came in. She was dressed prettily and had a broad smile. She came up close to where we were sitting on the davenport and stopped suddenly directly in front of us. Then she waited while looking intently at me first, then at Quinton. I began talking to her, but she just bowed again and again. Then her grandpa, Mr. Schulte, took over. It was so funny up to this point. He was a good interpreter as he asked the questions and the little girl, or we, would answer in our own language.

The Schulte home was on the second floor of a red brick building. The first floor contained a Bible bookstore, which they owned. That evening both Mr. and Mrs. Schulte took us up to the third floor to a bedroom. There was a single bed at one wall and another single bed at another wall. We were amazed to observe the beds. There was a huge round pillow filled with feathers on the bed. That was all. They showed us where the bathroom was, smiled and said goodnight.

They did it so quickly that I thought it was a joke, knowing we were ignorant of this mode of sleeping.

We were too embarrassed to ask how it was to be used.

So I hurriedly got into my pajamas and pulled this way and that until the huge ball was as long as the bed.

It was a chilly, rainy night.

I climbed in and pulled it around me. It was so soft and comfortable. I was surprised. I told

Quinton to hurry and try his.

We agreed it was wonderful, and we soon fell asleep. In the middle of the night, I suddenly awakened. I was much too warm. In the darkness I rummaged through my suitcase to get a light nightgown. *"What is the matter? What are you doing?"* asked Quinton. I told him. He agreed but went back to sleep.

Mrs. Schulte took us shopping the next morning. She wanted us to see the beautiful Bavarian dish store. It contained very beautiful, expensive ware. I settled for a pretty twelve-inch tall vase. It laid on my lap on the plane all the way home. All these years, everyone thought it to be special, not knowing the price of it. It cost me four dollars.

I was extremely happy to make these trips, but we did not have much spending money. From Switzerland we bought music boxes for our children. Quinton had often brought me gifts from different countries when he traveled alone and I stayed at home to care for our family.

* * * * *

From there we flew to London for the weekend before returning the United States.

We lingered quite a while for our luggage. Quinton found his, but mine didn't show up. The crowd got thinner until almost everyone was gone.

Then I saw a suitcase sitting against a wall across the room. We rushed over to it and both thought it was my Hartman suitcase. But when

we looked it over, the tag was not mine. We hurried to tell an official there, before they all left
the room, that this was not mine but one like it.

They found the owner's name, destination
and called him. He said he was seventy miles
away from the airport at his daughter's and that
they had just arrived. The officials asked him to
open the suitcase that he had and see if it was
not filled with women's clothing. Sure enough,
he was amazed when he opened it.

He wanted Quinton to come and get it. "No,"
Quinton said. He had no car and did not know
where he was. The official said, too, that it was
the man's mistake. He took our suitcase.

So the airport official told us to go to the hotel,
which was just across the street from Hyde Park,
and they would bring it to us.

Quinton insisted I needed clothes from that
suitcase early in the morning, for tomorrow was
Sunday and we were going to church.

It was delivered to our room at nine o'clock
that evening. We then relaxed and went to bed.

The highlight of our stop in London was to
hear Dr. John Stott, the world-renowned preacher. Quinton and I had read some of his books.

When we arrived inside the church, an usher
said Dr. Stott would be preaching that morning
to doctors. The church was full of doctors. It
didn't take Quinton but a moment to show him
his card with Dr. Quinton Everest on it. Before
he could explain, the usher said, *"We have a good
place for you,"* and proceeded to take us two-
thirds of the way to the front. Doctors and wives
and more doctors and wives, downstairs and in

the balcony.

As Dr. Stott announced his subject on abortion with such forcefulness, we understood why the doctors were invited. He awakened the group to the scriptural stand on the subject. We knew little on the subject in those years, but it was becoming prevalent in England.

Dr. Stott met each one of his congregation at the close of the service to present them a copy of it, and as we met him, we asked if we could have an extra copy for our Christian family doctor, Dr. Robert Thompson. He pleasantly gave us a second one.

After lunch at the hotel, we were introduced to a university student who gave guided tours to tourists.

The young man was very bright and knowledgeable. He took us to Westminster Abbey where we saw the burial place of Robert Livingston, which is in the center aisle of the Abbey. The covered area is of bronze. It has printed on it his life and death record.

He took us to the changing of the guards, the Palace, and to 10 Downing Street where Quinton took my picture standing side of the mounted police; then on to Big Ben.

We enjoyed the afternoon, but we had had two very full weeks; so we were glad to go back to the hotel for a rest and then to dinner.

This was not a pleasure trip, but there was pleasure in it.

The next day we were on our way home with a plane full of people all going to Chicago.

Eight or ten people were all dressed in black,

looking very tired and very weary. Maybe they were sick; maybe they were fleeing persecution, but all looked very sad.

As our plane neared the terminal, someone came to the plane and gave the stewardesses a medicated, moist cloth for each of us to scrub our hands and faces. It was a command. I concluded there were sick people aboard.

When we pulled up to the airport, we saw many people waiting for this group with tears and greetings.

* * * *

How good it was to be home again, sleeping in our own beds, lounging on the screened-in porch, cooking what we wanted to eat, mowing the lawn, cutting our own flowers for bouquets, calling our children, yes, and visiting with the office girls.

Of course, this lasted only a few days, and we began the next schedule of meetings, radio rallies, revivals, camp meetings.

* * * * *

Twice Cynthia asked me to come to California when her babies were born. Christine was born when Mike and Cynthia were living on a seminary campus. Three years later, Ryan was born. I flew out alone for these occasions. Both times June was a very hot month.

One night it was especially hot. Christi and I were sleeping in the same room in twin beds with a table and lamp between us. She was squirming, and I was fanning with a piece of paper.

351

"Christi," I said, "do you want to fan? I'll give you something to fan your face. That will make you feel better. And if you lie real still, be very quiet, you won't get so hot."

"Do you remember that Grandpa is on his way to Pasadena? He is driving our car pulling a little trailer behind it that has our davenport on it. Maybe he is tired, too. But you will see him tomorrow. I think you will go to sleep if you think about Grandpa because you love him."

"Yes, and I'm going to think about Jesus, too," she said, "because He's my friend."

Words from a three-year-old child.

Neither one of us said another word. We both fell asleep.

Chapter Twenty-Two

We visit my Swiss ancestor's farm in PA.
—the massacre.

As I grew older, I thought more and more about my ancestors immigrating to America from Switzerland. I wanted to know and see the farm they bought when they came here.

When I was quite young, my father showed me a Hostetler Family history book. He wished I would read it sometime. I did and hoped that we could some day take time to go to the farm in Pennsylvania where they settled.

After our son Q.J. was married and pastored in Philadelphia, we periodically visited them. He and his wife Shirley sometimes took us to historical places. It was always a delight to be in that area.

Once on our return trip home, I asked my husband to go a different way. It took us north a bit farther, but I had, all my adult life, wanted to see the land on which my ancestors lived.

* * * * *

I am well aware of the toil, blood and treasure that it cost my forebearers to leave Switzerland to come to the new land of America. My family history book tells me this.

Their farm, possessions and everything was

left behind.

After saying goodbye to many friends and relatives who were dear to them, they sailed away on the ship, Harle.

One hundred and fifty-six men, sixty-five women, one hundred sixty-seven boys and girls, counting our ancestor, his wife and three-year old son John, were on this boat.

A journey from Switzerland to America required about fifty days or more.

They traveled up the bay at Philadelphia. It was the year 1736, September 1st.

Having left his beautiful native country of Switzerland with its lakes, valleys and picturesque mountains, he looked for a beautiful location. The choicest land within fifty or sixty miles of Philadelphia being already occupied, he went some distance to buy desirable government land.

William Penn had bought land from the King of England, but when our ancestor arrived, his possessions had passed to his sons. So it was from Tom Penn that he purchased five hundred acres of land south of the Blue Mountains.

He made a good selection of land with a rapidly flowing creek, which heads in the mountains.

Perhaps not a tree or a bush had been previously removed. The buildings were built in sight of the never-failing stream, which furnished fresh water for the family and cattle.

As I stood on this ground, in my sixties, I was so awed and excited to view the place where my ancestor in America was to raise his family in freedom.

But it was not to be without great suffering.

However, for about twenty years, their lives had been peaceful with the Indians because of forts built every so many miles apart with soldiers always on the alert for the farmers' safety.

After years went by and there were no more incidents of Indians kidnapping children and adults, or people scalped, the forts were forsaken.

Then one fall evening the family invited young people to come for apple peeling to prepare for making apple butter the next day.

About midnight, the young people left for home. Our ancestors were already asleep when the dog made an unusual noise. The son Jacob awakened, opened the door to see what was wrong, when he received a gunshot wound in his leg. He managed to lock the door before the Indians could enter.

The family was on their feet instantly. Eight or ten Indians were standing near the bake oven discussing their next move, perhaps. The family could not be seen because there were no lamps lighted. Joseph and Christian picked up their guns to defend the family, but their father strictly forbade them to kill even for the family's protection.

The Indians immediately set the house on fire. The family fled to the cellar. The house became so hot that they tried to put out the fire by sprinkling apple cider, from barrels, on the fire.

Then all was quiet for some time and thinking maybe the Indians had left, tried to escape through a dark cellar window. But the Indians were waiting, scalped the mother and killed the wounded son and a daughter. The cellar was filled with fruits, vegetables and meats. Indians sometimes stole the farmers' food to feed their own families.

The father, Joseph, and Christian were kidnapped. They were bound and forced to walk fast. Before being bound, they had gone through their peach orchard, their father instructed the boys to gather as many as they could and give them to the Indians.

This gracious act surprised the Indians, and they stopped beating them with switches, clubs and tomahawks.

They walked many miles, the father calculated, toward Detroit. He instructed his sons, as they traveled, never to forget their faith in God, and if they were separated and forgot their language, to at least remember the Lord's Prayer in their native tongue.

When they arrived at their wigwam village, they took them to the river and performed a ceremony of washing out their white blood.

They gradually dressed them as Indians. Jacob, the father, had a beard. They pulled out the hair one at a time. The hair on his head was pulled out the same way except for a tuft, which was long enough to braid.

In time they trusted the boys and their father to daily hunt for food. They were sharpshooters; the Indians were hungry. So they allowed each of them so many bullets each morning and commanded them to bring back meat. Each one was sent in a different direction. Each night they had to give an account of each bullet.

After a long time, the father was trusted; so he started to store an occasional bullet in a tree trunk far from their wigwams.

The time came when the father made his escape.

But his two boys were living and growing up as Indian boys and never were released until they were in their twenties.

As the father started out, he prayed for direction, for he was uncertain which way he should go.

He stopped to make a wooden raft after a couple of days and paddled down a river. But he wasn't sure.

One night he had a dream. In his dream he saw his murdered wife who told him he was on the right course and how to continue.

He made his way back home but sorrowed for his wife and sons.

Many years later when the sons were in their early twenties, the Indian chief in their area wanted to sign a peace treaty with the governor of Pennsylvania state. But the governor refused unless he made it possible for all the kidnapped children and adults to be released to their homes within two years.

The chief came back in two years ready to sign, but the governor had scores of names that were not returned. The chief had to finally acknowledge it and tried again. That was when Christian and Joseph Hostettler were released.

What a family reunion! But it was hard then

357

for the boys to make the adjustment of living in a wooden, closed house and wearing other clothes.

The boys claimed that after the Indians adopted them, they were very kind and tender to them. Christian and Joseph sometimes went back to visit them.

Christian became a Christian at a revival meeting and gave up the farm life to preach. He also had two sons who became preachers.

There are many interesting stories of many of our people down through these six or seven generations to be read in our Hostettler family history book.

The earlier men were mostly farmers or ministers. One of the family members was a circuit rider who traveled day after day from Kentucky north as far as Wisconsin stopping in every community preaching in schoohouses, homes or any place he could find someone to listen to the Gospel. People were hungry for news, fellowship and the Gospel. Many hard, rough men were saved and the lonely pioneers were glad to give him a bed, breakfast, pack a lunch for him and feed his horse. He went back and forth for years, encouraging and strengthening the saved and reaching out to the unsaved.

It was a rugged life, but in his lifetime, he baptized three thousand souls. He gave his life for others. His life story was written in Madison Evans' book "Pioneer Preachers of Indiana."

As the family grew and spread out over the states, having large families with courage and good minds, it resulted in contributing much good to their communities and their nation.

Many have been farmers, teachers, preachers, university presidents, state senators, United States congressmen, artists, many doctors, engineers and plain workers in all kinds of trades.

I am blessed to know that they have been a great benefit to our God and country.

As is always the case, there were a few who were not willing to take God into their lives, which caused heartache and tragedy. "Trust in the Lord with all your heart and lean not unto your own understanding; acknowledge Him in all your ways and He shall direct your path."

Now I was standing on the ground I had wanted to see all of my adult life.

I looked all around. We had come down a long tree-lined lane.

Suddenly there was a wide lawn, and a house that was rebuilt around the original stone wall that was on the inside, a fireplace for cooking and heating. This stone wall was the only part of the original house.

On the lawn nearby was a well-built stone monument about five feet high and three feet wide with a bronze plaque

My ancestor's home.

imbedded in the stone recording the massacre of the Hostettler family on September 19, 1757.

Then we went back to the main road, turned left into another lane that went a short distance farther south than the original family home.

This was a lovely large stone house of John's, the little three-year-old boy who traveled with his parents to America.

The night of the massacre, he heard a commotion and then saw the burning house and barn of his parents, brothers and sisters.

John wanted to help. He was so frightened he took his wife and baby, hid them a little way back of their house in the bushes while he went to see what he could do.

He stealthily crossed the field, but as he came nearer, he saw that his father and two brothers were being kidnapped. He returned to his wife and baby to care for them.

John was my ancestor.

Barbara had gone home with friends that night; so she had no knowledge of the tragedy.

The Indians fell in love with Joseph and Christian. They planned to wash the white blood out of them so as to have them as brothers. Furthermore, the two boys and their father Jacob were all sharpshooters. The Indians needed them to hunt meat for their families to survive the winter months.

From John's house, we walked to the beautiful creek that ran through the farm. The water was very clear as it rippled over many large rocks.

In the early days, Indians used creeks and

rivers to travel from one area to another.

I stood in amazement at the mountains, the stream that flowed from it, trying to relive that historical story of my ancestors. The blue mountains were very visible from the farm looking to the north.

Chapter Twenty-Three

*Grandpa Everest's death, Hawaii meetings,
and one more trip to Europe.
I meet Princess Grace, and our
international excerpts.*

Quinton arrived home at midnight from a North Carolina crusade. He was very tired so immediately went to bed.

About one o'clock the phone rang. His sister, Bernadine, was calling from a nursing home where their father had been living for a few years. Previously he had lived in her home until he had so many small strokes the doctor advised them, that since they had small children, it would be better for the family and grandfather, to be taken care of in a nursing home.

Bernadine was calling to say that he had a severe stroke that evening. She was called by the nurse and staying at his bedside. She felt he would not last long. Would Quinton come right away? He jumped out of bed, dressed and left the house in a very short time.

I felt sorry for him, but I appreciated how he felt about his dad.

For some time, his father could not read or enjoy much in this world anymore. His memory was poor, but he always asked Quinton when and where was his next meeting away from

South Bend. So Quinton always told him. He seemed to memorize it and would say when he expected Quinton to come home, and Quinton would always plan to go see him. It was about eighteen miles from our home.

Quinton arrived in time to stand side of him, with Bernadine on the other side. He prayed and talked to him. Quinton was always glad he made it in time.

He had been a faithful Christian ever since Quinton was two years old. He was an elder in the Elkhart Missionary church and taught a Sunday School class for many years.

Quinton's mother had died about ten years previously. His mother always baked the communion bread. When I became a pastor's wife, I used her recipes and baked those little squares for twenty-two years at Gospel Center Church. In those days, we did not buy it because the church felt the communion bread should be baked without leaven by Christians.

* * * * *

We kept in contact with our children and grandchildren. We wanted to be available to help them in time of need.

One morning Sharon called about six o'clock in the morning. She sounded very distressed and asked me if I could come get her and the children. Lightning had struck their house and caused her husband Gary to roll out of bed. The neighbors took the family to their home. The fire was so fierce that the baby was scarcely rescued. In five more minutes they could not have reached him, so the firemen told Quinton. All things were burned or ruined by smoke.

They were cold and in their night clothes. I grabbed blankets, scarves and clothes for Sharon. Quinton and I hurried out to Roosevelt Road and took Tami, Gary, Jr., the baby, and Sharon with us. Gary, Sr. needed to stay for a little time with the firemen.

They lived with us at the parsonage for six weeks until they found another home.

We enjoyed having them, and we got along fine.

We were looking for a property of our own, also, since Quinton had just resigned from Gospel Center Church to continue with the growing radio ministry.

When we found a house in Swanson Highlands, Sharon told us they had settled on a house three blocks from ours. We were so happy about that.

* * * * *

Some months after that, we were invited by our pastors in Hawaii to go there to conduct meetings.

Up to that time, the pastors were from the States, who had been educated at Fort Wayne Bible Institute.

Don Rohrs and his wife, Faith, were some of the first missionaries to answer the call. It was a great challenge. Many of our church people were Japanese, some Hawaiians.

By the time we were there, our Missionary churches were on three islands – Oahu, Hawaii and Kauai.

Quinton had meetings at one church; then would go to another.

The first time in Hawaii we lived with the Rohrs. They had a guesthouse built next to the parsonage in Honolulu. They were most gracious. Their beautiful girls were so courteous, too. We certainly enjoyed our stay. Much could be written of the things and places they showed us and the good fellowship we experienced.

We also stayed in the home of Pastor and Mrs. Ed Terrui on the coast of Kauai. Each morning after breakfast he always asked what we would like to see or do that day. We didn't know much about these islands; so we left it up to him. We loved the islands and the weather, but one night there was a terrible storm with terrific winds. The news on television told exactly where it hit the island. It was up the coast about twenty miles.

The next morning, Pastor wanted to take us up to see the damage. When we arrived at the edge of town, a sign said, *"Go no farther."* Rev. Terrui went on a little farther, then stopped. He said the van might get stuck. So he turned off the engine, got out and talked to the first man he saw, who was a policeman.

The officer told him he had twenty-five years of police work there and had never seen anything like it. The waves had been fifty feet high. The homes along the coast were destroyed. By the time we got there, he said they were twenty feet high.

* * * * *

365

We were called to go a second time for a Prophetic meeting. On the island of Kauai, the churches combined for the services. In one churchyard was a large sign with these words in large letters – *"Come Hear Quinton."* Unique, but the church was full with good results. It encouraged the people and the pastors.

I found that the husband of the organist was a distant cousin of mine from Middlebury, Indiana. We visited in their home. It was built on a high cliff with mountains in the distance. He had built an extra room on the house so she could have an organ.

* * * * *

On this second trip we were entertained in the Wendall Sousley home. His father was Sunday School superintendent, elder of the church and building treasurer for Gospel Center. He also helped in our radio work as a board member, and he sang in the radio choir. So we were acquainted with the Sousleys.

Mrs. Wendell Sousley was choir director, Sunday School teacher, as well as hostess of the parsonage.

One morning I saw her ironing. I asked if there wasn't something more I could do for her than just wash dishes.

"Well, there's a whole basket of papayas that need to be cared for."

I said, *"I'm eating all I can. They are my favorite fruit. Tell me what I should do and I'll take care of them."*

So she had me peel, dice and pack them in

bags to be frozen. Every morning I was cutting a long papaya lengthwise and eating a half. Several people brought in much fruit. The last day of the meeting was on Thanksgiving. The people brought dishes of all sorts – fish, even octopus, casseroles of all kinds, fruits and vegetables. They are wonderful cooks. We had Thanksgiving dinner in the park.

We had come not on a pleasure trip, but there was much pleasure in it. Quinton was only promised the price of his fare to and from Hawaii. (This was a mission trip.) But they took an offering the last day. It made up all of Quinton's fare and a little more; so they said that could help to cover mine.

* * * * *

When we arrived back at the parsonage, the phone rang. Rev. Sousley answered it. The mayor of the island had recently been saved and had enjoyed these special meetings. In fact, he told Quinton, in my hearing, that he had gained much knowledge in the meetings.

On the phone he asked Rev. Sousley if the Everests' tickets were paid in full. Of course Rev. Sousley said, *"No."*

He asked how much was lacking. He was told. Then he said Rev. Sousley should meet him in an hour in front of the bank. He would give him a check for it.

I wrote him a thank you note when I got home. God again met our needs!

* * * * *

We had always lived by *"what wilt Thou have me do, Lord?"* When calls came in, He provided not only the money for our mission trips but also the strength and spiritual stamina we required.

As a full-time Christian, let us not offer Christ that which costs us nothing. As we aged, we rejoiced to suffer something for Jesus.

The more we learned and understood the sufferings of our dedicated brothers and sisters who work and pray vigorously for the spreading of the Gospel, we understand our responsibility, at least to a certain degree, of God's call to earnest prayer. In remote places, where missionaries and Christian literature has never entered, is where radio is most important. As you give and pray for people who are hearing God's Word of salvation in their own language, just take time to imagine what it would be like to hear for the first time. Then how anxious they are to bring others to listen to the radio, too.

* * * * *

For the third time, Dr. Paul Freed invited us again to come to the European Christian Broadcaster's Convention.

This time one of the board members of the Worship Hour broadcast, on hearing we were about to leave again, told Quinton he had a strong desire to accompany us. This certainly was a pleasure for us. Of course, he would take his wife along. This couple was Ancil and Virginia Whittle of Goshen. They laughingly said that they would help carry our luggage.

Trans World Radio chartered a plane that was

painted red, white and blue. On the side in very large letters was printed, *"United States."* The year was 1976. Many Trans World board members were on this trip also. Some we had known for years, but some we had never met before.

We refueled at the Azores. At three o'clock in the morning, we could see only a bit of the plane's lights on the water. No land could be seen until after we landed. We got off the plane and strolled around.

A week after we returned home, a newspaper article told of a large plane that missed the landing there and crashed in the water. We flew on to Nice, France, where a bus was waiting to take us to Monte Carlo.

We checked into the beautiful new Loew's Hotel built partially over the Mediterranean. We were all guests of Trans World Radio. Quinton and I were far down the hall from the elevators; so Virginia took me down to the desk where she asked if this elderly couple could have their room changed to one nearer the elevator.

"Of course. No problem."

So that made it next door to the Whittles. Quinton laughed when she told them he was elderly.

They gave us a delightful tour before dinner.

When we came back to the hotel, it was time for the evening meal; so we hurried to our room to freshen up.

"Look," I said, *"here on the dresser is a card of invitation by Princess Grace to a concert of chamber music tonight in the ballroom of this hotel. I suppose*

Ancil and Virginia received one, too."

They did, and Ancil was quick to say, *"I'll pay the tickets, only four dollars each."*

* * * * *

Sessions did not begin until the next morning. What a lovely evening it turned out to be.

We were to have two free meals each day. That first evening meal was so delicious with all the fresh fruit you could imagine covering a large, long table. We learned that the fruit was raised in Israel.

All at once everyone was talking and leaving their tables. Then we heard some say, *"Look out the window. The limousine is driving up at this door. There, Prince Rainier is getting out."*

Then he gently helped Princess Grace and a woman companion to alight from the car.

We hurried to the door—for our table was not far—and got a close look at them.

Ancil said, *"Maybe we'd better quickly finish eating and hurry to the ballroom. Hope we aren't too late for tickets."* We ate just a little more and rushed down the hallway. But Ancil was on ahead to see if the tickets were sold out. As we rounded the corner, he waved the tickets at us.

We found good seats about two-thirds back in the room, but we were on the same side as the instruments. This small group was promoted by Princess Grace and leaving the next morning for the United States. It was lovely music. And then at intermission, the excitement began for me.

As Princess Grace started slowly back the center aisle, she took note of each person who was standing next to the aisle, first on one side, then to the other. She would pause and say *"good evening"* to each one. Sometimes the person would kneel down to bow low, but most just bowed and said a few gracious words.

All at once I seemed to realize I had that opportunity, too. There was no one sitting at the end of our row of seats. So I just slowly, very slowly, stepped to the aisle. Oh, so very quickly, a man in a dark suit stood at my shoulder. I was aware that it might be a secret service man; so I did not turn my head. I stood very still until she reached me. I smiled broadly and said, *"Good evening, Princess Grace. I'm Mrs. Everest from the United States. We have a mutual friend."*

She stopped and smiling said, *"And who could that be?"*

I said, *"Dorothy Hartman."*

She raised both hands up high and as if she forgot her station said, *"Oh, good old Philadelphia!"*

Dorothy and Grace had gone to school together in Philadelphia and their mothers were very close friends. But Dorothy had a very genuine conversion to Christ and married a fine Christian young man. Both were very brilliant and felt called to the mission field. They went to Brazil under our Missionary Society. Quinton was president for twenty-three years and had the privilege of interviewing them.

I was saddened when a few years later the car of Princess Grace went over the high cliff. She died as a result. We traveled that mountainous

road a number of times when we would go up to
the top of the mountain where the Hitler radio
buildings are, which are now in the hands of
Trans World Radio. The road has a number of
hairpin turns where the cars, especially our bus,
had to back up several times to adjust to the
sharp curve.

* * * * *

The sessions of the convention was much the
same as other years. But there was much enthu-
siasm and discussions of how to extend more
time into countries like Romania, Bulgaria, and
many others. Some new broadcasters were
there. Many experiences were told by speakers
with fire in their souls, which stirred our hearts.

Dr. Freed asked Quinton to greet the people.
He gave Trans World thanks for giving him an
outlet for his messages to over eighty countries
and more from which we received letters. He
also wanted to encourage them in their work for
God and for souls. Again, it was difficult to
leave these dear servants of God.

* * * * *

When we left France, we were told that our
plane's radio back-up system was not working.
They would be flying to Ireland, then Iceland,
and on to Kennedy Airport in New York, making shorter hops.

We were allowed off the plane in Ireland. The
gift shop in the airport was one of the largest
and most interesting I've ever seen. The woolen
garments were so attractive, and the crystal was

beautiful. Evidently they were less expensive than in the States, for the women were busy buying all the time we were there.

The plane could not be fixed in Ireland; so we proceeded to Iceland. It was 3:00 a.m., but the sky was light and the air was cold. The women had packed their heavy sweaters. We had stopped quite a distance from the airport; so everyone took off running.

We arrived in New York with no trouble but with little sleep. They took us by bus to sleep two hours at a hotel. What a relief, but we were rudely awakened to be ready to board a bus in a very short time.

The whole trip with the experiences of the convention was a great blessing, especially with the fellowship of so many of God's people.

*   *   *   *   *

I feel it is very appropriate to add some of the excerpts of letters we received at our office in South Bend, Indiana, from many countries concerning Quinton's messages on "Your Worship Hour" broadcasts.

Many prayers have accompanied our office girls' replies to those letters.

> **GRENADA:** *"I am a listener to your broadcast. I was not a Christian."*
> *"But one Sunday evening while listening to your program I found Christ as my Savior. I thank God for His goodness to me and for Pastor Everest. Please keep praying for me."*

GUYANA, S. AM.: *"I am a policeman over here. Many times my life is at stake. It was while listening to your broadcast over Bonaire that I settled the question, and thank God there are no regrets."*

MICHIGAN: *"I was working while listening to your program. I stopped and knelt down, confessing my sins and asked God's forgiveness. A great burden was lifted. Words are not adequate to tell what joy and happiness I received from that broadcast."*

ENGLAND: *"I have been listening to Pastor Everest every week for many years. I find his preaching brings the Lord right into my kitchen."*

ENGLAND: *"We listen to your messages and have been encouraged that you speak very plainly to sinner and saint alike. It is a joy to know that these messages are being beamed across the world in these days."*

PENNSYLVANIA: *"I truly enjoy every word as I feed upon it. God speaks through you in a wonderful way. Thank God for your obedience to His call. The singing and the piano music is so beautiful to worship with."*

ONTARIO: *"We did very much enjoy your program Sunday night. The message you gave caused me to search my heart. We need messages like that."*

DENMARK: *"This morning while casually turning my radio I came across your program for the first time and enjoyed it very much. Please send me your sermon book and any other literature, which would enable me, a sinner trying to find his way back to God. Please remember me in your prayers."*

TURKS ISLANDS: *"Your service today was a real blessing to me and the contents seemed so relevant to my little island. It is a very hard thing to make an outward confession of the Love of Christ. During your sermon I decided to make heaven my aim, and if I lose friends in the struggle, I will."*

ENGLAND: *"As a pastor, I find the broadcasts a great help to myself, spiritually, especially before leaving home to face my own congregation. I feel I have been fed and blessed."*

CUBA: *"I am still listening to your broadcasts every week. It strengthens and renews me, keeping me closer to my Lord."*

GERMANY: *"For years your program has proved a great blessing here in Germany."*

SCOTLAND: *"I am at this moment off the west coast in my ship. I much appreciated your message which I heard clearly this* *morning on things that really matter."*

VENEZUELA: *"We missionaries enjoy your program. We need this inspiration. We need to hear good preaching in English. Trans World is reaching countless souls for Christ. Their hearts are being prepared before we reach them. May the Lord bless you and supply your needs to keep your good program, 'Your Worship Hour,' on the air."*

And so thousands upon thousands of letters came for over fifty years of broadcasting of "Your Worship Hour."

URUGUAY: *"Last night after returning from the interior, I tuned in to Quito and heard "Your Worship Hour" very clearly. As a missionary I can tell you that this is a great blessing to me. Your message entitled "Fact Of The Atonement" was a tremendous inspiration."*

YUGOSLAVIA: *"We are very glad to have permission to write to you. Maybe I will never see you here on earth, but up yonder we shall meet. Thank you for sending me your book "Man's Death and Destiny." I will try to study it from the beginning to the end. If you distribute the next series of sermons based on I Samuel, don't forget me. We will continue to pray for you. Excuse my poor English. I have learned it myself without any school. I know it is a gift of*

God that I can use it for His Glory. I was just married and am 25 years old."

HOLLAND: *"Just a few weeks ago I came to know of TWR. Your program is a very great blessing to me. I was thrilled that you preach prophesy the radio, which is a great privilege and we pray for "Your Worship Hour.' "*

WISCONSIN: *"I am a Roman Catholic nun who listens faithfully to your broadcasts. They are tremendous, and I am certain they have helped countless people. Most assuredly it has helped me, and I wouldn't miss them."*

MISSOURI: *"My husband has been sick for some time. He was bedfast for six months and you will never know what your programs meant to us during that time. We are praying God will keep you on our station."*

NETHERLANDS, ANT.: *"I have been listening to your program and enjoy it immensely. Before the 28th of July I was a heavy drinker, living without God. Now I'm living on a plantation and am usually alone at night. Now I've discovered Christ and am really never alone. I lay in the dark with tradewinds moaning through my little shack listening to your program, and I feel happy. After listening to 'Future Space Dwellers,' I go outside and look at the sky* *which is beautiful at night here."*

* * * * *

When we went back home to South Bend, we were weary but very inspired and refreshed in our spirits.

Again and again the verse in I Samuel 12:24 would come to my mind. *"Only fear the Lord and serve Him in truth with all your heart for consider how great things He hath done for you."*

This was my lifetime verse given to me at age eighteen.

I told the office girls that they should never feel bored in the work they were doing day after day. The result of their work was rewarding for the multitudes of people throughout the world.

The mail must be read, checked for offerings and prayer requests, letters to be answered, mailings to be ready for the post office. At ten o'clock each morning they stopped working to gather in the main office for prayer. Each request sent in by listeners was remembered before the throne of grace. Sometimes there were half days of prayer.

Beside the regular office girls, there were twelve or more regular volunteers who came in for a few days each month to prepare the mailing of the sermon books.

The office personnel was made up of trustworthy Christian people. We had great respect for them. The head secretary had great responsibility when Quinton was away in meetings, but they were always in touch by phone.

Burdens became very heavy at times. Many

were the answers to prayer concerning souls in distress, wisdom to know what stations to take on, and of finances. Always God surprised us with answers greater than what we had asked. It was His work of the Kingdom and not a man's work. To Him is the Glory! The greater the results were, the more we realized it was through the power of the Holy Spirit that people were turning to Christ. *"He that winneth souls is wise,"* the Bible says. So God does work through people to accomplish His purposes, but it is to build up the Kingdom.

* * * * *

Now we are ninety!

Quinton preached quite frequently at 87, but the time came, as it does to all of God's servants, that the work of the Lord must be carried on by others who are strong and ready to take up the work that the elderly have laid down.

Every phase of life has its advantages. We do not live in discouragement and say, as many do, that we are "over the hill" or going down. We are going farther up each

Our 70th Wedding Anniversary

day.

We have much yet to learn.

We have great burdens of prayer.

We have a family of 42 to keep in contact with. We dearly love each of our family and appreciate what we have learned from them.

There are many opportunities for acts of kindness to others, although we are limited in strength to help in physical ways.

We suffer at times, but not greatly.

One of our joys is our ability to read many valuable books. We constantly are learning. We study the Word of God daily, and we are so blessed by it.

Our friends are many. Praise God for all those who pray for us. Thank God for the many, many people we met in our travels who said that they would not think of retiring at night without praying for us and our family.

What a covering of God's protection over us through the years! If you, our readers, were some of them, we say God will reward you, and we thank you!

At age 85, we decided to sell our home in South Bend. Hubbard Hills Estate, a senior citizen's retirement home in Elkhart, is where we now make our home. Quinton was on the board from its beginning twenty-one years ago. Last month he resigned.

About six months ago a new wing was built on. Because the hallway was built right through our apartment bedroom, we were told we could have our choice of the new apartments. We selected the far end one since it had a large window in each of the three rooms. It overlooks the Hubbard Hill Village, which is made up of duplexes. There is a group of large trees between us, occupied by squirrels, other small animals, birds of many kinds, and wild flowers in the spring. A few times we have seen deer. A small path runs through the woods with a small stone bridge down in the ravine.

However, we are not in Heaven, our real Home. We are reading the book of Joni Erickson Tada, Heaven. It is tremendous. I love to think of our prospects of Heaven more and more. I sometimes find tears beginning to trickle down when I think of really seeing Jesus. And of seeing my mother who prayed for me as a little girl. God did answer her prayers. She was a fresh thirty-three-year-old woman, and I am ninety. What a marvelous transformation God will perform, giving us glorified bodies. What joys I am looking forward to.

And what about my mother's other two girls she prayed for in her last hours here on earth? My older sister, Mary, is ninety-three. I am ninety. Myrtle, my younger sister, is eighty-seven. Each of them is in nursing homes in different towns. Mary is blind and in a wheelchair or bed. Myrtle has lost her muscle strength and can barely talk and cannot walk or help herself.

Last month, Myrtle's daughter, Elizabeth, and her husband, Dick, came from Cleveland, Ohio, to visit her mother. Then they brought her here to get me to accompany them to Wakarusa where our sister Mary is. The nurse had Mary prepared for this visit of three sisters. This had not been possible for several years.   Mary's daughter, Carol, was present also.

We recalled the many years of our youth when we sang "specials" together in church and for the Literary Society, especially Mary and me. In our high school years we sang in a mixed quartet.

For many years we sang in the Worship Hour broadcast choir.

When we agreed we must leave Mary, I suggested we have prayer. While I was praying, Mary was crying, laughing and rejoicing. I said to my sisters, *"I wonder if Mama can see us now!"* Thank God for the hope we have in Christ Jesus. Life has been sorrowful, exciting, surprising, joyful, and full of friends who helped us on our way. *"He holds us in His hands, and binds our feet to the path."* Psalms 66:9, from the Living Bible.

* * * * *

I wrote this poem about my own family.

Friends

My best friend is Christ who forgave my
sins
I have another friend my heart did win.
He taught me how to laugh and cry
And then rejoice as years went by.
Our children four brought work and fun.
Then they left us one by one.
They, too, have found the Saviour dear
Which took away all anxious fear
To give them joy to serve each day
Where e're the Spirit leads the way.
These four have twelve to boost our num-
ber.
These twelve have fifteen to put to slum-
ber.
But I have more to say!
There will be sixteen any day!
It seems like quite a bunch we've raised
But we rejoice that most are saved
To live and glorify God's name
And never on His Name bring shame.
And we look forward to the time
We'll be united in the sky
To praise the Lord forever more
Without a sigh, without goodbye!